A Larrikin's Life in Lyrics

By
Tony Gibbons
aka
Tony Johns

Contents

Preface ... 5

Chapter 1 - 1960's-1970's
The Tenambit Tiger ... 9
The Boy Next Door ... 9
6 View Street ... 13
Confined Spaces ... 14
Pet Cemetery ... 15
From "King of the Dogs" to "King of the Lizards"! ... 17
Kids in the Hood ... 18
Above the Law ... 19
Lake Toddles ... 22
Other Ways to Cool Off ... 25
The Other Side of the Tracks ... 28
Winter Games ... 31
Go the Tigers ... 32

Chapter 2 - 1960's-1970's
School Daze ... 35
Cloaked in Mystery ... 35
The Chicken Farm ... 37
Grandma's Feather Bed ... 39
The Lemon song [Devil's Music] ... 45
Straying from the Fold ... 47
The High School Years ... 50
From Sisters to Brothers ... 50
The Band! ... 54
The Year my Voice Broke ... 57
Studio Time ... 60
Senior High ... 61
Pure and Simple ... 69
Big Harry's Place ... 74

Chapter 3 - The 1980's
Tony Who? ... 85
Movin' Away ... 88
The Hunter Hotel ... 89

Pete's Wine Bar	100
The Hill	**102**
New Friends	108
Old Friends & New	110
Time to Party	112
Hittin' the Road	**117**
Surfers Paradise- Life is a Cabaret	128
That's Entertainment	**131**
The Power of The Press	131
Feelin' Festive!	136
From Dirt Tracks to Rock City	**142**
Welcome to the House of Fun	150
Handing Over the Reigns	163
Europe & London 1984-1985	**181**
Helmut's Pub, Hopfgarten	192
Solving a Problem like Maria	198
Burning the candle at both ends	201
Returning to the Motherland	208
Hendon NW4	212
Sept-Dec 1985 Back in Newcastle	**219**
The Boy's Back	220
1986 Austria & Greece	**231**
Back in Europe - January 1986	231
Rhodes, Greece	245
Turning up the Heat	254
Sept'-Dec' 1986 Darby St. Newcastle	**263**
The Boy's Back [Again!]	263
Darby's Pies	265
January-April 1987	
Hopfgarten	**268**
Winter Season #3 in Hopfgarten	268
May 1987-Dec'1989	
Newcastle/Sydney Merry-Go-Round	**273**
Kitchener Parade. The Hill. Newcastle.	273
The Way I live [Album]	281
Wentworth Avenue. Hillsdale. Sydney.	289
Dangar Street, Wickham. Newcastle.	296

The Tex Pistols [Ye-ha!]	297
The End of an Era-Painting the Town Yellow	306

Chapter 4 - 1990's

Adopting to Adapt	309
Austria Calling	313
Domestic Bliss	318
Sophie and the Seven Dwarfs	320
One Day Away	323
Scottish Superstition	325
Man's Best Friend	329
The Valley album	332
Circle of Life	336
Tree Change?	338
Hard [studio] Time	340

Chapter 5 - 1998-2018

From Dream to Nightmare	347
Spasmodic Dysphonia	347
The human voice is the organ of the soul. [Henry Wadsworth Longfellow]	349
Financing the Nightmare	354
A Point to Prove	359
Investing in the Future.	361
The "Natural" album.	365
Coming Back To Life	365
One Night Only!....Gratitude, Justification and Closure	369
Creative Isolation	375
Listen	376

Index of Songs 380

Acknowledgements 383

Timeline 384

Preface

If a person's life could be depicted in a painting, mine, as I neared the age of 40, was a picture of contentment.

Content and secure with my chosen career in music and song which had filled my life with so many beautiful people and wonderful places and which was now supporting my precious young family.

It was then that an illness called Spasmodic Dysphonia took away my ability to sing, ruining my musical career and shattering my life's picture of contentment into broken pieces - like a jigsaw puzzle scattered on the floor.

Approaching my 60's I began gathering up those broken pieces of my life, trying to make sense of them, reconnecting them to, hopefully, put that jigsaw puzzle back together - to restore that picture of contentment.

The pieces of the puzzle were the songs I'd written.

The restored picture is this book.

Tony Johns 2022

A Larrikins Life in Lyrics

The story of Tony Johns, Newcastle based, Australian singer/songwriter, his journey through life and the music business, as told by the lyrics of the songs he wrote along the way.

Copyright © 2022 Tony Gibbons

All rights reserved. This book or any portion thereof may not be reproduced or used in any manner whatsoever without the express written permission of the publisher except for the use of brief quotations in a book review.

ISBN: 978-0-6454362-1-1

Cover design and typesetting by Graham Davidson
Published 2022 by Rack & Rune Publishing
raxkandrune.com

ELVIRA EDNA MARGARET GIBBONS
26th May 1933 ~ 22nd February 2020

Dedicated to
Elvira Edna Gibbons 1933-2020
"The perfect mother"
The only person who didn't need to read this book to know who I really was!
Although I'm sad you didn't get to read my book, there are some things a mother just doesn't need to know about her son's life!
All my love forever.
Tony x

A Larrikin's Life in Lyrics

Chapter 1
1960's-1970's

The Tenambit Tiger

The Boy Next Door

It was **1963,** and while everyone was wondering "who shot JFK?" I was wondering "who shot *Me*?"

I had recently turned 5 and was in the backyard, weaving my way through the wet clothes and sheets that my mother had just hung on the clothes line to dry. The clothes line was two wires, strung from one side of the yard to the other, attached to wooden crossbars on posts. They reminded me of crucifixes, so I called them "Jesus" posts. We hadn't followed the trend, at that time, of buying a Hills Hoist, but that was soon rectified after one of my sister's friends almost sliced her top lip off on one of the low hanging wires while playing "chaseys"!

Emerging from the camouflage of damp clothes, I walked past the framework of the cubby house that my father was building for us

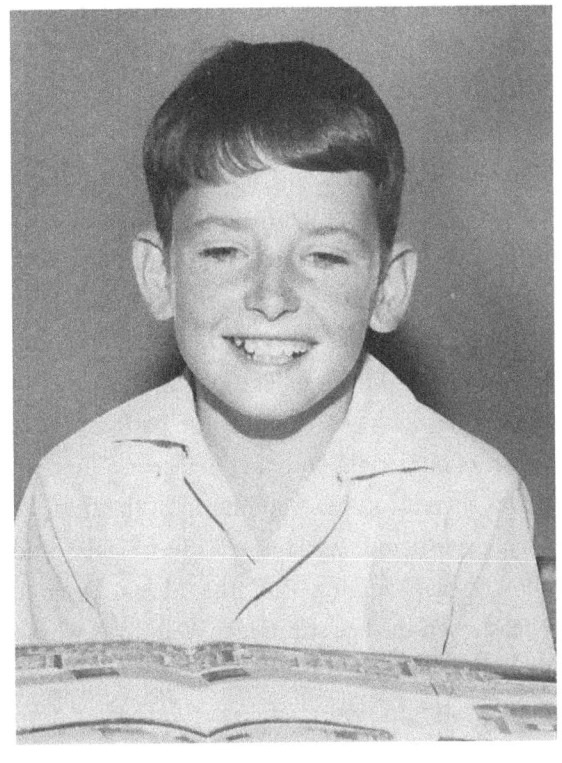

in his spare time, and hoped it would be finished soon. It seemed to be taking forever to complete but that was because dad was doing shift work at the nearby coal mine called Bloomfield-which I always thought was such a pretty name for a dirty, black tunnel! One night, after having my bath and I was in my pyjamas ready for bed, Mum drove me out to Bloomfield Colliery to pick Dad up from afternoon shift. He got me out of the car and, to mum's dismay, took me down the mine shaft in the little train carriage they used to descend into the dark depths of the earth. When we'd gone down about a mile below the surface, Dad walked me to a fresh coal face and turned on the excavating machine that ate into the wall of the tunnel. The noise it made was frightening and, along with the stifling heat and humidity, I found it a very unpleasant place to be. Any chance of me considering a job in the coal mining industry was well and truly snubbed out that night as we returned to my waiting mother's horror, both as black and grimy as the coal itself!

Behind the cubby house construction site was the wooden paling fence that ran like a border wall, separating all the houses and their backyards for the complete length of our block. Careful not to get any splinters in my hands or feet, I pulled myself up onto the top railing and then proceeded to clamber along it, like a cat, to the corner of the yard where the back and side fences of our neighbours met in a cross junction. It was there I sat, perched on top of the massive corner post and, as loud as my lungs would allow, began singing Puff the Magic Dragon. That's when the bee stung me! Well that's what I thought it was. I had the sharpest, most burning, searing, stinging sensation in the soft part of flesh just below the inner ankle of my right foot. As I screamed in pain, howling, with tears pouring down my cheeks, I lowered myself down from the fence and hobbled back towards the house and my mother's comforting arms. As I approached the wall of hung washing, I noticed an older boy climbing back into his yard from the adjacent corner junction of fences. He was carrying an air rifle - which we called a slug gun. They fired small lead pellets that were usually only lethal to birds and small creatures such as mice and lizards. He lived in the house down the back from us, diagonally adjacent to our backyard. I'd seen him from our back verandah, shooting his gun in his back yard on other occasions. I figured he'd got bored, shooting cans and bottles, and had found a live target...Me!...I also wondered if my singing performance had driven him to commit the crime! A teenager toting a rifle, probably wasn't a fan of Peter, Paul and Mary!

I never fully convinced my mother of the "Sniper" theory, especially as my wound did look a lot like a bee sting - or maybe she just didn't want to stir up trouble with the neighbours by accusing their son of my attempted assassination!

That incident remained a mystery to me for the rest of my life - but now as I approach 60, and cynically ponder the shortfalls of my career in music, I wonder if it wasn't an omen, or "warning shot", to stay out of the entertainment industry.

Although I wrote this song when I was in my early 30's, it was strongly influenced by that cubby house that my dad built in our backyard. It symbolises the pride I felt in my new role as patriarch and my hopes to be as good a provider as my own father.

I Built this House

I built this house with my own hands
You picked the site and I drew the plans

I built this house from the floor to the roof
My calloused hands and raw knees are proof

I built this I built this house
I built this I built this house

I built this house to keep you warm
To keep you dry when there's a storm

I built this house out of your dreams
My love supports the walls and beams

Somewhere in the cobweb covered memories of my mind
Smiling now as I begin to see
Children playing games in the backyard
In the cubby house my dad built for me

I built this house down by the clothesline
My cubby house kids are in there all the time

I built this house with hammer and nail
My thumb survived to tell the tale

I built this I built this house
I built this I built this house

*

6 View Street

Despite the shooting incident, my early childhood days, spent playing in our backyard at 6 View street, East Maitland, were pretty much idyllic.

Our yard was a safe haven and sanctuary where, over the years, my sisters and I and our friends played games of chasey's, hidey's, cricket, netball and football - the ball games resulting in broken walls and windows on more than one occasion! I also use to perch myself on the front fence and serenade the kids coming home from school each afternoon, and, as far as I remember, survived those performances, unscathed!

Our house was a fibro, two bedroom cottage, initially. It was, what was called, a Housing Commission House which, back in the 1950's and '60's, could be rented by young, working families, with the option of some of the rent going toward a deposit to eventually purchase it. My father, John, worked as a coal miner, and later as a painter and docker at the Newcastle State Dockyard. My mother, Edna, was a shop assistant in the meat department of the latest Coles New World supermarket in Maitland. They eventually bought the house and renovated it - to add another bedroom for my sisters. They also clad the exterior walls to give it a unique look- unlike the other commission homes which all looked alike, apart from their pale pink, green, yellow and blue paintwork.

My sisters, Pam and Lynette, were older than me by 6 and 4 years respectively. Being in their early teens at that time, they seemed almost like adults to me - so I filled most of my infant days playing by myself around or under the house. While mum and dad were at work, the girls often supervised me and allocated chores- such as shelling the green peas out of their pods into the pot for dinner. I didn't mind *that* job, and usually ate more peas than what made it into the pot! They also took on the task of disciplining me when I occasionally stepped out of line. I can't remember what crime I committed - the time they locked me in the toilet - but I didn't facilitate my early release by screaming a barrage of the latest swear words at them that I had just learnt from some of the neighbourhood kids! Luckily, they released me - just as I was planning to escape through the glass slates of the louvre window!

Left: Lynette, Pam & Me

Confined Spaces

One of my favourite pastimes was crawling around under the house - building roads with my toy D9 grader for my matchbox cars, or digging channels and holes to create mini rivers and dams. Fifty four years later, I found myself back under that house - cleaning it up when Mum needed to be moved out to a nursing home. To my surprise, those roads, riverbeds and dams were all still there! Some of them dangerously threatening the integrity of the brick pier foundations of the building! Of all the fun filled days spent down there in the cool dirt, the one that stands out in my memory is; when I crawled right back to the lowest part - furtherest from my mother hanging the washing [again!]- so that I wouldn't be caught playing with a box of "Redhead" matches and some old newspaper! As I lit the paper, the smoke immediately headed down toward my mother - and the sacred, wet washing! Panicking, I started shovelling dirt on the flames with my bare hands, pounding out the fire. This created even more smoke! Then my blood ran cold, as I heard my mother's voice calling out "Tony, what are you up to under there!" I replied as calmly as I could "nothin' Mum" and to my absolute amazement she was satisfied with my response and didn't enquire further into my activity. Averting the catastrophe of burning our house down - I had completely gotten away with one of the most dangerous and stupid stunts I'd ever pulled! Unfortunately, I think I learned little from that incident, because it seemed to set a precedent, in my coming years, of narrowly surviving *many* idiotic activities that I would undertake along my life's journey!

Pet Cemetery

It was common for people to keep chickens in their backyards at that time, and most of our neighbours did. I have an early childhood memory of my dad holding down a chook and cutting it's head off with an axe - then, watching the headless body running wildly around our yard, spurting blood from it's neck, as my sisters ran and screamed hysterically away from it! Whether this *actually* occurred, is a matter of contention with my mother, but maybe dad did it when she wasn't home - to avoid her displeasure! Anyway, that was my last recollection of us having chooks in our backyard. There *was* an array of other animals, such as pet cats, guinea pigs and dogs. One of the cats was an albino kitten we called Pinky, which died not long after it was gifted to us by a friend of my sister, Lynette. That friend became one of my most influential mentors in my musical career and remains a friend to this day. His name was Mark Tinson, now a highly regarded musician and producer, who I'll talk about in more detail later. My favourite pet was a black, curly-haired, poodle-cross, bitsa, called "Zeus", which I referred to as "King of the dogs - *dogs* being *Gods* backwards". He met his untimely end, out on View street, under a car, while I was inside my room studying for the HSC exams. I felt responsible for his death as I'd been playing with him that morning but forgot to shut the yard gate. I interrupted my studies that afternoon to write this eulogy for him;

Zeus

I had a dog now he's dead
In the morning when I'd wake up he'd be there on my bed
A car ran him down
I dug the grave and laid him to the ground

After I'd filled in his grave
I wanted to cry but had to be brave
He was only a dog just a pet
But he's one little dog I will never forget

Oh why do we miss him so
He brought so much light to this dim world of mine

Sometimes when I'm alone
I hear him bark and I hear him groan
I see him crying at the back door
But when I open my eyes I see him no more

Oh why did he have to go
He'll live on in my dreams
But until I forget
My heart will bleed

From "King of the Dogs" to "King of the Lizards"!

Before Jim Morrison was tagged "The Lizard King" and Alice Cooper paraded on stage with pythons, *I* was walking around with "Bearded Dragon Lizards" on my shirt and head! They were the most unusual pets ever to reside in our backyard. I collected them from a small area of bush down the road, adjacent to the East Maitland Golf Course. I housed them in a corrugated iron enclosure in the corner of our yard-furnished with hollow logs and branch cuttings. They would puff up and open their yellow mouths wide-to scare off predators - but I got quite comfortable walking around with one or two clinging to my shirt front. I even tied string around their neck and walked them like a dog - but stopped doing that when I found one had accidently hung itself by falling out of our peach tree. The iron enclosure collapsed one day and all the lizards escaped, and for years after, my mum would tell me about all the sightings of *them* - by the neighbours!

Kids in the Hood

My circle of friends, at that time, was within throwing distance of my backyard. Dallas and his little brother, Rob, lived right next door; while Robert and his little brother, Michael, lived two houses down. Next to them was Marshy; and one house up from him was Jacko. We usually commuted between our houses by climbing over fences - or running through neighbour's yards and stepping through gaps in the fence where palings had fallen off. One, *ingenious*, form of communication, that we developed, was a *modification* of the "old-Milo tins joined by a piece of string" phone device. Instead of string, we used copper wire [source *unkown*-but *suspect*!], strung along the backyard fence tops, then into our respective bedrooms, where it was attached to the Milo tins. The clarity of reception was pretty good - considering the distance of *six backyards*! The only problem was not knowing when someone wanted to call you on the *"Milo Line"*. So we'd go outside and yell - as loud as we could - to "pick up your Milo tin"!

Above the Law

We were a creative bunch of scallywags! The night we all slept in a tent in Jacko's backyard is legendary. There was probably a dozen of us sleeping over that night. The usual gang, plus a few ring-ins from surrounding streets, including two particularly mischievous characters, Wally and Meyny. As the night got late and we started to get bored with "shadow plays" on the tent wall and ghost stories, someone suggested we do a prank on passing traffic out in the street. The plan was to wrap a shoe box in gift paper, tie string to it and place it in the middle of the road. When a car stopped to pick up the box, we would pull it off the road, with the string, into the bushes where we would be hiding. To add spice to the stunt, we decided to put one of my bearded dragon lizards inside the box! The main group took up position in bushes by the roadside next to the entrance gate of the catholic primary school. Across the road, perched 10 feet up on a tree branch, was me and Marshy. *We* had a birds eye view of the box in the middle of the road. The first car to stop, grabbed the parcel and drove off before we had time to pull the string. I cant imagine the surprise that person got when he opened the box to find my pet lizard inside! We then got another box and wrapped it in Christmas paper, to try again - this time without one of my lizards! Some cars slowed down when they saw the box but kept on driving, until finally, around midnight, a car actually stopped and the driver opened his door and leaned out to grab the package. The boys yanked on the string and the box skittled off the road into the gutter-to the sound of suppressed giggles coming from the bushes. From my vantage point in the tree, I heard the driver swear under his breath, and knowing he'd been scammed, he slammed his door and accelerated away. We all laughed at our success then eagerly awaited our next victim. It didn't take long for the next car to approach, but it came from a different direction and, to our surprise, pulled up - right under the tree that I was in! It was a police car! Marshy and I froze, as our feet, dangling down from our posie on the branch, almost touched the copper's head as he got out of the car. The gang across the road scurried out of the bushes and ran, like rabbits, up the school driveway, illuminated by the police car's spotlight. I heard the officer tell his partner to... "drive around the block"- to head off the kids on the other side of the school - and they sped away. Snapping out of our fear induced comas, Marshy and I jumped out of the tree and ran back to the tent to wait for our escapee felon friends to return. One by one they all did return, having devised a plan to scatter around the neighbourhood to throw off the cops. With tears of relief and laughter, we sat up for most of the remainder of that night - reliving our brush with *The Law* - occasionally stopping to watch a police car go past with it's spotlight coaming the empty streets!

Doin' Time

This song was inspired by a shady character who frequented many of the venues I performed at in Newcastle in the early 1980's. Known as "Tony the Pusher", he'd roam from venue to venue, up and down Hunter street, offering his variety of "medicinal" remedies that where concealed in the linings of the long trench coat that he always wore. Unlike my street gang in Tenambit, he *failed* to avoid the clutches of the law, and spent some time in the Cessnock Correctional Facility!

It's been a long time I had a bottle in my hand
It's been a long time I had a bottle in my hand
It's been a long, long sober time

It's been a long time I had a woman in my arms
It's been a long time since I had a woman in my arms
It's been a long, long lonely time

Cause I've been doin time, doin' time
doin' time for a life of crime

It's been a long time I had a gun by my side
It's been a long time I had a gun by my side
It's been a long, long peaceful time

Cause I've been doin time, doin' time
doin' time for a life of crime

It's been a long time since I've been home
It's been a long time Lord, since I've been home
Well I've spent so much time behind these bars
This jail's the only home I've known

Cause I've been doin time, doin' time
doin' time for a life of crime

Lake Toddles

Summertime in Maitland was unbearably hot-especially in our, tin roofed, fibro walled house, that had neither air conditioning nor insulation. I spent many long hot sleepless nights out on the back verandah-rather than in my stifling bedroom. During the day, jumping under the sprinkler in the back yard was the best form of relief - until my friends and I found Lake Toddles - a water hole in a Paddock, up the hill in Tenambit, not far from Morpeth. One of the older boys named it after his dog. I'm guessing it was a disused quarry that had filled up with rainwater. It had been cut into the side of the hill, leaving abrupt cliffs of about 25 feet high at the top end - which were great to jump off! From our homes, it was a fifteen minute bike ride; up past Tenambit public school and the corner shop, and down one block to where the street ended at a paddock. Climbing through the barbed wire fence and dragging our bikes under, we'd then follow the cow trails, through the waist high Paspalum grass, to "Toddles"- as we called it.

We'd congregate on a sandstone ledge to sun bake and watch each other jump off the cliffs. It was a country club atmosphere- in which we'd lounge about, taking in the fesh air, sunshine, and wonderful view of the farmland on the Hunter River flood plains. Swimming in the waterhole was a bit creepy- as the water was an opaque dark green colour that evoked scenes from a horror movie of the time, called "Monster from the Black Lagoon"! The mood would be lightened when one of the "cliff Jumpers" would surface from the murky depths, screaming in agony because they'd smashed their balls by falling awkwardly onto the waters' surface, and we'd all erupt into hysterical laughter! Others didn't time their run to the cliffs edge correctly, and instead of landing in the deeper water, would land in the mud and reeds at the cliffs base, sometimes stuck up to their thighs until they wriggled themselves free. How we didn't sustain serious injuries was a miracle. The day we decided to frolic around fully naked, turned out to be the most painful experience of all. Apart from my lily white arse getting so badly burnt [for the first time in my life!] that it blistered, the paspalum grass - cuts to my groin and scrotum stung like hell and brought tears of agony that night as I squirmed in my hot bath, vowing I would never go "Hippy" again!

My "Cliff Jumping" infatuation, set a reoccurring theme throughout my life - as I went on to continue jumping off *other* high places - such as the disused brick quarry, not far from "Toddles", called "Bakers". As we all began to acquire our drivers licences and cars, we'd drive there after a session at the nearby "Hunter River Hotel" and egg each other to jump or dive off the 40 foot precipice. I think it was a guy we called "Sheep", who impressed us most, by actually running off the cliffs edge and doing a somersault before diving into the water. He'd obviously had a few more beers, or joints, than the rest of us, who barely worked up enough courage just to jump!

It seemed that the high diving board at

Maitland Baths just wasn't high enough to satisfy my "Jumping Lust"- and I went on to christen other local structures such as; the Clarencetown Bridge and the high arched bridge that connects Tea Gardens to Hawkes Nest. The latter, being my *last* "bridge" jump, as it really hurt! - plus we saw a shark near the bridge just after I got out of the water!

In later years, I went on to do a *parachute jump* at Luskintre with my mate Gluey. Although it was a 2 day course that eventually lead to doing a "Freefall" jump, I was content to survive doing just the one, "Tethered", jump - in which a line connected to the plane, pulled your shute open as you jumped out. That decision was made after I almost landed on a barbed wire fence!

My last memorable jump was off a rocky cliff face on the Greek island of Rhodes, in a town called Lindos. It was the summer of the Chernobyl Nuclear Power Plant Disaster in 1986, and on that occasion I was wearing a very brief pair of "Speedo" swimmers. As I hit the water with my legs opened wide, I almost passed out from the resulting pain to my genitals. Considering the radioactive fallout at that time - together with my *ball crushing* leap - it's a wonder I was able to father three children!

The sensation of "Falling", intrigued me! It exhilarated me, while at the same time, terrified me. A reoccurring dream throughout my whole life, has been of falling and flying. I've heard it said, that if you hit the ground while you're dreaming of falling, you'll die in your sleep. To prevent that, I often say to myself that, "it's only a dream!", while I'm actually having that "Falling" dream!...and, so far, I've survived every one of them.

This song is a falling experience of a different kind - that I haven't always been so lucky to survive!

Falling

I'm falling for you, falling
into your arms that keep calling
how far will I fall this time?
Take my hand I'm blind or I just don't want to see
where your leading me
I hope it wont be

Where I've been before
I've always been the one to say...we can be no more
'till now I've pushed the past aside
hoping each and every tear had dried

I've told myself to let you go
before the whole thing starts to grow
into what I can't undo
but your something new and exciting too
and I'm falling for you

I'm falling for you, falling
I'm calling to you, calling
Calling you to take me by the hand
just take me as I am
and I'll take you anywhere with me

Come into my life and share some time with me
I'm not promising a future that might always be
Let's just see how we go
but right now I know
I'm falling for you

Other Ways to Cool Off

When lake Toddles became more well known - and over crowded with kids from rival gangs in the suburb - our alternative, and more productive way to cool off, was to jump in the creeks and dams at the local golf course - and retrieve golf balls - to sell to the passing golfers. It involved wading in brown, stinking water - up to our waist or necks - and feeling with our toes in the mud - for the white, egg sized, sunken treasure. The mud, our toes were sliding through, often came up to our knees, so we also had to feel for the golf balls bumping against our knee caps or thighs. Sometimes, that *bumping sensation* was also caused by a passing eel or turtle, and I was always amazed at our agility to leap from the creek, in a single bound, when that occurred!

Early in 1971, the Hunter River flooded the area, and the golf course was inundated. My start to high school, at Maitland Marist Brothers, was delayed by one week, that year, as the road to Maitland was cut by the flood waters- So I went down to the golf course to survey the damage. What shocked me most, was the vast numbers of eels that were left stranded on the greens and fairways as the flood subsided. I'm talking hundreds, if not thousands of them - and huge ones that reminded me of boa constrictor snakes! I shuddered, thinking of all the time I had spent in those murky creeks with all of those hideous creatures!

Our golf ball recycling business was quite lucrative for a while, until the resident golf professional demanded we hand over all the balls to him - as his shops' profits were being affected by our elicit trade - and the fact that we were trespassing on private property.

To compensate our loss of pocket money, I started a new venture - with my mate, Jacko- selling tennis balls - that we retrieved from the roof and gutters of the, nearby, Maitland Boys High School. My love of heights, and climbing skills, had me scaling the downpipes at the school - like a miniature Batman or Robin - and climbing onto the roof. Once up there, I would crawl along the gutters edge, harvesting the hundreds of tennis balls that had landed there from wayward handball shots. *Handball* was the game of choice at recess back then. *My* high school even had a, specially designed, handball court, that I often scrapped the skin off my knuckles - on it's concrete walls - and still have the scars! I cringe now, as I picture myself - leaning over the edge of a roof - three stories high - throwing tennis balls down to my mate - 30 metres below - in the cement courtyard! The first raid rewarded us with two garbage bins full of the rubber bounty! There were dozens of white and green tennis balls and numerous black handballs - The green balls being the most popular and profitable. I'm sure I used up *one* of my *nine lives* that day, especially when I manoeuvred myself, by my fingertips, to an isolated section of roof, clinging to the side of a four story brick wall....all for a cache of half a dozen green balls!

Getting back to the water sports....As we got older and gained more independence, we ventured further afield to find somewhere to cool down.

Swimming in the Hunter River, down at Pittnacree road, was one option - if you were game enough to negotiate the bull routs - the small fish with a poisonous barbed spike! - but the most popular alternative was a train ride, on the "Red Rattlers", to Nobby's Beach, in Newcastle. It began with a half hour walk to Victoria street station - followed by a bumpy half hour train ride to Newcastle Station - followed by a ten minute walk through the railway shunting yards - avoiding moving carriages and hostile rail employees - and finally, to the rock wall at Nobbies. After four hours of getting pounded by the surf - frying our skin to a crisp, using baby oil to accelerate the burning process - we'd head for home, repeating the whole journey in reverse. Sitting in the noisy, crowded carriages - our hair and skin caked in drying salt from the hot wind blowing in all the opened windows - the ride back was exhausting. By the time we got home - to where it was even hotter than when we left - we often wondered if it had been worth the effort!

This song was certainly influenced by those long, hot, summer train rides and reminds me of the days spent, sitting on my granma's back steps, counting the endless line of coal carriages passing by on the Northern Line en-route to Newcastle harbour from the upper Hunter Valley mines.

Train Ride '3801'

*Sunday morn, clear blue skies, I got you a big surprise
engine 3801 huffin' and puffin' and ready to run
"all aboard" yells the station master right on time
gotta clear the line*

What a way to spend the day in the country

*Look outside and say goodbye to the harbour, ships and seagulls high
Let the track take you back up the valley to Murrurundi
and along the way stop at Maitland Station for a while
We're gonna go in style*

*What a way to spend the day in the country
You're by my side goin' on a train ride*

*Next stop Singleton, Muswellbrook, Aberdeen for a wee quick look
We'll see a horse or two in Scone, Coal mines on the way back home
Dairy cows wandering all along the riverside
side by side*

*What a way to spend the day in the country
You're by my side goin' on a train ride*

You're by my side goin' on a train ride

goin' on a train ride

The Other Side of the Tracks

When "Marshy's" family moved to another suburb called "Eastville", the rest of the gang saw it as a chance to expand our territory. So we'd mount our bikes and ride down past the golf course, under the railway line, through a drain culvert, up the paddock next to the PGH brickworks, and along some streets, to his house - for a visit.

This was where I got my nickname - of "Dozza". It originated from a girl I met there, whose name was Dorry. She was taller than me, and possibly twice my weight, and I was intrigued at the fact that she did Ballet! This confusing and amusing tale, I told numerous times to my friends at school, who, to my dismay, eventually started calling *Me* Dorry! Kharma is a bitch! But I accepted the tag - as a type of penance for my disrespect for the young lady's chosen hobby. Luckily, I managed to convince my friends to address me by the abbreviated tag of Doz, and eventually, "Dozza". The later of which I am still referred to by many old friends, to this day!

"Eastville" was also a *Housing Commission suburb,* but predominately more so than ours - and was a bit more hard core. So Marshy, being a "local" now, was our ticket *in*. Giving us, but not guaranteeing, immunity from harm. My protection ran out one day when Jacko and I got isolated by a gang - led by a well known thug who'd spent time in juvenile correction centres - who tried to take my bike from me. I'd recently modified the bike with *coat hanger* handle bars and a *dragster* seat with a *sissy bar* - making it an attractive target for the teenage jailbird. As he stood over me, demanding I let him ride my bike, I went into "flight or fight" mode and punched him in the jaw. It stunned him, but only briefly, before he knocked me to the ground and rode off on my pride and joy. I don't know if my feeble punch played a role, but he abandoned the bike just up the street and walked off, laughing with his mates. With tears in my eyes, and Jacko consoling me, I retrieved my bike and quickly rode back home - to where Dad proceeded to give me an impromptu boxing lesson! My dad was a good boxer in his younger days, and could've pursued the sport professionally. That *trait* certainly didn't get passed on to my genes! The only other punch I ever threw in anger was at the Chelsea Picture Theatre in East Maitland, at a matinee, where I managed to get a good one in on a guy who was hasslin' me. Before he could return the favour, the manager threw him out of the theatre for being rowdy!

On the way to Eastville, near the railway underpass, was a cemetery. One night - on a dare from Jacko and the rest of the gang - Marshy and I, camped in it! There are cemeteries of many different denominations, located beside that Northern railway line - one of which boasts the grave of Les Darcey, the famous boxer from Maitland in the early 1900's. Whether it was from the need to show no fear for anything, or just our curiosity in all things macabre, we met there, just on dark, with our sleeping bags and torches. I still can't believe our mothers let us do it, but I suppose they thought we'd chicken out and be home by nine o'clock. We stayed in that cemetery until just before dawn, camped next to a tombstone that dated back to the late 1800's. We didn't attempt to get any sleep, and occupied ourselves by concocting stories about the people whose names adorned the gravestones around us. In the middle of the night, we played a prank on the occasional motorist - driving past on Raymond Terrace Road - by running between the graves with our sleeping bags thrown over us to resemble ghosts. I can assure you that none of those cars slowed down to take a better look!

As early morning approached, a damp fog began drifting in from the nearby swamp, and our mood became much more sombre and apprehensive. We started to feel the guilt of our inappropriate and disrespectful intrusion into this place of "final rest". Just then, our eyes widened and our jaws dropped, as all the marble headstones throughout the whole graveyard began to glow. It was an eerily beautiful scene, but it terrified us! We were preparing to run for our lives when we realised that the headlight of a locomotive freight train, coming slowly down the tracks behind us, was illuminating the graves shrouded in the mist. As frightening as it was at first, it was truly one of the most magical and surreal scenarios I have ever witnessed - and well worth the scare!

'Til this very day, I wonder if we weren't cursed for our sacrilegious activity that night. Those doubts were manifested in *this* song;

Haunted

*On a foggy Sunday evening driving home from work
I called my wife to tell her I'd be late
From a phone just east of Gresford in a town too small to name
Near a house where lived a girl I used to know*

*I'm haunted by the memories
the memories of my youth I hold so dear
yes I'm haunted by the memories
forever young as I grow older year by year*

*In a steel city backstreet on a corner is a pub
I played there every friday night for years
and they danced up on the tables and I sang the songs they loved
But now there's four guys playin' pool for beers*

*And the memories come back to haunt me
drifting in the way they always do
and the fragrance in the air sent to remind me
lingers like the jasmin in the dew*

*On a highway headin' north on a rainy afternoon
the sleepy town of Greta looks the same
Comes an image of a boy up a tree hummin' a tune
hidin' from his granma callin' out his name*

*I'm haunted by the memories
the memories of my youth I hold so dear
yes I'm haunted by the memories
forever young as I grow older year by year*

Winter Games

When the cold westerly winds funnelled down the Hunter Valley in wintertime, our gang hibernated in our cubby houses and tree houses. An architectural masterpiece of the latter was built by the Tenambit boys. It was a two story mansion high up in a huge old pine tree near the public school behind "Belly's"house. Our gang was lucky enough to get invited there sometimes, and we would marvel at its construction.

Not to be outdone, our boys came up with an even more ambitious building project.

It was to be our own estate, complete with streets and private dwellings for each of us, as well as public buildings in which to congregate for meetings or parties. The unique aspect of this megalopolis was that it was all to be located beneath a vast area of lantana and brier bushes that completely infested a gully around the corner from our homes - close to where the East Maitland Swimming Centre is today.

Using an assortment of our dads' gardening implements, we started by cutting holes into the mass of tangled bushes and eventually chiselled out tunnels, deep into the undergrowth. These tunnels would then be hacked out into larger areas, sculptured to form a type of cave with walls and ceiling comprised of dense vegetation. The tunnels or streets, as we called them, had a road base of compressed dirt, compacted from all our crawling around, like commandos, on our knees, elbows and bellies. We named each passageway after the person whose area it was to construct. So there was "Fletcher" street, "Parry" road, "Marsh" lane, "Jackson" avenue and so on. The dwellings and meeting places were lined with grass clippings or hay or cardboard - whatever was available to scrounge from around our homes or the local shopping centre.

The whole concept was remarkable - as we'd spend all day down there - where the rabbits and foxes lived - completely undetected by the passing traffic and nearby residents. Ironically, the street bordering that gully was called "Maize" street and that's exactly what our hidden suburb was - a labyrinth of adventure and privacy where we were free to secretly play and plan our next campaign.

Living today in an age of "helicopter parents", and computer addicted kids that are wrapped in cotton wool for protection, I'm so grateful to have grown up in the 60's. Allowed to take on the risk of cuts and scratches from those briar bush hideouts - not to mention the risk of snake and spider bites from the creatures cohabiting down there with us!

Still, we all survived that wonderful childhood!

Go the Tigers

As I approached my teenage years, the games began to take on a more serious complexion - and one year after Neil Armstrong took that famous step onto the surface of the moon - I stepped boldly onto the football field, with the under 12's, Tenambit Tigers!

It was Rugby League, and no place for the meek or mild mannered. So what was *I* doing there? At four feet-six inches tall, and four stone in weight, I was a fraction of the size of the other boys my age. I was still waiting for that growth spurt my mother kept promising me would happen - and I'm still waiting! Maybe I was trying to prove my courage, but more likely I was just running with the pack - happy to be part of the gang. My main concern was whether I had enough of the "Mongrel" in me, that it took to survive out on that battlefield.

As we ran onto the oval, wearing the black jersey with the big orange V - based on the Sydney Balmain Tigers uniform - I became "Tony The Tiger", from my favourite breakfast cereal [Kellog's Frosted Flakes], and I hoped I would have the courage of *that* tiger to last the whole game. I had two things in my favour; 1; I was a fast runner, so I could get away from danger quickly, and, 2; I was out on the wing - which usually meant I never got to hold the ball, as they rarely passed the ball that far along the back line - and therefore wouldn't be a target to be tackled. My greatest concern was if one of the players on the opposing team decided to run with the ball, in my direction, and it would be up to *me* to stop him! Once again, it was my father who - sensing my impending doom - gave me tips on tackling techniques. *They* turned out to be as useless as the boxing lessons!

Coincidently, one of the guys on our team that year who shared the arena with me, went on in life to establish himself as a talented and well regarded musician - performing with me on my last album nearly 50 years later. His name was Michael Hawke or Hawkie, as we called him. He, like myself, was diminutive in stature, and I wonder if he shared my concerns - of being pulverised - playing that sport!

I survived that first game, and went on to complete the season - in which we ran second last in the competition. The team we came in ahead of, was the Beresfield Bears. The day we defeated *them* has lived on in my mind and dreams - as it was the only time I scored a try. Late in that match, after every other player on my team had scored a try, someone yelled out " give the ball to Gibbo!" and, miraculously, for the first time that season, the ball got passed all the way along the back line to *me* out on the edge of the field. By the time it made it into my hands, I only had to take two steps to cross the try line and put the ball on the ground - without a single hand laid on me by the opposition.

The last game of rugby league that I ever played wasn't as triumphant. Our opposition that day was the East Maitland Griffens, whos star player was a giant of a boy they called "Matey". I got to know "Matey" extremely well that day. You could even say he left a great impression on me. I have an indelible vision of him barrelling toward me with the ball tucked under his arm, his other arm outstretched with his open hand - the size of an oven mitten - coming toward my face. As I squatted and braced for impact - with my arms out wide to encircle his tree stump legs that tapered down to his sprigged, size 12 boots - he shoved my head back like a bolt, and trampled over my prostrate body as if it was a crumpled blanket. I pictured myself being run over by one of those steam rollers with the square spikes on the barrel. It felt as though every drop of oxygen had been pounded from my lungs, and I thought I was never going to breath again. I was too numb to feel any pain, until my lungs finally expanded and sucked in some lifesaving air.

As I was helped from the playing field, I knew I'd given the game my best effort but realised "football" just wasn't my thing. The courage I'd drawn on to play the game would serve me well, later in life, and part of me would *always* remain - a Tenambit Tiger!

The Tenambit Tigers! (Front row; Me & Michael Hawk at either end)

My Fire Will Never Die

There's a fire in my life
and the flames can take their toll
sparks of ambition in my heart
start a yearning in my soul
a burning in my soul

There's a voice in everyone
and it's telling us to try
to give the most of what we have
to achieve before we die
and succeed before we die

Sometimes I feel like I'm wasting my time
but time is on my side
I'll do my best
no more no less
I'm not afraid to cry
My fire will never die

There's a fire in my life
burning out of control
and it's melting down my heart
Burning in my soul

Sometimes I feel like I'm wasting my time
but time is on my side
I'll do my best
damn all the rest
just leave me here to cry
The fire's burning in my eyes

Chapter 2
1960's-1970's

School Daze

Cloaked in Mystery

Sister Eugene was my first teacher. It's no surprise that I should remember someone who absolutely terrified me! Shrouded in long robes from head to toe - black in winter, white in summer - with braided cords around her waist and a huge black ivory crucifix hanging from them - she was a spooky image of an ancient monk in a horror movie!

Saint Josephs' Primary School, East Maitland, was run by the Catholic Church and the Sisters of Mercy nuns. The Church and presbytery, where the priest lived, was on one side of the school, and the Nuns lived on the other side, in the convent. My neighbourhood friend, Jacko, who went to a public school, referred to the nuns as penguins. So whenever I felt intimidated by them, I'd imagine them waddling along the ice somewhere in the south pole - and they didn't seem so scary any more. Another image, stuck in my mind - that made them seem less alien - was the array of underwear I saw on the cloths line in the backyard of the convent, the day I went in to retrieve an errant soccer ball. Flapping on the line, in the wind, like flags, were *rows* of huge, granny sized,

Me in front of the "Chicken Farm School" Hall/barn/ Church on First Communion Day

under pants, and on the next line, huge bras - or what we called "Over the shoulder boulder holders" - that could've easily held a water melon in each cup! Fortified with these humorous images, I managed to tolerate my *unease* with these female *caped crusaders*, for six years. The *following* six years, at High School, were the biggest challenge, dealing with the nuns' male counterparts, the *Marist Brothers*. It was strange how, during those *twelve* years of school - spent with all those *Brothers* and *Sisters* - I never really felt like "one of the family"!

In fairness to the Sisters of Mercy, it was mainly their *appearance* and *lifestyle* that concerned me as a young child. Apart from seeming stern and grumpy most of the time, they did have a caring nature, and I sensed they were good people. Fifteen years later, when I returned to the school to teach guitar, I was re acquainted with Sister Eugene and my former 6th class teacher, Sister Bonaventure. The *habit gowns* had been replaced with civilian clothes, and they lived and worked out in the community, making them seem much more personable. My *guitar teaching* didn't last more than a few months, as my discipline skills - with the kids - left a lot to be desired. Although I got on well with my students, there was more than one occasion I had to be rescued by the principal when the class erupted into chaos. I figured I was just making *music lessons* too much fun for them!

The Chicken Farm

Apart from my chilling encounter with the nuns my first year of school, in kindergarten, was unremarkable. My two main fond memories there, are of "Nap Time" and painting pictures. The *real* school adventure, began the following year, when I was relocated to the new infants school in Tenambit. It was called Saint Marys', and was just around the corner from my home. This meant I could walk to school every day, which I did with a proud feeling of independence. I enjoyed getting to school early - before the teachers and all the other kids - so that I could explore the grounds and buildings. You see, the *big attraction* of *this* school, was that it was an old Farm House! - With a barn! - That used to house chickens! The main homestead was a huge federation style building - that the rooms had been converted to classrooms and offices - and the bottom floor of the two story barn was an assembly hall - also used for church services on Sundays. The upper floor of the barn wasn't used for anything - but I would often hide up there, playing in the dusty remains of hay and chicken feathers!

The two years I spent at this school were probably the most enjoyable of my whole educational journey! Every day was like a "farm stay" experience! The playgrounds were like small paddocks where we could "freerange" enclosed by rustic, rickety, barbed wire fences. There were remnants of orchirds where we could pick mandarins, nectarines, peaches and mulberries and, best of all, there was rusty old farm machinery lying around to be played on!

In the centre courtyard was a huge Moreton Bay fig tree with a bench seat fully encompassing its base - that was always my first challenge to climb on arrival in the morning.

One day at lunchtime, I found a ladder, and climbed up into a Manhole in the ceiling of the homestead, with another boy. We were both severely chastised by one of the nuns who saw the ladder and climbed up to find us, sitting on the dirty rafters in the musty hot roof cavity. On interrogation, I said I just followed the other boy up there to see what he was doing, and she replied with the classic question…"would you jump off a cliff if the other boy did?" and I remember thinking…"of course not, that wouldn't be as much *fun* as climbing up into a ceiling!"

Two decades later my infatuation with roof spaces took a more sinister direction as-in the words of that nun-I, metaphorically, "jumped off another cliff" following the advice of a friend to grow my own crop of pot up in the attic! Probably the riskiest and most foolish activity I ever undertook that, thankfully, was a complete failure! My horticultural skills were as deficient as my ability to make wise, moral, life choices and subsequently the crop yielded no more than a small sandwich bag of weed that was about as potent as a handful of dried lawn clippings! My decision to abandon the project came late one night as I was putting my garbage bin out on the kerb for collection the following day. As I turned to walk back into my yard I noticed an eerie purple glow emanating from the rain gutters that enclosed the perimeter of my roof – caused by the ultra violet lights that were fuelling the growth of my plants up in the rafters. I instantly realised that if a police helicopter should happen to fly over my house at night my secret illegal activity would be obvious to them – standing out like a beacon in the blackened suburbs – looking like the fluorescent disco dance floor in the John Travolta movie, Saturday Night Fever! Motivated by paranoia I frantically proceeded to dismantle the operation and bring it all back down through the manhole in the bathroom ceiling. My final reckoning came when I slipped off the top of the ladder while carrying a thirty kilogram pot of soil and landed on my back on the tiled floor - narrowly avoiding splitting my skull on the porcelain toilet bowl. The pile of dirt that landed on the floor, before I did, probably saved me from breaking my back! As I lay there, stunned and winded, staring up at the manhole twelve feet above me, the prophetic words the nun had lectured me with [as a child] spun around my head like the stars and chirping birds in a Bugs Bunny cartoon scene!

I had my first "Showbiz" experience, in the courtyard of that quaint and unique little school. It was December 1965, and the teachers organised a nativity play for Christmas. I was one of the three wise men, bearing gifts for baby Jesus in the manger. It was a magical, warm, summer night, and standing on the stage that adjoined the homestead verandah, I nervously faced the audience of parents - sitting in rows of chairs under the Moreton Bay fig tree that had been adorned in coloured lights. I still sense the excitement I felt from that brief performance, and the audiences' enthusiastic applause and laughter, and am sure it planted the seed for my life's future career - in entertainment and all it's associated vices!

Granma's house circa 2013

Grandma's Feather Bed

I clearly remember my last day at Saint Mary's Primary School in Tenambit - a dark, stormy day, with torrential rain in the afternoon. The rain was so heavy I couldn't walk home, so my mother picked me up in our black EK Holden, with the yellow and black number plates CDS-127. [Funny how I still remember *that* registration number! Especially as I can't even remember my *current* vehicles' registration!]. As I stood staring out of the large front window of the homestead building, I was particularly excited this afternoon to be getting picked up. Not just because it was a rare event, and not just because it was the start of the Christmas Holidays, but because I was being driven to Greta, where I would spend a few weeks with my Grandmother. My dad's mother, Elsie, or as I knew her; "Granma Gibbons".

Going to Granma's, for me, was like going back in history to the early settler times. Even her house resembled an early settlers cottage - clad in rough weather boards, painted yellow, with a rusty corrugated iron roof that had a bull nose awning over the front verandah. Two rough brick chimneys clung precariously to the side of the house, near which, was a slightly leaning garage - come work shed - also constructed completely of corrugated iron. At the back of the house was a small laundry building, and way down in the middle of the large back yard was a cute little lavatory-housing a toilet seat atop a steel drum. My grandmother used to dig holes around the yard to bury the contents of that drum, until a collection service was arranged where a council worker would come and empty the drum into a truck - carrying it bravely on his shoulders! Although she had electricity connected to the house, we often lit candles and kerosene lamps for lighting at night - to play Eucha, Gin Rummy, Poker, or Dominoes - while listening to the Dad and Dave show on a Baker light Radio. We would go to bed after the card games and continue to listen to the radio. Her bed had ornate brass bed heads with decorative baubles that I would spin with my fingers as I lay at the foot of the bed with granma's feet beside me. There, I could look out the window at the stars and moon as I fell asleep. She would often warn me not to stare at the moon for too long or I'd get "Moon Blindness"! A condition that intrigued me and concerned me enough to follow her advice. I vaguely remember seeing feathers under the bed sometimes, and many years later when John Denver's song called Granma's Feather Bed became a permanent fixture in my repertoire, it always evoked that blissful childhood bedtime scenario.

On rare occasions, she would play the harmonica for me, and I would try to imitate her by playing tunes on a comb with Tally Ho cigarette paper pressed to it – buzzing the tune with my lips – it sounded like a Kazoo. My uncle Micky taught me that trick - and supplied the Tally Ho's - when he occasionally dropped in to see his mother. He would amuse me by singing funny songs, like…"aba daba daba said the monkey to the chimp" or "Hang down your head Tom Dooley" - in his gruff, low, voice, that was a mixture of Louis Armstrong and Lee Marvin. His unique timbre was attributable to the huge scare that ran across his throat, from ear to ear! He delighted in watching me squirm, as he told the story of the surgery he'd undergone [probably for throat cancer] and how the nurses would become sick when they had to clean and dress the oozing wound! I eventually progressed from Uncle Mickey's home made kazoo and taught myself to play the harmonica - backwards, apparently, with the low notes on my right leading up to the high notes on my left - but could never master the technique of using my tongue to create a rhythm, like my grandmother did.

There was an open fire place in the lounge room which burned continuously in wintertime, and she cooked on a wood burning stove in the kitchen. Hot water for bathing and washing clothes, also came from wood burning heaters. Washing clothes, involved transferring items from the hot copper tub into concrete basins, using a long smooth white stick - coloured by the years of use with bleach. They were then rung out, by feeding them through two rollers that had to be hand wound using a big winding handle. The clothes lines were similar to those in our back yard - two wires strung across the width of the back yard supported by "Jesus Posts" - except granma had fashioned two long tree branches, with forks at the end, to support the lines in the middle.

Her house was on the outskirts of town, on the other side of the rail line, not far from Greta railway station and the old "migrant camp" - used to house immigrants after the second world war. It was right on the edge of the Bush, and she had worn a track from her front gate into that bush from walking with her dogs - carrying bags of household rubbish to throw down a disused mine shaft that had caved in. I loved going on those bush walks with her and the two Golden Cocker spaniels named Tibby and Tammy. The collapsed mine shaft was about five hundred feet into the bush, and she would always tell me to be careful as we approached the circular, fifteen feet wide, crater, with it's sheer earthen walls that descended into darkness. She'd let me drop the garbage bags into the chasm, and it would seem to take an eternity to hear the thud as they hit the bottom of the mine shaft, countless feet below. I used to shudder thinking about my fate if I fell into that hole! The new Hunter Valley Free way passes right through that area of bushland now, and the engineers constructing the road had to pour concrete into the sink holes and mine shafts, that litter the area, to make the roadway more stable.

Our bush walks would then continue to collect kindling and firewood, listening to the magpies and bell birds, and watching out for snakes, lizards and the myriad of other "bitey" creatures! Twenty five years later, while taking my young children for walks in the bush near our house in Belmont, it's easy to see where the inspiration originated for this song...

Walkin' Track

At the end of the street is a walkin' track
Winding it's way through the memories that take me back
Hearin' birds in the trees doin' what they should
It's just a walk in the bush but it sure feels good.

Magpie high in a tree, skink lizard on a log
Tadpole swimmin' in a puddle, gonna soon be a frog
Skippin' stones on the lake as a yacht sails by
Headin' home as the sun sinks low in the sky.

Walkin' track from the ridge down to the water
Time out with the trees to put my life in order
And as I turn my gaze
From the sun's last rays
They point me back
Home along the walkin' track.

So many years since I moved away
I see the company had it's say
Filled in the gullies and they tarred the clay
The trees are gone but the memories stay

At the end of the street is a new estate
Cleared quarter acre lots and the views are great
I took a walk to the end of the cul-de-sac
I looked around but I couldn't find the walkin' track.

Walkin' track from the ridge down to the water
Time out with the trees to put my life in order
And as I turn my gaze
From the sun's last rays
They point me back
Home along the walkin' track.

One day, on a long walk to climb the nearby hill called mount "Molly Morgan", we came across a shanty hut made of corrugated iron and branches. Granma said it must have been made by the man who came knocking on her door a few days earlier, asking for food. She recalled how there used to be lots of drifters like him during the Great Depression. Recalling this, makes me realise the hard times she lived through in the 1930's and '40's. Her greatest hardship must have been the death of her husband, Hugh, at that time. He fell into a collapsed mine shaft and drowned in the water at the bottom. A search was mounted for him in the Anvil Creek area, not far from his home, and the incident was reported in the Maitland Mercury at the time. My family didn't tell me any more than it could have been an accident related to alcohol or possibly suicide. After all, it was during the great depression and he did have seven children and a wife to support. It's always been one of those "skeleton in the closet" mysteries, that most families have, and I'll probably never know the full story. My father was an infant at the time so he never got to know his father – a possible reason for his awkwardness in our relationship. I find it incredibly ironic that Granma threw her garbage down one of those mine *sink holes* that her husband died in! Maybe it was her way of cursing *them* for taking her husband! Or maybe she was cursing *him* for leaving her and the children to fend for themselves in those terribly hard times. Either way it now becomes clear to me why those bush walks had such a ritualistic and special purpose!

I never got to know my other grandfather either, as he died shortly after I was born. My mother always said I would've loved her father, Percy, as he was a beautiful soul and also a musician. He played piano for the "Silent Movie" shows that travelled from town to town in a horse drawn cart, performing in local halls in the 1920's. I was dumbfounded the day my mother confided in a whisper to me that Percy probably had a "lady friend" in each of those towns he toured through! This made me feel a great affinity with him because, apart from the mode of transport, it was similar to my performing life, spent on the road, playing town to town!

Another amazing story my mother often told me was how her father rode his push bike all the way from Greta to Tea Gardens, just to go fishing, so he could feed his family through the lean post depression years. It's a story I've always found hard to believe - as much as I also love bike riding and fishing - but I never argued the point with her, so as to leave him up on that pedestal where she had placed him in her heart.

Mum's mother, Pearl, for a brief time, lived right next door to granma Gibbons, so I would feel obliged to go over and spend some time with her too. She was a bit too stern for my liking and I wasn't sure if she cared for a lot of my company so my visits were brief. I sometimes wondered if she got jealous of my other grandmother who I obviously favoured. A macabre air of mystery intrigued me about her as the ring finger on her left hand was missing. The story she told of how she lost it, impressed me even more. Many years earlier, she was attending a function at the RSL hall in Greta that had an ornate iron picket fence at the entrance, and as she was exiting the building she slipped on the steps at the main gate. To save her from falling on the concrete path, she reached out for the top of one of the spiked pickets and her wedding ring got impaled on it. As she continued to fall, the wedding ring, bearing all her weight, sliced through her finger and all but tore it off! That story certainly earned her my admiration, and I'm sure my visit to her, the day she told it, was longer than usual!

Sadly, Pearl developed a type of *anxiety based dementia* that made her even less amiable, and although my mother cared for her for quite some time, she eventually had to be placed in a nursing home. I was mortified to learn that Electro Shock Therapy was commonly practised on disorders of the kind she had back then. Sadder still, is that, as I write this now, my *own* mother is in an aged care facility with a similar type of dementia. As I grieve for my mother, I also fear what might lay ahead for me or my sisters in *our* senior years.

Although the words of this song were written with Pearl in mind, I cant help but sense a feeling of foreboding - despite the fact that I wrote it at an age when I couldn't even imagine being old!

Perce Charnock standing in front of picture show truck. Rio Grand movie on poster.

BODY IN WELL

Search Party's Find

GRETA MAN

GRETA, Wednesday.
A search by 200 Greta residents ended with tragic suddenness at noon to-day, when, from a 40ft well, a mile from his home, the body of Hugh Gibbons (48), of Anvil Creek, was drawn to the surface with grappling irons.

Gibbons, who was a married man with seven children, had been missing from his home since 9.30 a.m. yesterday. When he failed to return yesterday afternoon, a search was carried out until dark.

This morning a search party of about 200 residents was organised by Constable Jones and commenced to scour the scrub country between Greta and Cessnock in an endeavour to locate the missing man.

A large area had been covered and many waterholes dragged before the well, which is situated between Greta and Allandale, was examined and the body recovered by Constable Jones.

Gibbons is stated to have been in ill health for some time.

Notice of my grandfather's death. Maitland Mercury Wednesday, 4th of December 1935

Too Old to Be

Who'll care for me
now I'm too old to see
Too old to be told
Too old to be

Living alone
in this shell of a home
sheltered by the walls
and the memories they've known

Why do I see you all turning from me?
my family and friends leave my life as it ends
Left to decay with the nurses you pay
what did I do, didn't I care for you?

Why are you so unkind?
Am I loosing my mind?
Where's all the love I gave you in my prime?
Please don't put me away
I'm so scared won't you stay
I won't keep you long
Soon I'll be gone

Once I was young, now I am old
Once I could tell, now I am told
Once I could sing, now only sigh
Once I could live, …...................

Who'll care for me?
Now I'm too old to see
Too old to be told
Too old
Too old
Too old
To be.

The Lemon song [Devil's Music]

The Farmhouse school in Tenambit, before more classrooms were built, only taught kids up to second class, so we were all sent back down to Saint Josephs' primary to complete years 3,4,5 and 6. It was a grim, unattractive place for me after the utopian environment at the "chook farm" school. It had a monotonous brick building, housing 5 identical classrooms, under which, were the toilets, lunch rooms and canteen or "Tuck shop" as we called it. The lunch rooms and toilets always smelt of stale sandwiches and disinfectant - which wasn't conducive to a pleasant dining experience at recess! Add that to the *legendary ritual* of drinking the free milk that had been delivered and left out in the sun for two hours, and it probably explains my obsession with food hygiene and refrigeration!

The primary school years rolled by, and although I did fairly well in scholastic activities, my fondest memories are of playing at lunchtime in the huge grassed area behind the main building. It was bordered by the adjacent public schools' playground where there would often be confrontational shouting matches between the opposing students. Each group yelling to the other…"go home Catholics"…and "go home Publics"—occasionally punctuated with a thrown rock or stick. Each spring, we would be attacked by nesting magpies in that playground - and many a pecked head had to be patched up in the sick bay. One time, after receiving a beak puncture to my scalp, I developed a forward tumble technique while running away from a "Maggie", which resulted in the soles of my shoes taking the brunt of the attack. This stunt received howls of admiration from my school mates and even from some of the kids in the enemy school yard.

My taste and interest in music began to develop in these years, strongly influenced by my sister, Lynette, and her growing collection of 45RPM vinyl records. Up until then I'd been singing along with The Beatles and The Monkees, mainly due to the TV shows and cartoons that had been developed around their fame and success. Lynettes' collection had an edgier sound to what I'd been hearing, and included; The Troggs, The Kinks, The Easybeats and The Animals - but the day she put on Led Zeppelin, playing "Whole Lotta Love", changed me forever! As Robert Plant's voice lasered my eardrums, and I asked.. "who is that *woman* singing", I couldn't believe it when she laughed and said.. "it's a guy!". That was it. There and then, I wanted to be a rock singer!

When you're in sixth class at a Catholic School run by Sisters of Mercy Nuns, and it's "show and tell" day - apart from bringing in a loaded shotgun - probably the worst thing you could bring is a Led Zeppelin album! The next worst thing you could do is play the record on the class stereo system with the volume up full boar so that the whole school hears the lyrics….*"squeeze me baby, 'til the juice runs down my leg"*!

My fall from grace with the nun's gained further momentum that year when I, along with a few other rebel boys, hid in our classroom while the rest of the school students and teachers boarded buses to go to the School Swimming Carnival over at Maitland Baths. Our absence was noticed at the pool hours later, and the school secretary, upon being notified to search the school, found us listening to my Led Zeppelin album in room six.

    At the end of that year, as I walked out of the schools' gates for the last time - books under one arm, Led Zeppelin under the other - I sensed I was moving on to a new experience that was *more* than just *starting high school*!

Straying from the Fold

Up until now I had obediently gone to church every Sunday with my mother and sisters, occasionally managing to stay home and read the comics from the Sunday papers in bed with my dad. How *he* was excused from church attendance always puzzled me.

I was beginning to question where I fitted in with the Catholic Religion and although I sensed my own spirituality, something inside me resented the "Man Made" aspect of Church. My unease and distrust of Institutions, in general, would play a role in my life's direction from that time on. Whether the church influenced this strange aspect of my personality, is hard to say - but it certainly determined the level of education and formal training I would attain in life, in what ever field I chose to follow. I always had a sense of my inner self being like a primitive, fiercely independent, *maverick* - wanting to achieve everything by himself – in his own way! Determined to do things *"My Way"*, I often visualised a Cave-Man trying to survive on his own and inventing his own methods to do so.

Even at a young age, something disturbed me about, what seemed like, an unnatural lifestyle choice of the cloistered. The celibate priests, nuns and brothers - so influential in my formative years.

As suspicious as I was of the clergy at that time, most of them seemed nice enough and approachable - apart from some of the older priests who I found to be more pious and arrogant. It surprised me when I heard of our parish priest being jailed for child sex offences. He used to visit our elderly neighbour when she was ill, and he seemed the most genuine of all I'd met. He later died in prison of illness himself. A recent court case saw charges laid against a senior clergyman for covering up that priest's crimes against a boy who attended my primary school a few years after I'd been there.

The closest I came to feeling like *"one of the flock"* was the time I helped out with "alter boy" duties at Saint Joseph's Church. It was like a *trial run* to see if I wanted to be a *regular* alter-boy, and I *did* feel very special doing it. Looking back now, I think it was more the *"Theatrics"* of being on a type of stage [being the alter] that appealed to me, more than the spiritual aspect of the event! It was at that time, after a bout of tonsillitis that had me absent from school for quite some time, I noticed everyone in mass making the sign of the cross in a different way to what I'd been taught. Instead of taping their forehead, bellybutton and left and right shoulder with their fore finger, they seemed to be touching their forehead, chin and heart with their thumb, using a circular motion as if rubbing something on those parts. This ritual was always just before my least favourite part of the ceremony - when we would all kneel down for what seemed like an eternity as the priest slowly rambled on and we all shuffled uncomfortably from one aching knee to the other! I often became nauseous kneeling there with my head resting on the back of the pew in front of me, giving the appearance of being deep in prayer but actually praying for the priest to hurry up before I passed out or vomited! Sometimes I would get up and walk outside for fresh air before either of those happened. So with the mystery of the new hand gestures [that was never explained to me] and my propensity for feinting spells, I began to loose interest in the Eucharistic formalities of the Catholic Religion and eventually stopped going to church - whenever it could be avoided.

It would be over ten years later that I managed to put my conflicted and rebellious thoughts on the Catholic religion into a song, called *"Pray in My Own Time"* and, although it simmers with teenage angst, it still basically sums up my feelings on the subject.

It was at church, however, that I really became aware of my singing voice. I loved to hear it echoing throughout that cavernous building with the incredibly high arched ceiling. At one of our school masses I completely opened up my vocal chords in one of the more anthemic hymns and went straight into the next verse as loud as I could, not realising that everyone else had stopped singing. As I clamped my wide opened jaws shut I heard my last words ["Oh Lord"] echoing right through the rafters and felt my *red* face burning with embarrassment as all the kids turned to look at me, giggling in their pews! Years later, at my gigs, I always preferred the reverb/echoe on my microphone to be on the "Chuch/Hall" setting!

In our later teenage years, a few of my old Catholic school friends would go to the midnight mass on Christmas Eve after "closing time" at the Hunter River Hotel, to belt out Christmas Carols. It was great fun singing all those old classic Christmas songs that reminded us of our childhood - although it did seem a bit sacrilegious to be up the back of the church as drunk as monkeys and as rowdy as football fans at a grand final! In years to come I would return to that church to sing wedding songs as a paid performer. My last performance there, however, was sadly to sing a song I'd written to honour my dad at his funeral. I'd pre recorded it to be played through the church's public address system as I knew I'd be too emotional to perform it live.

Pray in My Own Time

I was raised to bear my cross like every Christian boy
but I refused to play their game like a plastic wind-up toy
I turned my back and refused to drift along
but who can say I'm wrong?

Now I agree with the laws God made and I live the best I can
but if I don't chose to worship Him am I any less a man?
I didn't ask for life and I don't reach for His hand.
He should understand.

I'll pray in my own time
and if I'm heard or not how can I tell?
I'll build a church up in my mind
and if the Lord don't like it I can burn in hell

God gave us life and a choice to live the way we wanted to
but then he gave us laws on slabs of stone for us to pay heed to
and if you break his laws your chance with him is through.
What can you do?

I'll pray in my own time
and if I'm heard or not how can I tell?
I'll build a church up in my mind
and if the Lord don't like it I can burn in hell.

The Lord don't know what he's gonna do with my ungrateful soul.
Put me on his cross to feel the pain
that he went through, even though he knew
there would be many like me
who would not pay their fee

Now Sunday saints and weekday snakes can sit beside his cross
while I walk by and live my life prepared to pay the cost
I've found myself and don't need the faith I've lost.
I'll pay the cost

As I pray in my own time
and if I'm heard or not how can I tell?
I'll build that church up in my mind
and if the Lord don't like it I can burn in hell

The High School Years

TONY GIBBONS —
"The rest may reason & welcome; 'tis we musicians know". (Browning)

A member of the School Council, Tony's other involvements ranged over golf, debating and public speaking, and his interests extend to body surfing and music (including at least one appearance at a senior social). Future plans: accountancy and "good clean living".

From Sisters to Brothers

1971 saw me enter high school at Maitland Marist Brothers - relieving me of the strange ways of the "Nuns" at primary school but introducing me to the even more bizarre lifestyle and customs of the "Brothers"! The layout of the high school was similar to the primary school - in that it was flanked by the Brothers residents on one side and the clergy residents on the other, the clergy in this case being the Bishop of the Maitland Diocese. The church that bordered the school on the other boundary was referred to as The Cathedral, which impressed upon me the significance of this whole area of Holy real estate - The *Grand Central* of the Catholic Organisation for the Hunter Valley region. The actual school building was a two story brick structure that had undergone various additions, some of which were supported on concrete pillars and protruded out over the main courtyard. The concrete and bitumen surfaced courtyard was the main assembly and recreational area and often reminded me of the exercise yards I'd seen in old prison movies. Recess and lunchtime would see us loitering around the *tuckshop* or in the shade under the third form extension wing, while the more active would be down at the cricket nets that bordered onto High street or playing handball in the concrete handball court beside the brothers residence. On the blisteringly hot summer days we would just sit on the wooden benches under the trees in the corner near the Bishop's house. On days that the cricket nets weren't being used we'd go and stand at the back of the nets and look through the wire with our fingers hooked on either side of our faces pressed against the hexagonal holes, peering out into the street like forlorn prisoners longing for freedom. Ironically, directly across the road was the Doc & Doris Hotel which was the meeting place for the local *bikie gang - The Gladiators -* or, as we called them - *The Glads* - The image of a *bikie* being the epitome of unbridled freedom.

One hilarious school assembly comes to mind when the Glads were all gathered outside the pub - beers in hand, looking across High street at us being addressed by the principal - yelling out taunts and insults. After trying to ignore them for a while, he finally retorted very loudly and clearly over the public address system that we should take no notice of the *Gladioli's – his mocking term for their organisation* - and that we should strive to do more with our lives than what they have. Apart from being surprised at his defiance, we were even more excited to think that he might get a bashing from them for his disrespect.

Although the Nuns had ruled with a firm hand, it was mild compared to level and methods of discipline that the Brothers applied - which only served to fuel my simmering rebelliousness! I had my first taste of *"The Cane"* that year—receiving six burning whacks of it on the tips of the fingers of each hand - from Brother Bead, who was renowned for his lethal accuracy and athletic strength with the weapon! The searing pain from that corporal punishment lasted many days and I avoided ever being punished that way again, not by improving my behaviour, but by becoming more adept at not being caught!

The school had strict uniform and grooming codes, one being that the hair length was not to exceed the shirt collar at the back of the neck. My way of defying that rule was to simply keep trimming my hair length when it reached the collar but not to thin it out. As a result my head of unruly black curls just got thicker and thicker, eventually resembling a woolly helmet that tumbled over my eyes and ears! On one morning assembly when there was a *Hair and Uniform inspection* I, along with several other *mop head* radicals, were told to leave the school grounds and not return until our hair was cut. We were supposed to go straight to the Barber shop up the road, that was aware of the school's hair regulations, and get shawn. I misunderstood that instruction and caught the next bus home where I got my mother to simply trim the collar section of my locks as usual, and didn't return to school until the next day, where I was further chastised for not obeying the Principals instructions!

Brother Ralph usually did the "hair and uniform" inspection. He ran the Cadets at the school—which was akin to military training complete with army uniforms and even 303 rifles. He played the role of *sergeant major* superbly—with his robust physique, bulldog face and shaved head. We nicknamed him "Spike". He wasn't one to be *messed* with! The principal of the school was Brother Nestor - who was also not one to *toy* with! His notoriety came from his past experience of being a proficient boxer in his youth. There was a rumour that he had settled a disciplinary matter with one of the students - a tough kid from Kurri Kurri who also did boxing - by having a punch-up with him in his office. Wether true or not, it certainly made for a good yarn around the school yard and added to the contempt that most of the students held for him. I had a more *intellectual run-in* with him when I was in Forth Form. I was summoned to his office one morning after submitting an essay I'd written, outlining the shortcomings of the teaching skills of my economics/commerce teacher, Mr Blakeny. In it, I explained how he was just walking into the classroom and telling us to read a certain chapter of our text book, then write an essay about that chapter, while he sat at his desk, reading a book. I suggested that I and my fellow students would learn more on the subject if he adopted a more pro-active teaching style by engaging with the class more often. Part of my motive in doing this was genuine, but mostly I was just tired of writing essays in all of his classes. As I stood before Brother Nestor in his office that morning, part of me was fortified and defiant, but another part of me was "shitting in my pants" and terrified that I was going to receive a "*jaw breaking*" "*left hook*" from him. As it turned out, there was *no* physical assault, but as he spat out the words..."WHO DO YOU THINK YOU ARE!" - with pure disdain and anger that seemed to come from a very dark place within him - I reeled back, just as though his knuckles *had* ploughed into my face. That encounter frightened and disturbed me. Not because I was chastised and belittled. I fully accepted I was in the wrong. It was something sinister I saw inside that man, as his eyes bulged while he roared out his condemnation of me. It disturbed me so much that I never felt comfortable in his presence for my three remaining years at high school. Many years later, when I was in my thirties, I was shocked, but not totally surprised, to hear that Brother Nestor had been sent to jail for child molestation crimes that he had committed earlier in his teaching career at another school. It's strange how you can have a *gut* feeling about someone. You just *know* something isn't quite right or *real* about them. I wrote down my concerns about *this*, sometime during those senior school years;

Plastic Man.

*I know a plastic man
moulding his plastic plan
playing with his toys all day
but should people be treated that way?*

*Plastic people all the same
They're the toy
Life's a game*

*. Plastic smiles are fake
plastic friends are easy to make
mould yourself into the day
the plastic man likes it that way*

*Plastic is brittle and hard
or soft and bendable
we live behind a plastic fascade
love is mend-able*

*Plastic people all the same
we're the toys
Life's a game*

*I know a plastic man
moulding a plastic plan
I like to see
Plastic melt*

The Band!

1973 was *the* year of discovery for me. I was 14 and in third form. I was enjoying most subjects at school, especially Geography, Social Studies and English. I was interested in what was happening around the world - The war in Vietnam and why Australia was involved, the Cold War and the threat of nuclear war, the Space Race, Watergate and that sleezy president Richard Nixon - and, of course, Music - mainly Rock Music. Deep purple, Led Zeppelin, Uriah Heap, Black Sabbath, Billy Thorpe and the Aztecs were some of the favourites in my growing record collection. My life was exploding with information while my face was exploding with pimples. My interest in sport also widened, even to the point of riding my bike all the way to Maitland Park on Saturday afternoons to watch the girls' Netball and Hockey matches. No doubt encouraged by my growing attraction to the female figure - especially those long legs in those short sports skirts!

I'd heard that three boys in my year had formed a rock band but didn't have a singer, so I went along to watch them practise. Mark Johns [Johnsie] was on lead guitar, Glen Hill [Hilly] on bass and Terry Lantry [Tex] on drums. They were playing Honky Tonk Woman by the Stones - One of my favourites! - So I offered to step in and sing it. I knew all the lyrics to that one, and did ok, so they tried me on some more songs that I also knew most of the lyrics to - such as Tootie Fruity, Lucille and Hound Dog by Little Richard and, of course, Johnny B. Goode by Chuck Berry. Apart from *jumping off bridges*, it was the most liberating experience I had ever had! It was like riding a huge wave, propelled by the power and energy of those loud electric guitars and drums. I felt big - and strong - and untouchable. I was hooked. And, I was *in*. I was a singer in a rock'n'roll band! Ironically, that audition took place in a small class room located near the cricket nets that I used to peer out of and long for freedom. Becoming the singer in this band gave me *that* freedom! Even more surprising was that the school allowed us to use the classroom for practising at lunchtime. Not that they condoned the loud, unruly rock music [Devil's music!] and the long hair that came with it, but I can only figure they were giving the appearance of being supportive of an interest in the arts, albeit one of the lower forms! If anything, I felt like we were simply tolerated by the school's administrators but certainly not encouraged, to any degree. I looked on with a tinge of jealousy a few years later when another group of young boys formed a rock band and were actually supported and promoted by the school - to the extent of buying them equipment and entering them in competitions. But it *was* a change for the good. The guitarist in that band was Michael Punch. One of the most talented, skilled and unassuming musicians I know. Almost ten years later I shared the stage with Punchy and his band - The Colours - along with Tony Heads on keyboards [another mentor of mine and family friend who sold me my first P.A system], Dave Carter on bass and Craig Lancaster on drums. We did a brief tour of Hunter venues with *me* as the *featured artist* but I felt totally inadequate amidst that array of talent!

Regardless of the lack of support from the

school, our band, called "Atacama", at first, and eventually, "Khan" - names derived from our geography and history classes - battled on, under our own steam. We bought our own equipment and instruments with our pocket money or loans from our parents. We arranged halls or garages to practise in. We booked our own gigs and, since we were too young to drive, our parents or older siblings provided transport to our rehearsals and gigs. We even caught a train to Newcastle one time to hire some speakers from Mick Sampson (BAEZ Amplifiers) to use at a Maitland Town Hall dance, returning them the next day, also by train! The hired speakers were lucky to survive that gig, as were we, due to the fact that the *Glads* showed up, ready to smash some heads - the *band* being the prime target! We were tipped off by a friend, who new some of the bikies, and made an early exit via the rear stage door. Surviving that night taught me a valuable lesson in learning to read the audience! A skill that, in my later years as a solo performer, far outweighed my singing or instrumental ability but was an integral part of my performances. I spent much of my performances getting to know my audience and letting them get to know me. The real me. Strengths *and* weaknesses. Not some fake *Ëntertainer*" personality. I figured it would compensate for any deficiencies in my musical ability and take some pressure off me - and it worked. Most of my audiences were very kind to me and I often left a gig feeling like I'd spent an evening with friends.

On another occasion, we played support act to a local band that was making a name for itself in Sydney. They were called "A Rabbit" and their rhythm guitarist was Mark Tinson, my sisters friend. We saw it as a great opportunity to make a name for ourselves, so, to stand out on stage, we had our mothers make special costumes for us - made out of brightly coloured fabrics such as satin and velvet, into tightly fitting pants with bellbottoms and long flared sleeves on the shirts. My shirt had a sparkly lightning bolt sewed to the front—like David Bowie's Alladin Sane. Contrary to "standing out", we just blended in with the main act, as their costumes were the same as ours - but more professionally made! - so we were quickly forgotten when we left the stage after our short set. We stayed to watch them perform and were awed by their power and ability to totally rock the place, which, by the way, was the Maitland Town Hall, again, and the Glads did make an appearance, again, and I'm fairly sure there was an all-in brawl - *again*!

Maitland Town Hall also had a more romantic connotation for me around that time. At the side of the main building was an old wooden stable with a loft above it. Each morning before school I, along with some of my mates, would meet up with some girls from the nearby Dominican Convent Girls High School and climb up into the loft and pair off for a bit of kiss and cuddle. Innocent fun at our tender ages of 14 and 15 but a crime of severe consequences if the Nuns or Brothers had found us out! Our biggest crime, however, was in pretending to be gentlemen, standing back and allowing the girls to climb the ladder to the loft, before us, watching them ascending the rungs in their skirts!

We were a devoted bunch of young "rock stars" - rehearsing most weekends and school holidays. Apart from blasting the neighbours in my dad's garage, we hired halls, such as the Kitchener Community Hall near Cessnock. It's remoteness was an advantage to make as much noise as we wanted, but the ninety minute drive - once to drop me off in the morning and then to pick me up in the afternoon - on a Sunday, must have been a pain in the arse for my parents. Another venue we practised in was the hall behind the Methodist Church, across from our school. It's biggest disadvantage was it's proximity to the Doc & Doris hotel and that the Glad's would come over and start requesting songs. Another lesson in pleasing the crowd! - to avoid a bashing or having our equipment trashed! Our guitarist, Johnsie, was somewhat of a prodigy. Not so much due to natural ability, but his intense determination and focus on mastering what he played. I was in awe of his intensity and still am. He went on to teach himself piano and saxaphone, and became a much respected and *in demand* session guitarist in London and Sydney. "Tex", our drummer, played hard and loud - emulating John Bonham from Led Zeplin - and to enhance his style he had an oversized drum kit - specially made out of stainless steel - with two huge kick drums that reminded me of shiny canons. They were deafening, and the thud from them passed straight through my back and into my chest cavity as I stood in front of them - screaming my lungs out to Eric Clapton's "Layla" - trying to make myself heard. Terry went on to play in various bands in Newcastle - such as Catch and The Young Guns - and is now running a premier booking agency called Eastern Acoustic Organisation. Our bass guitarist, "Hilly" was the entrepreneur of the group. He organised gigs, equipment hire and costumes. He had a very *bohemian attitude* towards life, and went on to play in the *punk and new wave scene* around Newcastle and Sydney.

Before I acquired my own PA system, I would borrow "Willie" Walkers' bass amp to sing through. Willie was in Mark Tinsons' *earlier* band called *"Blue Grass"*, and I would wake him up early on Sunday mornings, on my way to Kitchener, to ask for his amp. His mother would show me to his room where he would simply groan and point to the amplifier and nod to signify I could take it - and *get out*! I would gratefully acknowledge him, and leave quickly - with the massive box - so he could sleep off his hangover. 45 years later, in 2018, I was reacquainted with him on stage at Lizottes Restaurant in Newcastle - at a *Blue Grass* reunion - to play harmonica - and we laughed as we reminisced about those Sunday morning rendezvous!

The Year my Voice Broke

A bass amplifier isn't the most efficient public address system! - and I really had to push my voice to be heard above the two electric guitars and that monster drum kit. This, also being my time of puberty, when my voice began to break, didn't help either. I simply screamed my way through all those voice breaks. Alice Coopers' "School's Out" was a particular challenge! I had singing lessons a few years later and the teacher couldn't quite figure out what was so unusual about my voice. She said I was somewhere between a Baritone Tenor and a Bass Baritone, but when I explained my earlier years of screaming through that puberty period she understood why I sounded peculiar. She also said it was wrong for me to sing through that stage of adolescence and that I probably hindered the full development of my voice. I remember, at that time, hearing of a young, well known singer called Jamie Redfern having problems with contractual obligations because *his* voice was changing as he came out of puberty, and needed time off to let his voice fully develop. He was a major draw card on Johnny Young's TV show called "Young Talent Time" and was eventually recruited by Liberace, the flamboyant piano playing American entertainer, who took him back to the States to perform in Vegas with him. 25 years later, when *my* voice completely malfunctioned due to a medical condition called Spasmodic Dysphonia, I approached another singing teacher who, coincidentally, happened to be the sister of my earlier teacher, and she agreed my problem may have stemmed from those teenage "rock singing" years!

Subsequently, singing was never easy for me, or particularly comfortable. It required immense concentration and passion to overcome that "breaking" sensation - which it continued to do, on occasions, into my 30's. The fear of this happening, made me very nervous as it was extremely embarrassing. I still cringe remembering a solo gig at Donny Graham's "Log Cabin Lounge" in the early 1980's. Donny being the former manager of the infamous Star Hotel where "The biggest Riot in Australian History" occurred on its final night of trading in September 1979. His next venture was just down Hunter street at the Bellevue Hotel where, similar to the Star Hotel, the public bar catered to the merchant seamen and all other sorts of Newcastles' shadiest characters, whilst the lounge bar, whose walls had been lined with rustic bark slabs, provided entertainment consisting mainly of solo or duo singer/guitarists. I figure Donny thought he couldn't possibly have any more riots with that kind of laid back, easy listening music. *I* featured prominently in the line up of musicians who performed there, sometimes appearing 3 or 4 times in one week. Among the regular line up were Jus' Gordon and Jim Overend, who I have remained friends with and who still perform locally and abroad. Jim was present on the night I almost died of embarrassment while soaring through one of my favourite blues numbers called "Walk On" by Sonny Terry and Brownie Magee. My voice broke so sharply, it sounded like I'd sat on a pitch fork - "*pitch*" being the operative word! - and a shrill screech blared from my throat - instead of the lyrics.. "*walk on*". It made me want to "*walk off*" that stage and never return, and it invoked a vulnerability within me that remained as a chink in my performing armour for the rest of my career. I eventually adopted a technique akin to meditating, while I sang, to overcome or control this insecurity - which is described in this song that I wrote at that time.

For all the anxiety and frustration that my quirky singing voice caused me, it still took me somewhere very special, mystical and sacred. And that was the attraction. The addiction. And the journey there, felt like I was Flying!

When I Close My Eyes To Sing

Here tonight alone with you again
I'll play my songs and sing the best I can
the only way you'll know it
the only way I'll show it
is if I close my eyes to sing

'çause when I close my eyes my soul guides the song
it leads me to your heart where I want to belong
then you'll get to know me
and what I've come to bring
when I close my eyes to sing

in the darkness I'm free without a care
please don't think me rude
I still know your there
close your eyes and you may feel it too
I really hope you do
it's something we could share

here tonight alone with you again
to play my songs and sing the best I can
but most of all I'm sharing part of my life
please take it in
when I close my eyes to sing

Studio Time

Hoping to take the band [Khan] to the next level, we went to a recording studio to make a demo. To prepare for this, we spent a whole weekend practising in a shed on "Hilly's" uncles' farm on Raymond Terrace road, near Thornton. Even sleeping on the floor between our amplifiers and drums. Total devotion! Livin' the dedicated life of "rock musos". Johnsies' older brother, Steve or "Sohj" as he was known, arranged the recording session at Bert Moonan's studio which was a room at the back of his house in Wallsend. Bert was an accomplished bass guitarist and singer, and a total gentleman, who went on to a career in radio marketing. It was fairly intimidating having all those older and experienced musos looking on - while we played and "doubled tracked" our way through the session - but they were very supportive, and complemented each of us on our abilities. We managed to record a few songs in our short time there that night, my favourite being "The Ocean" by Led Zeplin - an ambitious effort at our age and level of experience!

At our rehearsals, while we were taking a break from learning songs, the boys would show me chords and riffs on the electric and bass guitars, and Terry taught me how to play syncopated rhythm on the drums. Skills that would serve me well, later in my years as a solo performer - playing guitar and harmonica and eventually programming bass and drum patterns into drum machines and sequencers, when they became popular equipment in the '80's. Later in my high school years I even scored the position as the drummer for a *musical* that our class performed and toured the region to other schools. Admittedly, the band was playing along to a backing track, as I recall! Never the less, I was absorbing all these different musical experiences to add to my arsenal of tricks in future years.

Senior High

YEAR 12, 1976

In 1975, when I went onto 5th form, I entered a new phase of my musical journey. Mark, Glen and Terry had left school at the end of 4th form to enter the workforce, so the band folded. My next band formed when I became friends with Giles Smith or "Jynx" as we called him. He came to our school after leaving a boarding school in Armidale, and lived in Cessnock where he was friends with Johnsie. He had a defiant attitude and a larrikin outlook on life, no doubt fuelled by his strict discipline at the boarding school. He was an accomplished bass player and guitarist and had great taste in a wide variety of music, including rock, funk and jazz. I was stunned the first time I went to his house, as there were wild animal heads such as antelopes and boars, mounted on the walls. His father, who owned a panel beating business in Cessnock, was a game hunter who went on overseas trips to shoot wild animals - and bring them back, mounted or stuffed, as trophies. Ironically, after he retired from the car smash repair business, he set up a zoo on his property at Nulkaba which, today, is the well known *Hunter Valley Zoo*. Sometimes we would have a jam in his father's workshop [Smith's Smash Repairs], near the Cessnock Hotel, with Johnsie and Tex - setting up our amps and drums and microphone stands amongst the twisted car wrecks and greasy machinery. The noise we made in that huge corrugated iron shed would echo down Vincent street, attracting locals - usually friends of Jynx and Johnsie – who would invite themselves in for an impromptu performance, and request songs. Still, it was a more relaxed atmosphere than those previous rehearsals in Maitland - with the bikies as our critics!

We only did a couple of gigs with that line-up, before Tex was poached from us by a well known local band called "Catch" [Jim Overend was their singer], and Johnsie moved away for work commitments. That left Jinx and me - still keen to have a band - but lacking a drummer and lead guitarist. At that time, Tony Heads staged a lunchtime concert in our school library - performing on his Hammond organ - with Pete Sheen on drums. It was an impressive performance, with a big sound for just two guys, particularly when they stunned us with "Fanfare For the Common Man" by Emerson Lake and Palmer. Jinx and I already knew Headsie - as he was a friend of my sister, a local music store owner, and mentor to many young budding musicians around Maitland. He introduced us to Pete [Sheeny], who showed an interest in filling the spot in our band as the new drummer. Inspired by the simplicity of Headsy's duo, we decided to play as a trio, with me on bass [under Jinx's guidance], and Jinx taking on the role of rhythm and lead guitarist. Pete was an amazing, free flowing drummer who seemed to make it easy for me to take on the new role of bass guitarist - as well as having to sing the lead vocals. Jinx didn't shy away from his responsibility as lead guitarist, ambitiously attempting the lead guitar solos to some exceedingly challenging songs such as "Still Alive and Well" by Johnny Winter. I have fond memories of rehearsing in an old church at Woodville - a tiny village, nestled in the farmlands between Maitland and Paterson - and driving there in Jinx's old Commer Van that his father had salvaged for him from his wreckers yard. Not so fond, is the memory of running up the back of a car as we drove onto, the single lane, Dunmore bridge, over the Paterson River near Woodville, and being thrown, knees first, against the windscreen - hearing all our amplifiers in the back of the van being smashed against the partition behind our seats. The amplifiers survived - my knees recovered - the Commer van hardly got a scratch[built like a tank!] - but the car we hit, had it's boot crushed! I think Jinx talked his way out of that mess by using his "Panel Beater" *father* as an escape route! We only did one gig - as that band - which was a school dance, held in the hall below our classrooms of the old cathedral building beside the banks of the Hunter River. Our time together as a trio barely lasted a few months but the experience and knowledge I gained from it was invaluable, not to mention, wonderfully enjoyable.

My main reason for staying on in senior high was because it was co-ed. That meant the girls from the Dominican Convent School - intending to go on to 5th and 6th form - came over to our school for the final two years of high school. The promise of mixed classes was incentive for other boys like me, who considered themselves to be young Casanova's, but, who also had no idea of what career they wanted to pursue if they left school after 4th form. Those two years were relatively enjoyable. The girls added a more sociable aspect, and the teachers treated us more as adults - reinforcing the fact that we were *there* because we *wanted* to be there and not because we *had to*. Subsequently, there was less pressure to finish assignments, as there were no penalties. Just reminders, that *"the time we were wasting by not doing the work, was our own!"*. Because "The Band" *thing*, with Jinx, had fizzled, it was *now* that I began to develop my acoustic guitar playing skills and song-writing - even drawing inspiration from topics we were studying in the curriculum - such as *this* ancient Greek tragedy by Sophocles ;

Oedipus Rex

Is life for real and what it seems
are plans secure or only schemes
do we live life to find the end
or look for the place to begin

Look at yourself and where you stand
security is your demand
but is your life so self secured
do not buy what you can't afford

Look for the truth it's in your will
never resting never still
your eyes are open but blind are you
Death will come whatever you do

Look for your father where is he
Mother / wife where is she
Oh your brother, he is your son
Oedipus what have you done

Now blinded but you see
you see the truth. Misery
You will not die but live in shame
Oh Oedipus....such a cursed name

Certainly not a song with the greatest commercial value - or catchiest title! - but it was a start for me, and it kept me from daydreaming in the classroom while staring out the window - watching the Hunter River flow slowly towards Horshoe Bend. Needless to say, the "*romantic poet*" in me churned out a number of gut wrenching - or should I say "*nauseating*" - songs of unrequited teenage love - most of which, I'll spare you the agony of reading. Two of my favourite *ballads,* at that time, were "Changes" by Black Sabbath, and "Thank you" by Led Zeppelin. The later, I wrote out the lyrics - to pass time after finishing an exam early - and sent them to a girl I was *sweet on*, who went to the Lochinvar Convent High School. It had the desired effect, and earned me a special place in her heart - encouraging me to emulate that style of writing in my own songs.

The girls who came over to our school in 5th and 6th form, came for academic reasons - not romantic ones - so our mixed classes had a very platonic vibe. *That* didn't stop a few of the boys getting up to a bit of mischief. In particular, when, in maths class, I and two of my mates - Mick and Tom - would ask one of the brighter girls to come over and help us out with particular problems - admiring her long legs as she leaned over the desk to explain things. She was much more adept to dealing with *deviations in mathematical formulas* than she was in dealing with *deviant seventeen year old boys*!

One romance did bloom and flourish, however, in those senior years. It was the pairing of our two school captains. Mick and Jenny were two of the most caring and genuine humans I have ever had the pleasure to know, and was delighted to see them marry, not long after finishing school. They remain married to this day. A rare achievement in these days of spiralling divorce rates, and testament to their enduring love and stoic personalities. I admired long lasting relationships, and was aware of flaws in my own personality traits that made it difficult for me to sustain them;...as expressed in *this* song;

Sad Song of Joy

*Smile, you made me smile
while I was crying while I was dying
Sing, you made me sing instead of sighing
instead of dying
instead of trying so hard to love*

*A breath of fresh air fills my soul, makes me whole
when you be near to me
Be dear to me make me glad to be your friend
lets not pretend.*

*To love and be one in all we do
it's up to you
While I sit and choose which words to use
to describe, to depict
to predict my love of you*

*But something has changed it's all rearranged
My plan has gone wrong
This is just a song of dis-pare
Do you really care?
Where you ever there?*

*The years have aged my mind
They've made me blind
Did I really see
the smile of a girl being near, bringing life to me
making me sing
instead of sighing
instead of trying so hard to be loved*

In fairness to my two mates in that maths class - whom I labelled as deviates - they also went on to marry *life-long* partners - who attended our school but who were in the year ahead of us. Surprising me with their penchant for older women!

Although the academic pressure increased in sixth form, we were revelling in our new found freedom of obtaining our drivers licences. A common topic of debate was why the girls seemed to pass their driving test on the first attempt, while many of the boys had to do the test three times before they passed. The boys argued that the length of the girls' skirts played a significant roll in persuading the driving instructor to be lenient in the test. Many of us drove to school now, instead of catching the school bus. Most of us borrowed our parents cars but some were lucky enough to have their own vehicle that their parents had bought for them. Unable to contain my excitement, the day I proudly drove my fathers Mazda 808 station wagon into the seniors playground - showing off, by doing "*doughnuts*" in reverse gear - I hit one of the 5th form students, smashing the rear taillight and knocking him to the ground! Luckily, he wasn't seriously injured, only receiving a bruised hip and grazed knees. I worked off the cost of replacing the tailight by washing cars for the local Rally Driving Legend, Ken Tubman, who lived up the road from me, in Tenambit. He was famous for his rally driving skills - winning the Redex Trial in 1953 and the World Cup Rally in 1974 - but, obviously, his driving skills hadn't rubbed off on me while I was rubbing off the beads of water on his Peugeot with a chamois.

More *infamous* than my playground "hit and run" incident, were the lunchtime meetings we would have in the back of Jinx's Commer van. He would park it under the trees at the end of the playground by the river levee, where, one by one, we would discretely jump into the side sliding door for clandestine gatherings - that involved various activities such as guitar jams, gossiping about students and teachers and, although I'm a bit vague on this, occasionally passing around a joint. An image comes to mind of seeing *that van door* sliding open and six or seven students, girls and boys, clambering out, coughing and cackling with laughter, shrouded in a haze of smoke that bellowed from within. Some of the teaching staff must have also witnessed that event because "*gathering in parked vehicles*" was on the agenda of the next school council meeting, and was subsequently banned.

In an effort to reduce my *study load* for the Higher School Certificate exams, I chose only four subjects - being English, Maths, Economics and Geography - and began memorising the notes I had prepared for them. My memory served me well, but the subject matter in the exams didn't match my notes – resulting in my overall score being just above sixty percent. Luckily, the average scores that year were low, so I still managed to qualify for university. My results, however, made me question my intelligence, and I wondered if I hadn't just *memorised* my way through high school. This wasn't a good state of mind to enter Newcastle University the following year - to begin a Commerce Degree - and after buying all the text books and signing up for all the classes, I pulled out, after only three lectures. Three hours of university education! It had to be some kind of record! That fear I had of institutions - as well as knowing I couldn't bluff or memorise my way through such a heavy course - had me running out of that lecture hall, and straight to the university bar, to celebrate my departure from academia. Two of my drinking mates that day were Mick and Tom - from my high school math's class - who both went on to, eventually, obtain degrees in economics, and have successful careers in accounting and management. Part of me was disappointed in giving up so soon, and part of me felt a degree of shame in letting my parents down after all their financial and moral support - but another part of me just *knew* this wasn't my destiny. A few years later, I was back in that bar – performing a set of my own songs!

I still clearly remember the anxiety I felt as I walked out of Maitland Marist Brothers High School on our last day, having no idea of what career I wanted to pursue, and terrified of the pressures that university studies would place on me. The only thought that eased my anxiety was imagining a life involved in music and entertainment. I had no clear image of what form that life would take, at this stage, but it slowly revealed itself over the next three years - that I spent in a kind of limbo.

Pure and Simple

It was at this time that I formed a *Folk style* duet with a dear friend of mine, Helen, who lived down on Morpeth road, and I have the fondest memories of rehearsing in her garage - stopping to have lunch with her beautiful parents, Nance and Tom, while overlooking the farmland through their back door. Part of that land was used for the Maitland Jail prisoners to grow vegetables. Remnants of the old Morpeth railway line could be seen among the undergrowth just over their back fence. Helen had a gentle - caring, free spirited, partly hippie – personality, and a soulful, velvet, singing voice to match. Our duo, which we laughingly named "Pure and Simple" after a popular cooking oil, performed regularly at friends' parties and eventually had residencies at the Cessnock Hotel restaurant as well as The Happy Valley Restaurant in the vineyards - which was owned and operated by the "internationally acclaimed" chef, Robert Molines and his wife Sally. Performing our *laid back* style of music in that restaurant was *as good as it gets* for an entertainer. Couples having romantic candlelit dinners smiled in approval as we harmonised to songs by Neil Young, Bread, The Carpenters, Joni Mitchel, Bob Dylan and others of that 60's and 70's folk era. We also managed to slip one or two of my original compositions into the set list, just to try them out in public. Helen always encouraged my song writing - and was particularly fond of this one.

Cold Again

In a world of see and touch and feel
I knew a girl and saw she was real
I touched her lips and her long dark flowing hair
but yearned for her soul I knew was there

I lived for her or did I live at all
She couldn't see in my eyes what she meant to me

She drew my soul into her heart
then just called me a friend tearing me apart
but life goes on
for me everything's gone wrong
My life is so sad
I'll always miss what we never had

For all the heartbreak she caused me, I'm intrigued now, that, I can't remember who I wrote that song for!

The ambient atmosphere within that cottage style building in Pokolbin - surrounded by gardens and grape vines - was dream like, and in our breaks, Robert would insist on us sitting down to try some of his latest culinary creations along with a glass or two of the best wine the region had to offer. All this, and we got paid! - in cash! - at the end of the night! I took a greater proportion of the fee - as I provided the transport and the amplification equipment - and although I can't remember the dollar amount that I paid Helen, I do remember it was considerably more than the waitresses earned - which wasn't bad, considering she was still at school in 6th form. The enjoyment I got from this gig - with all it's comforts and perk's, as well as a reasonable financial reward - started me thinking about "performing" as a full time job. Helen eventually moved to Gosford to pursue a career in nursing, so I concentrated on refining my repertoire as a *soloist*. We kept in touch, and occasionally reformed the duo to play at friends' parties or weddings. After a break of over ten years, we were re united to perform at the wedding of Grant Walmsley, the guitarist/songwriter in The Screaming Jets. Before their meteoric rise to fame, they had been under the same management as me, with Peter Anderson at Rock City Promotions. Grant had heard and liked my songs from my album, *The Way I Live*, that I'd recorded in Pete's adjoining recording studio, Studio 21. I was very flattered that Grant thought so highly of me to book me for this occasion but I also felt totally inadequate for the event. Helen and I had never even performed the songs from my album, so we just winged our way through the night. It was intimidating - playing to an audience comprised of so many high calibre musicians - but I eventually relaxed, realising they were simply enjoying not being in the spotlight themselves, and hanging out with mates - hardly noticing what *we* were doing on stage.

Helen and I also performed at local venues at that time, including regular gigs at the Belmont 16 Footers Club and the *new* Queens Wharf Brewery - where we played to over a thousand people crammed onto the wharf, one news years eve. We eventually went our own ways - as I concentrated on my solo career and my second album called The Valley. It would be fifteen years before we reunited musically - to perform at a series of events that Helen had organised to gather all our friends, both old and new, including musicians - for a concert and party. Helen pulled out all the stops for these concerts, building stages and sets - including a spectacular laser light show provided by her talented brother, Johnno - that she held on her own property at Lochinvar, and also at a vineyard in Greta. Money raised from these events was donated to the Black Dog Foundation in honour of our friend, Paul Mahony, who played guitar and sax at the first concert but sadly, took his own life shortly before we were due to gather again for the next one. The loss of such an amazingly talented and beautiful, gentle, soul, devastated all of us, and although I didn't know him closely, the empathy I felt for him is uncannily expressed in these lyrics - which I wrote over twenty years earlier...

Am I really on My Own

*When friends just go their own way
and exclude you from their life
sit alone in silent exile
tend the wounds and clean the bloody knife*

*Am I really on my own?
I've never been so alone
What's the use in trying to go on?*

*Frustrated by security but afraid of liberation
Lost and searching for purpose here
but no one to give hope or inspiration*

*Am I really on my own?
I've never been so alone
What's the use in trying to go on?*

*Walk with me a while and share our pain
Bleed alone together
maybe from this moment we will learn and gain
and rid our lives of this sadness forever*

*Help me God, what's going on today?
Too great the distance between what we live and say
We're all so lonely but we laugh to hide the pain
and the laughter's weak like sunlight glimmering through the rain*

*Am I really on my own?
I've never been so alone
What's the use in trying to go on?*

Helen even had T-shirts made to commemorate each of these events - using the proceeds to pay the professional musicians and caterers, and cover other costs - as well as donating to the Black Dog Foundation in honour of Paul. One of the shirts - representing the show we did at Tellace Estate Vineyard at Greta - had a cartoon drawing of a boy running along the road with a wheel on the end of a stick. Helen's partner, John, designed the shirt - based on a story I had told him, about running along the road that Tellace Estate was now situated on, from my Grandma's house, not far away, merrily pushing the wheel on a stick that she had made for me as a small child. As I performed that afternoon, surrounded by good friends and family - as it was also my mothers 80th birthday - overlooking the vines and nearby bushland, I felt as though I'd come full circle - returning to that magical place of my *childhood*, to play *music...* the magical *essence* of my *adulthood*.

Big Harry's Place

Not long after dropping out of Newcastle University I found employment at the BHP steelworks as a junior clerk. The local's called it *Big Harry's Place* - and with over ten thousand employees, there weren't many Novocastrian's who didn't have a family member work there at some time in their life. I was initially placed out on the plant in the "Machine Shop", a large iron clad workshop full of lathes and grinding and drilling equipment. It was a very noisy and dirty environment - even the enclosed office within it - but a haven, compared to the coke ovens and blast furnace departments. I must have looked amusingly out of place there, walking around in my pleated trousers, collared shirt and tie, surrounded by an army of tradesmen in greasy overalls and hard hats! Someone had told me to dress that way, especially to wear a tie, as it would enhance my chances of promotion. I initially doubted that advice, as I got heckled by some of the workers calling me a "Company Man" or "brown Nose'r". It was a very "us and them" mentality at the steel works - with the "workers and unionists" versing the "management". A situation I was familiar with, as my father was a staunch union member - affiliated with the powerful Waterside Workers Union - while he worked at the Newcastle State Dockyard and later at the Floating Dock as a Painter and Docker. He was often at home on "strike" - over disputes with "management" - and I was alerted to his devotion to the union when I'd hear him address his workmates as "Comrade". I was caught in the middle - both at work and at home - as I was neither unionist nor management, and I learned to *tread lightly* when discussing the benefits or disadvantages of "strike action" with Dad - as *my* perspective came from what I'd studied at school in Economics Classes, and *his* was from experience on the factory floor as a "down trodden worker"! Polar opposites, with very little room for compromise in between.

My attire did earn me that promotion however, and within a few months I was transferred to the Main Administration building where I became the new "Mail-boy". It didn't seem like much of a promotion, especially being referred to as "Boy" when I delivered the mail and office memorandums to all the departments in the building as well as out on the plant - where I was driven around by a Hire Car driver - but it did bring me into contact with the top executives, and before long my smart appearance caught the eye of the Head accountant in the Cost Department and I was promoted to the position of Cost Clerk. This made things even more awkward for me - travelling to work in the car pool with my mates who were tradesmen out in the plant - as in their eyes, I really *was* becoming a "company man". Cost clerks were usually employed as trainees who were doing a part time degree in economics and, knowing I had begun that course, the boss said he would support me if I wanted to resume studies. The longer I stayed in that job, however, the less I wanted to go back to studying economics, and the more I began planning for a life in music. A critical moment in deciding that I didn't want to be stuck in a *nine to five* office job for the rest of my life was the day I was assigned to filing duties. The company owned a huge old federation style house in Mayfield which was used for storing records and files relating to steelmaking costs - dating back to the factory's inception in 1915 - and I spent the whole day transporting boxes of documents there. It was an enjoyable task, especially as it got me out of the office for the day. The Cost Department office was one of many departments on the first floor of the Administration Building. The whole floor was a massive area filled with desks grouped in clusters to represent the various departments, separated by low partitions. It reminded me of a gigantic classroom and it made me feel like I'd simply transitioned from the classrooms at high school to this one. It made me feel like nothing had changed and was never going to change for the rest of my life. Some of the men in the desks around me were nearing retirement age and had sat at those desks for most of their working life. Proof of this, hit me right between the eyes, that day in the "records" house, when I stumbled across some beautifully *hand written* "cost" records from the late 1930's. They were steel making costs relating to military supplies for the second world war. *That* was interesting enough, but what *astounded* me was that I *recognised* the handwriting in one of those thick dusty ledger books - that resembled ancient bibles. The faded blue ink columns of weights, times and pounds, shillings and pence - probably applied with a "Fountain Pen" - were the scribings of Les Wanless, the elderly man who sat in the desk behind me, back at the admin building. I suddenly realised he'd been sitting at that desk, collating endless amounts of figures, for over forty years! The thought of *Me* sitting at *my* desk for that long was akin to being buried alive, and the prospect of living out the rest of my years like this was as repugnant as the stale, musty smell of the decaying paperwork stacked to ceilings of that Crebert street mansion.

So, once again, just like at high school - staring out the window, watching the Hunter river go by - I found myself staring out of the window of the BHP Administration Building, watching the traffic go by on the Industrial Highway, formulating these lyrics..... and my escape plan.

Restless Man

Looking out my window I see the world go slowly by
seeing my reflection, seeing me start to cry
Stop, I'm being left behind
Someone give me strength to try

My stomach's in a knot, I'm not sure which way to turn
Hold down my steady job or drift toward where my heart yearns
To play my songs night and day
To earn my living that way

I'm a restless man turning in my sleep
wanting to live a life where I'd sing to earn my keep
Instead of pushing pen in an office 9 to 5
Where I've seen men do that until the day they die

Friends help me sing my songs, on them I do depend
To push me on, make me strong so that I'll never bend
and I'll need them for all time until my tragic end

To the only girl I loved I said goodbye
and though she thought she knew me
She'll never know why

I'm a restless man too scared to turn around
and face the truth with my feet firmly on the ground
to tour the land and find out for myself
If they'll applaud or leave me on the shelf

And if I fail and loose it all I'll hang my head and cry
But deep inside my soul will rest for I'll know I tried
At least I tried

The future's so uncertain but means more to me than yesterday
If I can't achieve my only aim there's no need to stay
please somebody hear my cry, give me a break

I'm a restless man turning in my sleep
wanting to live a life where I'd sing to earn my keep
Instead of pushing pen in an office 9 to 5
Where I've seen men do that until the day they die

For *me*, the *entertainment industry* seemed a more appropriate means of employment compared to the *steel industry*. My brief time in the workforce, surrounded by so many sad and bitter people, made me realise that this *work thing* was a real *drag* and a life sentence of regret, so I aimed to make *my passion for music* my job. My income. Music would become my alternative employment and, in pursuing the art, I would use it to pursue income. However keen as I was to be free of *Big Harry's* clutches, I knew I had to set myself up financially to ride out the initial stages of being self employed, so I volunteered for *overtime* at every opportunity. Some of that *overtime* would find me hidden away in the huge storage vault located in the basement of the admin building, writing out the chords and lyrics for songs in my growing repertoire - and sometimes even practising them on the guitar I had smuggled down there and hidden on the upper shelves amongst the old ledgers and records. The increased wages helped me to buy my first car, a 1974 model Chrysler Valiant Gallant station wagon. It was my *Mini* version of the popular, Holden Sandman Panel Vans that all the cool surfers - or *weeds* as we called them - were driving at that time. I smile now to think that my mother even sewed curtains for it, while I installed a mattress and pillows to come in handy - as I told her - if I needed to sleep over, after too many drinks at the pub or parties. She feigned acknowledgement of the practicality of these accessories but I suspected she really knew what I got up to in my little *shaggin' wagin'*, late at night. I lost my virginity in that car, parked in the bush - just behind the football oval where I use to play as a Tenambit Tiger. As with my football achievements, my first score, taking a long time to achieve - over in an instant, and only with the willing assistance of my more experienced playmate. My victorious demeanour was quickly extinguished the following day by the intuitive look of disapproval from my mother, when she asked me, who had I gone out with on the previous night. It seemed to me she knew more about some of the girls in my neighbourhood than I gave her credit for! The next major acquisition that year was my first proper PA system - a 200 watt Yamaha mixer/amplifier and two column speakers - which I purchased from Tony Heads' music store in High street, Maitland. *Headsy* was the *go to* man for musical equipment and advice, and being a family friend, he also suggested the latest Sennheiser microphone to my mother, as a gift for my 21st birthday. My first guitars ranged from a nylon string classical, to a steel string Ibanez accoustic, on to an Ovation, and eventually settling on a Maton C.E.90. The latter of which, I sacrilegiously painted bright red a few years later - as a promotional gimmick - much to the disgust of some of my *guitar purist* mates.

The vault, where I conducted my clandestine rehearsals, was once used by the Paymaster to store the cash for the employees wages but as the plant grew, the monetary logistics were undertaken in the basement of the Commonwealth Bank building in Newcastle. It was here, once a fortnight on Wednesday morning that, up to thirty clerks, myself included, from the admin building, would be transported to the banks' basement vault to count upwards of three million dollars cash to be distributed to the thousands of employees on Payday. How my eyes would bulge when I watched those stacks of bundled notes wheeled into the room on several luggage trolleys escorted by armed guards with sawn off double barrelled shotguns! It would take us most of the morning to count those bundles and even longer the next morning to divvy the money into the employee pay envelopes back in the paymasters office. I was severely reprimanded on one occasion for clowning around with another young clerk at one of those pay counting sessions and inadvertently shorting someone's pay by twenty dollars while the other clerk overpaid someone by the same amount. We were warned that any future discrepancies, caused due to misconduct, would be deducted from our own wages. Accountancy was a well oiled machine at the BHP Paymaster's office, and it intrigued me that out of all those millions of dollars, a $20 discrepancy could be accounted for and tracked back to it's source - regrettably me! Another interesting, but unrelated, calculation I have made, is that in the whole of my working life I will never earn the amount of money I saw in that vault on that Wednesday morning. Another interesting side light is that the Paymaster, at that time, lived a few houses down from me, in View street. Apart from occasionally "*car pooling*", his proximity to me had no influence on my future income earning capacity. *His* neighbours were the Bell Family, which included Michael Bell the acclaimed artist/cartoonist and John bell, founder of the Bell Shakespeare Theatre company. View street! – the hub of *finance* and the *arts*!

At the time that I was planning my escape from *The Big Australian,* one of my office co-workers announced *his* departure from clerical duties to pursue a career in music. Like me, he too was a guitar vocalist but had mainly played bass guitar in 50's and 60's style rock and roll bands. In the office, he was affectionately known as *Flash* - a good natured, irreverent title - relating to his slightly ample physique and unkempt presentation, as well as his lackadaisical attitude to work. He too, spent time as a junior clerk in the mail room where he earned a notorious reputation - after it was discovered he'd been throwing the mail down the elevator shaft, instead of delivering it! He was a likeable larrikin, and thinking back about him now conjures up images of John Bellushi as Jake in The Blues Brothers movie. Just before he resigned I made the mistake of doing a gig with him in the hope of gaining some of his senior entertaining experience. It was at an Asian restaurant in Charlestown, and we performed as a duo, playing various 60's and 70's songs by The Beatles, Credence Clearwater Revival, Roy Orbison and others of that era, as well as some classic rock and roll numbers from artists such as Buddy Holly and Elvis. Actually, Flash reminded me of Roy Orbison, as he had a wavering high falsetto type voice and often wore dark sunglasses. The latter, probably being due to his propensity for coming to work with a hangover. Our *one and only appearance together* started well enough - as we took turns in singing the lead vocals and harmonising - but it was when Flash began engaging with the audience, in between songs, that things began to go awry. It was as if he had a grudge to settle with the audience, berating them if they didn't applaud after each song, and snapping at anyone who asked for a song that wasn't in our repertoire, but the clencher was when he yelled over the microphone to a man dining with his family that..."HEY IF YOUR NOT GOING TO EAT ALL THAT MEAL, I'LL FINISH IT FOR YOU!". Shortly after that comment the manager asked us to pack up our gear and go home. After I had loaded my equipment into my car I found Flash hiding in the toilets where he passed my pay to me under the cubical door, explaining that it was all he could get for me - as the Chef had run at him with a meat cleaver when he'd gone to ask for our *full* performance fee! It was a scene that could've easily been written for the "Blues Brothers" movie.

I unintentionally got even with Flash - for subjecting me to such an embarrassing showbiz debacle - a few weeks later, when I borrowed his car, one lunchtime, to take my guitar for a service. The strings on my Ibaneze accoustic guitar were buzzing because the frets on the neck needed reshaping, and Flash had told me about an elderly man from Merewether who was very good at doing this. His name was John Thomas and I guessed he must've been in his late sixties or early seventies. He was a kind hearted, softly spoken gentleman who had performed as a jazz guitarist until retiring into his suburban life as a Luthier. I particularly remember watching his large arthritic hands and fingers, lovingly manipulate the thin guitar neck, as he played a series of intricate jazz chords and riffs with effortless ease and compassion, and thinking to myself..."yes, that's what I want to be doing when I'm his age!" I only had 30 minutes to get to Merewether and back to the office before our lunch break ended, so I borrowed Flash's V8 Holden Sandman Panel van, thinking it would help me achieve my deadline. I was surprised that he eagerly lent me his proud possession and took it as compensation for the traumatic gig I had recently endured with him. I thought it odd for him to own such a cool vehicle especially as he was a far cry from the image of a bronzed aussie surfer with which these cars were usually associated. I also found the car to be a lot less powerful than I had expected. In fact, pressing down on the accelerator as far as I could, barely saw me attain a speed of more than 60kms per hour all the way to Merewether. I began to suspect that the car had a mechanical fault and that maybe Flash had set me up again for some kind of disaster. This was confirmed as the car came to a groaning halt out the front of John's house as stinking white smoke began to billow out from beneath it. Thinking it might be ok once it had cooled down, I took my guitar into John's house where he reminisced of his years playing in dance hall orchestras and Jazz bands in Newcastle and Sydney throughout the 40's, 50's and 60's and explaining how he would fix the buzz in my guitar strings. On returning to the car I found it would not start at all and realising I only had five minutes to get back to the office I went back into John's house to call my office on his *home* phone. You must remember this is long before mobile phones had been invented, so I couldn't call Flash directly, but instead, I had to call my boss in Cost Department and explain my situation. Luckily, Mick Goldman - the chief accountant of Cost Department - was an understanding man, and although he was a giant of a man who reminded me of Lurch in the Adams Family television show, he had a gentle nature that endeared him to all who served under him in the office. *Company policy* frowned on employees leaving the Steelworks site at lunchtime, so I was lucky not to be severely reprimanded for my little excursion but, "Goldie" - as we called him - arranged for one of the clerks to come and pick me up, bringing Flash with him to sort out the car's mechanical problem. As it turned out, the car's problem was easily fixed, much to my utter humiliation and embarrassment, by simply releasing the handbrake! Unlike the *few* cars I had driven in my short time as a motorist, the handbrake on the Sandman didn't have to be in the "*UP*" position to be activated, and when I saw it in the "*DOWN*" position I presumed it was already "OFF". That was not the case, and I had inadvertently driven 10 kms with the accelerator flat to the floor while the handbrake was fully on! This had caused the brake pads to almost melt onto the wheel hubs and I was lucky that more serious damage hadn't occurred. I compounded my ridicule by telling the rest of the clerks - back at the office - that I *had* noticed a little red light *glowing* in the dash board but couldn't work out what the symbol was that it was indicating - and passed it off as a *low oil warning* - suspecting Flash hadn't maintained the car properly. I never lived down that incident and for the remainder of my time as a cost clerk I was referred to as *The Handbrake Boy*. Consequently, to this very day, I have an, *OCD-like,* obsession of fumbling with the release catch of the handbrake - whilst I'm driving - to convince myself it is *off*!

Although this incident would have made good fodder for a humorous song, I eventually penned another tune relating to my other constant calamity involving auto mobiles. I never again forgot to check that the hand brake was off - but I kept forgetting to take the keys out of the ignition before locking the car!

Key To My Cart

I went down to the beach my baby and me out for a day in the sun
surfin' and swimmin' and lyin' on the sand I didn't realise what I had done
when it was time to go home we thought we'd go to a bar
I said "give me the keys, I don't know where they are"
and that's when I saw them, locked up in my car

I locked my keys in the car and I sure ain't goin' too far
standin' here pullin' out my hair wishin' I'd carry a spare
well I'm bangin' on the window, kickin' in the door
I'm a fool I've done it so many times before
I always know where my keys are
They're locked up in my car

One night at the drive-in my darlin' and me started thinking 'bout something to eat
so we locked up the car and walked down to the shop but I left my keys on the seat
when we got back to the car and she saw what I'd done
she threw me her food and decided to run
and left me standin' there glowin' like the midday sunday

I locked my keys in the car and I sure ain't goin' too far
standin' here pullin' out my hair wishin' I'd carry a spare
well I'm bangin' on the window, kickin' in the door
I'm a fool I've done it so many times before
I always know where my keys are
They're locked up in my car

it's causing me worry I'm losin' my pride
I can't get a girl to stand by my side
not to mention just to go for a ride
I'm seriously considerin' suicide

well if a mule is stubborn it has to be said
I'm the biggest ass that's ever been
five times this week I've done the same thing
jumped out of my car and locked the keys in
I can't understand it and I don't know why
and every time I do it I break down and cry
I think I'll sell my car and give a motor bike a try

Because I locked my keys in the car and I sure ain't goin' too far
standin' here pullin' out my hair wishin' I'd carry a spare
well I'm bangin' on the window, kickin' in the door
I'm a fool I've done it so many times before
I always know where my keys are
They're locked up in my car

My last twelve months, working in that, supposedly, secure office job, seemed to drag on slowly as I tapped meaningless figures into the electric calculator on my desk - as if playing a soundless mini keyboard instrument - and writing the results on a spreadsheet that blanketed my desk. The spreadsheet would consist of thirty or more columns across, and maybe forty lines down, all full of figures which I then had to add - across and down - to give me my final result in the far right hand, bottom corner. This - equally meaningless - figure, I would then show my boss, who would either agree with it or ask me to change it, to suite his calculations. Myself and the other ten clerks in our department would toil away for weeks on these spreadsheets which, within ten years of my resignation, were calculated by one desk top computer! *Computer technology* was in it's infancy while I was employed at the BHP steelworks - where a whole two story building, called *The Computer Centre,* was dedicated to collating and printing all the results submitted by the army of clerks, like me, who worked endless hours on those spreadsheets. I'm amused now, remembering how I would load my station wagon with boxes of hand written data and drive across to the Computer Building to unload, then repeat the process a few days later, bringing boxes of neatly printed computer calculations back to the administration building for the bosses to examine. My time in that office work, although uninspiring, did, however, teach me valuable accounting skills that, to this day, I utilise in maintaining my business records. I still keep *hand written* ledgers relating to my business expenses and income, in addition to maintaining them on a computer accounting programme, and quite often, if there is a discrepancy, my *handwritten* records are usually the more accurate figures!

I was fully aware of the risk I was taking in leaving such a stable job but was equally determined to make music and entertainment my new source of income and employment. Unlike many of the musicians around me at that time - who accepted the premise of the "Starving Artist" - I was determined to make *my* musical career choice an economically viable one.

Walking out the back door of that administration building - for the last time - was like walking into another dimension. A whole new life. A rebirth. It was as if my life had just begun! It felt like *freedom,* but at the same time, I felt a huge weight of responsibility, and even some guilt. Responsibility, to the future well being of myself, and guilt, for turning from the course that my parents had set for me by providing my education and all my other worldly needs - 'till now. They had struggled and worked hard all their lives - to set me up for a life that was hopefully better than theirs - and I felt like I was putting all of *that* in jeopardy. They showed concern at my radical decision to leave full time employment - but never spoke out against it - and I tried to imagine the worry they must've been feeling for me at that time - in *this* song;

Be More Than We Were

He's mad he'll loose all he has
why wont he leave things as they are?
There's no future in leaving a job
to sing and play guitar

it's sad he's lost in a dream
he thinks he'll succeed on his own
but illusions of fame and success
don't assure him of a throne and wont build him a home

do as you must but don't count on us
and of one thing be sure
be more than we were

we've heard him he's really not too bad
he sings from his heart
but talent is made of more than that
he needs to learn more he's so far from the start

he might get a break but it's his life at stake
and this we'll pray for
to be more than we were

it's just so hard for us to bear
to see him throw his job away
the future we prepared
all those years we cared are gone

the game is far from being clean
they'll use him then throw him in the street
he's too soft to bear how it will be
the hardship he'll meet, the cruel pain of defeat

we've warned him and yet
his mind it is set
on one shinning lure
to be more than we were
be more than we were

TONY JOHNS

?

WHO

Tony Johns
GUITAR VOCALIST

Chapter 3
The 1980's

Tony Who?

I may have been born in 1958 but my life began in 1980. I finally had a sense of who I was and what I'd been put on this earth to do. I was free of the conventional shackles that school and being a part of the workforce had previously placed on me and I was now my own boss. I was a solo performer who sang and played guitar and harmonica to *popular* songs as well as my own tunes, some of which *also* became *popular* to my audiences! Music and entertainment was my business, and, to reinforce that fact, I gave my business a name, and that name was TONY JOHNS. There were other reasons for not using my real surname of *Gibbons,* such as reducing my income tax. I'd always begrudged how much my income was reduced by tax while working at the BHP steelworks, and with my new pseudonym of *Johns* I could control how much income to declare, especially as most of my performances were paid in cash. My *little tax minimising scheme* came to an end 20 years later when the Goods and Services Tax was implemented and cash payments all but ceased. I also declared more of my earnings later in the 1980's when I applied for a housing loan. I had a clear conscience about paying as little tax as possible. It's not like I had a secret stockpile of cash hidden somewhere. Most of my income was recycled back into the economy buying musical equipment, hiring musicians and engineers for recording sessions, paying for fuel and transport for touring gigs, paying rent and eventually paying huge interest to banks for home loans - especially when the rates were up around 17% in the early 1990's!

I chose the name of Tony Johns also because it was two common names that were easy to remember and they were my first two Christian names. I did have a slight reservation for using my real surname of *Gibbons* for fear of slandering the family name if things went bad for me and also the connotation of being associated to the gibon monkey and the risk of being nicknamed *The Funky Gibon!* [*The Goodies- 1975*]....*a tag with which one of my mates [Baza] still affectionately addresses me.*

So, after many weeks of *cold calling* every pub in the Newcastle and Maitland Yellow Pages phone book, I did my first gig, under my new title, at the Merewether Beach Hotel, with a stark, red and black poster advertising me as;

Tony Johns

Who?

Tony Johns

I think the *question mark* was just as much for *me*, as anyone else, in getting used to my new name and my new life!

As Shakespeare said…"what's in a name?"… the following song relates to all the pick-up lines I heard in night clubs that I had started to frequent after my gigs. The name Jacqueline was to honour the birth of my sister's new baby daughter. I never recorded this song but used the music from it to use in another song called "Train Ride 3801" which didn't impress Lyn[my sister], who remarked sarcastically upon hearing the new version that it use to be her daughter's song!

The Name Game

What's your name? What's your game?
Say your name and I'll say it again
it's Jacqueline, she looks keen
Jacqueline where have you been
all my life I've been waitin' for you

How do you do? How old are you?
Thirty two! Now don't be blue
you couldn't be that, matter of fact
if your that I'll eat my hat
you don't look a day over sweet sixteen

I've got a million lines in my mind to use
that's the aim-playin' the name game

do you smoke? Do you coke?
No you don't? well I'm your bloke
but if ya do tell ya true
I wouldn't mind havin' a line with you
But I don't need drugs cause you
put me on a natural high

Where's your home? Where's a phone?
I'll call a cab and we'll be alone
for the night, you'll be alright
I only wanna kiss and hold you tight
I'll respect you in the mornin' light

I've got a million lines in my mind to use
that's the aim- playin' the name game

Movin' Away

My enthusiasm for looking for new venues to play was only matched by my enthusiasm to perform, so the work started to pour in. I began to move away from singing in restaurants, and targeted pubs for work as they paid better and I could interact more with the patrons in a more casual atmosphere. One disastrous gig at a restaurant in Kurri Kurri, called the Spire Motel, helped me make this decision when the manager asked me to wander between the tables while serenading the diners. As I preferred the safety and comfort of sitting behind a microphone, the act of strolling around and singing right beside people made me very nervous which affected the quality of my singing and coordination, and on more than one occasion I turned around awkwardly and hit people in the back of their heads with my guitar neck. One man stained his shirt while trying to sip his soup as my guitar thumped into his skull! My pay that night was a free meal and a few glasses of wine and I wasn't asked to do a return performance. Another restaurant in Maitland, called *The Coach House,* had me climbing up a ladder to play in a loft that overlooked the diners - twenty feet below. I enjoyed the isolation and protection of that stage and performed well there and was even complimented on my singing by a well known celebrity of the time called Chelsea Brown - an American actress, known for her appearances on Rowan and Martin's *Laugh In* TV show - who had recently settled in Australia to be caste in the controversial TV soap opera called Number 96. Coincidently, at that time, she had been given skiing lessons in Thredbo by an Austrian ski instructor who, a few years later, would be my boss in an Austrian pub where I performed for four winter seasons. When I asked the owner of The Coach House restaurant for a pay rise he warned me that I would price myself out of business. I resigned that night, and within a week I was earning twice the money at pubs in Newcastle, such as the Gates Hotel in Adamstown, the Merry Magpie wine bar and the Hunter Hotel in the Newcastle mall.

Merry Magpie Wine Bar poster complete with red wine stains !

The Hunter Hotel

Negotiating my performance fee with publicans was probably the biggest challenge in my music business! Although they generally paid me more than restaurant owners they were still reluctant to part with their takings. A classic example being when the manager of the Hunter Hotel [Macca] suggested I open my guitar case on the floor at my feet for the punters to deposit money into to show their appreciation of my performance. At the end of my gig the barmaid would count up the coins and notes scattered within my guitar case and then contribute the shortfall from the till to make up my asking fee. It was a very clever ploy as, some days, - when the drinkers were exceptionally generous [or pissed], Macca's contribution was a mere fraction of what the audience had given me. It wasn't the only unique aspect of *that* gig – busking in the public bar – as my stage was also like no other I had graced. It was the bar!

High above the bar staff, beer taps and boozers – most of whom sat with their backs to me, looking out the window into the mall, watching the endless parade of young women walking by, shopping or walking up to Newcastle beach in short skirts and bikini bras – perched on a stool, I serenaded and solicited donations. Appropriately known as "The Fishbowl" that bar was my training ground – learning to satisfy such a diverse audience. Mr Bojangles and some Elvis kept the old, early morning, drinkers and shift workers happy while the younger crowd, priming up for "Heroes" playing in the back bar that afternoon, were happy with Locomotive Breath [Jethroe Tull] or some "Stones". My original compositions were well accepted too – especially my drunk driving song [PCA the Easy Way], which I wrote on the train to the gig while my licence was suspended! The more the drinkers liked me the more they donated into my guitar case which made Macca happy because it saved him more money – and he gave me more gigs which made me happy! [A Laissez-faire economy!]

Counting the money in my case after one of those gigs I found two crumpled pieces of paper; The first, was an "I.O.U. $1" with an indiscernible signature from a punter who had, obviously, liked my music but who had spent all his money on his last beer! That was hilarious – and I kept that note[and still have it-allowing for inflation, it could be quite valuable if I ever find that punter!]. The second note was much less amusing. It was a warning from a disgruntled *Christian* who had heard me sing my song called "Pray in my own Time" and it said..."God won't go to hell but you will if you don't take Jesus as your saviour!". I always knew that song was bound to upset some of my audience but I wonder if some of the hell I went through later in my life would propitiate that person!

Catching the train one Saturday morning and walking from Newcastle station up to the Hunter Hotel – for, what was to be, my last gig there – I found the windows and doors had been boarded up and a sign attached to them, saying the pub was closed.

Before taking up the licence of the Cambridge Hotel [at the other end of Hunter street] Macca had decided to not trade on his last day - at the Hunter – in order to avoid a possible riot like the one at the Star Hotel. Particularly as "Heroes"[who played on the night of the Star Hotel riot] were scheduled to also perform that day!

***

By the end of that first full time year as an entertainer I was doing up to six gigs per week, often earning two to three times more money than what I had previously earned per week at the BHP steelworks. The financial success of my new career eased my feelings of doubt and guilt for leaving that full-time office job and I proudly boasted my earnings to my parents to help reassure them I had made the right employment choice. It also put me in a position to be able to afford to move out of my parents home and into a place of my own - completing my quest for total independence and freedom.

A series of unfortunate events played a part in deciding when and where I would make my move to relocate.

It began with the tragic death of a friend who crashed his motor cycle into a bus in a horrific accident. Bob was part of a large group of friends I had been hanging out with at that time, most of whom lived in a historic three story building in Melbourne street, East Maitland, that had been converted into apartments. The diversity of tenants and the crazy things that went on in that building always reminded me of the infamous TV show called Number 96. It was a convenient distance from our favourite pub, The Hunter River Hotel. The infamous "H.R." was our sacred watering hole. Our *social central* where we'd all gather on weekends to party. I probably spent way too much time there, with my mates, in the first few years after finishing high school, playing darts with Jol [the master of maths in calculating our scores] or watching Tim terrorise the pin-ball machine in the foyer or demolishing a kilo of prawns with Steer and the boys in the beer garden on a Saturday afternoon. Not to mention the endless hours of playing pool in the lounge bar - where we all considered ourselves to be budding Eddie Charlton's with the cue stick!

It was after many long, boozy, nights at the H.R. [which was so much like our version of Arnold's Milkbar in the TV show-Happy Days!] that we'd all stagger back to Bob's large, one-room, apartment to "party on!". He was a wild bloke with a good heart—a bit like The Fonz in Happy Days—and always had a supply of weed for us to smoke while we drank our takeaway grog—usually comprising of a mixture of cans of Tooheys Old beer, a flagon of Mcwilliam's Port and a bottle of Bacardi Rum. Needless to say, we woke up sick and sorry the next morning, on the floor, while Bob, seemingly unaffected, made us coffee and toast with a contented smile on his face. His death had a severe impact on all of us and his funeral day was one of the saddest of my life. As we drove home from the cemetery in Wamberal, on the central coast, all bawling our eyes out and consoling each other, I realised the true fragility of life, and sensed the need to grasp every opportunity that life might offer.

Bob's Funeral

I didn't know you well but well enough to grieve here in pain
to see you laid to rest, never to see you again
Good bye my friend
we have lost a friend

As we stand around,our words drowned by our tears
realising now how close we were over the years
the memory of his smile appears
goodbye my friend
we have lost a friend

With him gone the space is too wide
where he stood in our lives but now a memory inside
let's close this gap, come closer to each other
and let this justify the death of our brother

He was wild but his freedom was admired, and envied by me
he was not the one to keep his soul locked in it's shell
He gave it to us all
that's how we knew him and loved him so well

I didn't know you well but well enough to grieve here in pain
to see you laid to rest, never to see you again
Good bye my friend
we have lost a friend

While writing this chapter I stumbled across my old booking diary from that week - when Bob had died - and I was amazed to see just how many gigs I was doing at that time. I had residencies at the Beach Hotel in Merewether on Sundays and Wednesdays; every Tuesday night at a gay wine bar in Hamilton called "Pete's"; alternating Thursdays at the Delaney Hotel in Cook's Hill, the Chelmsford Hotel at Kurri Kurri and the Hunter Hotel in, what is now, the Newcastle Mall; Friday nights at The George and Dragon Tavern in East Maitland and Saturday nights alternating between the Merry Magpie Wine Bar in Hunter street Newcastle, the Hunter Hotel, weddings, and parties all over the Hunter Valley - and eventually settling into a residency that lasted three years at the Belair Hotel in Kotara. In the month of May 1980, leading up to the day of Bob's funeral on the 29th, I had played twenty five gigs, even playing on the very night of his funeral. I still remember the feeling of consolation, singing that night gave me, in dealing with the grief of his death.

Two days after the funeral, on saturday the 31st May, I had the rare opportunity of having a day off. One of only five Saturdays that year that I didn't have a gig booked. As I lay in bed that morning, luxuriating in the knowledge of having the day free to wind down from the hectic schedule of the previous month and the strain of sadness from the previous week, I heard the home phone ringing in the lounge room. I heard my mother answer the call then knock on my bedroom door to tell me it was for me. As I sleepily stumbled to the phone and put it to my ear I heard the bright and dictatorial toned voice of my old school mate, Mearsy, say... " we're going wine tasting at the vineyards today, be dressed and ready, I'll be there in ten minutes! "

It's hard to believe that *one day* could be so pivotal in my life and career, but *that* Saturday certainly was!

The term "going wine tasting" is a classy way of saying " we're getting on the piss!" Subsequently, my recollection now, of that day, is fairly sketchy - as it *also* was on the following Sunday morning - when I woke up on the floor of a friends apartment.

Telling the story of how I ended up on the floor of that apartment seems to make more sense if I tell it in reverse - so here goes;

1. My girlfriend and I had been given a lift to this apartment - in a police car - and dropped off there at about 2am Sunday morning.

2. My girlfriend and I had been offered that lift by police officers at Maitland Police station where I had been giving a statement as to why I was driving a car while being intoxicated with alcohol - and I was explaining to the officers that my reason for being so intoxicated was that my girlfriend had been nagging me too much. [Our relationship was short lived after that night!]

3. We had been taken to that Police station about midnight, after I had been pulled over by a patrol car in the car park of the East Maitland shopping centre – where, upon being asked to step out of the vehicle, a bottle of beer fell out of my lap and smashed on the ground at the policeman's feet.

4. At 11.30pm that same patrol car had felt the

need to pull me over after they had observed me driving my car around a corner by mounting the footpath rather than staying on the road.

5. Prior to driving on the footpath, I had been drinking with my [ex] girlfriend at the Hunter River Hotel, at about 10pm – trying to convince her to go out with me again- after our recent break-up.

6. Prior to drinking with my ex girlfriend, I had been dining at a Chinese restaurant in East Maitland with my old school mate "Mearsy" and other old school friends - with whom I had spent the day "wine tasting" at the Cessnock Vineyards. To compliment our Chinese banquette, we toasted with a bottle of Mateus Rose' and a few beers, at about 7pm.

7. Before arriving at this Chinese restaurant we had stopped at a few Pubs in Maitland to celebrate our "wine tasting" day, with a few beers, at about 5pm.

8. Before driving to Maitland for a few beers we had spent the whole day driving from one vineyard to another, around Pokolbin - tasting the wines they had to offer at their cellar doors.

9. At about 10am that morning, after receiving his phone call, Mearsy and I had driven around Maitland picking up some old school friends - to go "wine tasting" in the Vineyards.

An agenda for a day out such as this was never going to end well and I'm so grateful that no one was seriously hurt, apart from Elizabeth, my unfortunate ex girlfriend, who was caught up at the *bad* end of it - who, by the way, has never let me live it down! This, however, occurred at a time when "breath testing for drunk driving" was in it's infancy and the usual test for sobriety, up 'till then, had been to walk in a straight line with your fingers touching the tip of your nose. There was also little or no education on drink driving, and many drivers would joke about how they managed to drive home, while drunk, by driving between the two lines in the centre of the road - which was a distortion of the *single* centre line that their blurred vision was comprehending!

Three weeks later, on Monday 23rd June 1980, on a crisp sunny morning, my mother dropped me off at the Maitland Courthouse, where, despite having glowing references - including, ironically, even one from the publican of the Beach Hotel - my licence was suspended for three months and I was fined $300 for drunk driving or P.C.A.

I was so humiliated and ashamed of myself that day!- berating myself incessantly - and travelled to Newcastle on the train that evening, with my guitar and bag of leads, to attend my gig at the Hunter Hotel. Not only was I ashamed of my reckless behaviour in my car on that fateful night, but I'd jeopardised my burgeoning career by loosing my licence – essential for driving myself to gigs. I also felt I'd brought shame to the family name, but was amazed at the support and empathy my parents showed me - especially when my mother offered to drive me to some of my gigs. I swell with admiration and gratitude, thinking of how she sat - knitting in the car - in the car park at the Bel Air Hotel, every Saturday afternoon, for three hours, while I performed inside. It was reminiscent of those earlier years—driving me to Kitchener to practise in my school rock band, every Sunday—and I'm eternally grateful to both my parents for their support of my musical journey.

I had plenty of support from my friends, at that time, as well—volunteering to be my Chauffeurs—to get me to my gigs, but unfortunately, they would all inevitably start drinking at the venue and risked being booked for drunk driving as well. This worried me - as I didn't want to be the cause of *them* loosing their licences. To lessen the risk, I rotated them as much as possible, but one friend in particular, Gerard—who was one of the biggest drinkers of them all—*kept* volunteering! Ironically, Gerard lived right near the corner where the Police had seen me driving on the footpath!

The Hunter River hotel was just around the corner from that notorious footpath that had led to my demise and it was almost like salvation when I returned there to perform my song depicting the incident. The same lounge bar where I used to play pool was packed with friends and fans of the song. So packed that they covered up the pool table for people to sit on! There were even people sitting, crossed legged, on the floor at the foot of the stage, singing along to it and other tunes in my repertoire as if at a sing-a-long by a camp-fire. Actually the open fire place in the room had a fire burning in it so the crackling of the glowing embers and the aroma of pine scented smoke enhanced that atmosphere. It is one of the fondest memories I have of performing! It felt as though the whole town had come to support me and my songwriting path-patting me on the back as if to say "local boy makes good!" and justifying my career choice! I still feel that sense of support and admiration whenever I meet up with old friends from Maitland—it's wonderfully humbling and heart-warming!

P.C.A. The Easy Way

Well I'd been drivin' my car for five years then
and I'd been drinkin' at the pub for more
but in all those years of drunken driving
I'd never been caught by the law
"till the night they caught me drivin' on the footpath
with a bottle of beer in my hand
I told them I'd been drownin' my sorrows
but they just didn't seem to understand

Well that day had started so fine
we toured the vineyards and tasted the wine
then just to make a day of it all
we did a 27 hotel pub crawl
at the local I won me a heart
but drivin' her home I wasn't so smart
and so my story tells
apprehended by officer Wells

for havin' the prescribed concentration of alcohol flowin' around in my veins
now I can't drive my car I ain't goin' too far
travlin' on buses and trains

Well I admit I was drunk
I'd even go so far to say I was blind
and when I breathed into that plastic bag
you should have seen those little crystals shine
So he drove me to the police station
I said "lock me up and throw the key away"
but he said "sit down there you ain't goin' nowhere
'till you listen to what I've got to say"

he said you've got the
prescribed concentration of alcohol flowin' around in your veins
you wont be drivin' your car you won't be goin' too far
travlin' on buses and trains

Well I was too drunk to know my name
too drunk to fell the shame
too drunk to know or care
why the hell I was even there

So I hired me a lawyer and I went to court
hopin' for a second chance
and I was so damned scared you could see my knees
knockin' right through my pants
The judge knew I wasn't all bad
he even told me that it made him feel sad
to give me a three hundred dollar fine
and three months suspension for the crime

of havin' the
prescribed concentration of alcohol flowin' around in my veins
now I can't drive my car I ain't goin' too far
travlin' on buses and trains

Don't have the
prescribed concentration of alcohol flowin' around in your veins
cause when you can't drive your car
you won't be goin' too far
travelin' on buses and trains

You know that I won't ever
drink and drive again

One for the road.

A sobering experience recalled in debut single

Tony Johns under the grip of the law — Sgt Ron Wells.

MOST songwriters are usually eager to relate their experiences in song, but few are likely to shout to the world about a personal run in with the law.

But not Tony Johns.

He's documented his experiences in a new song titled *P.C.A. (the Easy Way)*, telling us all about how he was arrested in East Maitland in 1980 and charged with driving with the prescribed concentration of alcohol in his blood.

The song is Tony's debut single and was launched last night to thunderous applause at the Ambassador Restaurant.

The young singer-composer is now hoping the song gets picked up by Newcastle's radio lads. And while this is all happening he intends keeping busy promoting the single, recording a new single and eventually an album.

Back to Tony's debut single.

After his arrest (by Sgt Ron Wells, of Maitland Police), Tony was fined $300 and banned from driving for three months. He wrote the song while he was suspended.

The song is a timely message but one that's also 'light-hearted and very commercial', Tony said.

He says he learnt his lesson and hopes offers give some thought before they take to the wheel after a night out drinking.

The Police officer who booked me on that night had quite a reputation, in Maitland, for apprehending drink driving offenders, so this song really hit home for a lot of locals - and boosted my reputation as an entertainer as more people heard it. Ron Wells or "Wellsie", as he was affectionately known, was also a good sport, and he even agreed to having a *[tongue in cheek]* photo taken with me for the local newspaper to promote my song - that I released, as a single, a few years later. The picture was a mock up of him arresting me, standing in his uniform behind me with his hand firmly grasping my shoulder. I got to know him better when he dropped in to my parents house to see how I was coping a few days after the incident. He seemed genuinely concerned that I wouldn't re-offend, as he appreciated the impact that loosing my licence would have on my career. Not fully accepting my fate, I had a few drinks, in defiance, at the HR, a few days before my court appearance - and nearly died of heart failure when I realised the car following me home that night was "Wellsie" in a patrol car! I sighed with huge relief as I pulled into my parents driveway and he drove on past. I could've well gone over the limit again that night and I'm sure he was just letting me know he was watching me. It was *that night* I decided to leave Maitland and move to Newcastle and to stop driving when I'd had a few too many!

Pete's Wine Bar

Although the move from Maitland to Newcastle was only a short, thirty minute drive the social and cultural gap was much wider – as I soon found out when I was hired to perform at a small but notorious wine bar in Beaumont street, Hamilton, called Pete's Wine Bar.

Despite the audience being one of the most appreciative of all the venues on my calender-showering me with generous applause after every song-I suspected my engagement there was more about being eye-candy for the, predominantly, male audience rather than my musical abilities. I rarely had to buy myself a drink as I sat at the bar-in my breaks-being chatted up by the inquisitive clientele, who, after being informed of my heterosexual preference, would politely leave me alone. A middle aged businessman still bought me a bourbon and coke when I told him I was *straight* and despondently mumbled to himself..."what a shame" as he moved along the bar to the next eligible young man. My brief tenure at that wine bar was an invaluable social education that enhanced my appreciation of the gay community. The frank honesty and humour of the homosexual friends and acquaintances I encountered along my life's journey endeared them to me most.

Moving Away

The room in which this song was born is the home of my new life
where maternal apron strings lie cut by my ambitious knife
where I run my life and my life runs me
running further from my home
from father, mother, friends and childhood memories I have known

I'm moving away, leaving my home
Moving away
Trying to make it on my own

For 21 years I had it sweet, I had it all laid on
I'd come to take for granted what they'd given me for so long
A mother who gave of all she had, for giving was all she knew
A father working all his life but now their struggle's through

I'm moving away, leaving my home
Moving away
Trying to make it on my own

I've got to prove the life I've chosen will ensure
security and peace of mind
To pay the bills and cure the ills that lie before
and heal the scares that lie behind...me

I don't expect to find it easy, a struggle would make it real
wisdom from experience from the pain I'm sure to feel
It's done at last I'm on my own, my future sings to me
the melody of my soul, my song of destiny

I'm moving away, leaving my home
Moving away
Trying to make it on my own

The Hill

With regular gigs at the Beach Hotel in Merewether on Wednesday nights and Sunday afternoons, I'd got to know a few of the locals there and was especially surprised one day when Mark Richards, the world champion surfer at the time, said "Hello Tony" as he walked past me on his way to the bar. The Sunday afternoon sessions were the most "chilled" gigs I've ever played, set up with my guitar, harmonica and speakers, in the rounded corner of the public bar that looked out over Merewether Beach, Dixon Park and Bar Beach - and all the way up the coast to the headland of Tomaree at Port Stephens - with the big blue Tasman Sea as my backdrop. The audience was also fairly chilled, and comprised of local surfies - and *wanna be surfies* from the outer suburbs - but whatever their preferred sporting activity, most of the guys were there to perv. To perv on the magnificent array of beautiful women, many of whom were wearing nothing more than skirts or shorts and the bikini tops they had been wearing that day at the beach below. My repertoire of songs - by Neil Young, Poco, America, The Eagles, Bob Dylan, James Taylor and Don Mclean - set the ideal mood, for all those tanned and salt encrusted bodies, to mingle, as the sun set over the billowing chimney stacks of the BHP steelworks to the west, in Mayfield.

As much as performing, I enjoyed watching the passing parade of beautiful bodies, and the clumsy attempts of the guys hoping to win a heart in this seaside social sideshow;

Merv The Perv

His name is Jack but we'll call him Merv
'cause all that he does is stand there and perv
he doesn't say much he's a bit lost for words
he just sips his drink and watches the birds

Merv the perv the man with the optic nerve
just havin' a look a bit of a captain Cook
he'll moan and sigh as the ladies walk by
but he won't say a word 'cause he's too shy

He checks out the chicks as they walk through the door
and wonders how each one would look in the raw
his eyes open wide take in every bit
of the view up a skirt or the flash of a tit

Merv the perv the man with the optic nerve
just havin' a look a bit of a captain Cook
he'll moan and sigh as the ladies walk by
but he won't say a word 'cause he's too shy

He's on the alert his judgement is trusty
He'll spy a bita skirt thinking she's not too dusty
He's hunting for beaver and loaded his gun
and sure would love to give his ferret a run

Merv the perv the man with the optic nerve
just havin' a look a bit of a captain Cook
he'll moan and sigh as the ladies walk by
but he won't say a word 'cause he's too shy

As a child he remembers pinching the bras and nickers off the neighbour's clothesline
and peeping through the keyhole of the bathroom all the time
at his sister who was nine

It's an Aussie tradition for the boys and the men
to be having a beer and a perv now and then
the big hairy eyeball is a natural reflex
so Merv have a good perv on the opposite sex

Merv the perv the man with the optic nerve
just havin' a look a bit of a captain Cook
he'll moan and sigh as the ladies walk by
but he won't say a word 'cause he's too shy

Geographically and demographically, Merewether was *The Beautiful place to be*, so that's where I aimed my flat hunting expedition. Unfortunately, it was the suburb that everyone else had their sights set on, therefore making accommodation scarce and expensive, so I settled on a moderately priced, one bedroom apartment in High street, on The Hill, in Newcastle. My Flat was part of a Heritage style mansion that had been divided into three self contained apartments, one of which was located in the converted attic space. A guy who I'd known from Maitland moved in upstairs shortly after me and we became drinking mates, spending a lot of nights, out on the prowl, at the local pubs and nightclubs. Bobby was a smooth talker with the women and a handy accomplice in the *night-life*. If I was performing at these venues, he'd introduce me to the girls he'd been chatting with - saving me a lot of groundwork - and we'd all go out to a night club after my show. He'd previously worked as a green keeper, and we had a running joke - about being a *grass cutter* - if either of us tried to chat up the same girl. He was an exuberant character and I spent many a sleepless night listening to his amorous antics, above my ceiling, after he'd had a successful night, trawling for a catch, out on the town.

The Hill was a historic suburb of Newcastle that featured some of the cities' most prominent buildings of architectural significance, as well as magnificently landscaped parkland on the coastal headlands that offered outstanding views in all directions. From my home I could walk fifteen minutes in any direction to go shopping in The Mall or Darby street, or have a swim at Newcastle Beach or Bar Beach, stopping to admire the scenery at Susan Gilmour beach - the unofficial nude beach! A favourite past time, was hitting old golf balls off the cliff in King Edward Park - near the WW11 gun emplacement bunkers - and watching them disappear into the foaming waves, far below, crashing onto the rock platforms near the Bogey Hole. Inspiration for new songs to write came easily as I strolled along the cliffs edge, near Strezlecki Lookout, just on dusk, watching the sunset bath the city, suburbs and distant valley in an orange haze, while the darkening wide blue pacific rolled hypnotically behind me. I sometimes took a bottle of wine to enhance the atmosphere, and was lucky not to fall off the edge of those loose precipices - that have now been made safer with an impressive stainless steel walkway called The Newcastle Memorial Walk. I have the fondest memory of sharing a bottle of wine, one evening, with a neighbour who I became acquainted with at that time. She lived in one of the Converted Mansions, in "The Terrace", that backed onto my house. We met at the back fence, one day, while hanging out our washing, and would visit each other-by climbing through a hole in the fence - to borrow some sugar or a cup of milk. We had a brief affair that was mainly based on our need for companionship, as we were both new to town and still coming to terms with living away from our parents homes. We shared that bottle of wine and our life's stories, late one afternoon, while sitting on the concrete roof of one of those war bunkers in King Edward Park, and gazing out over the ocean. I returned to that same bunker to sit down and write this song, months later, when our lives had taken different paths that were never again to cross.

A Loving Friend

How do I say we're only friends?
how would she feel if I ever do?
but saying it would be where our friendship ends
so I'll leave it for now and try to think it through

How do I say I don't need you near?
How can I pull away when her hand holds mine?
It's hard to act surprised when she drops by
and lately she drops by all the time

Can lovers ever be friends?
Or is loving where friendship ends?
Bedroom friendships are rare
"one night stands" the label they bare
it seems so unfair

I hope she understands the way I feel
and maybe even share the thoughts that I conceal
The nights and days we've shared I treasure and see before
The days and nights ahead as friends
Friends but nothing more

Living on The Hill was a wonderful place to be introduced to life in Newcastle, and the walks and bike rides to the beach and city certainly kept me fit - especially the return trips, up roads such as Memorial Drive and, *the near vertical,* Brown Street. One night after a few drinks with friends who lived near The Mall, I breathlessly staggered up Brown Street, stopping for a rest at a stone tower that looked liked it should've been part of a medieval castle. I was to learn later, it was an old Leading Light Beacon Tower, built to guide the ships into the harbour. I was also to learn later that it was at this landmark, that night, that I lost a piece of jewellery I'd been wearing, every day, since I began my full-time musical career. It too, was a symbol of direction for me.

Lucky Charm

*I used to have a lucky charm on a chain around my neck
a Stirling silver miniature guitar that would protect
me from harm or fear of danger far or near*

*Lucky charm to bring me wealth, romance and everlasting health
but in your absence do I find
your power was all in my mind
all in my mind*

*Strange how this small thing
had power such to bring
reality to my dreams
substance to my schemes*

*Well I lost that lucky charm but now that it's gone
seems to me it's luck ran dry
but I'm alive and doin' fine*

*Lucky charm to bring me wealth, romance and everlasting health
but in your absence do I find
your power was all in my mind
all in my mind*

New Friends

I enjoyed living on my own, but rarely felt lonely.

The only unpleasant and lonely moment in my new home was the day I woke up to hear the devastating news of John Lennon's murder - which I regarded as an affront to all that is good about music in life, particularly as I had just begun *my* musical sojourn.

On the other hand, the most bizarre and erotic event to occur at that address was on the cold and stormy night that frantic knocking woke me, at midnight, to find a voluptuous, leggy redhead standing at my door, pleading for me to let her stay until the storm passed. I'd met her, only a few days earlier, when she moved into apartments just around the corner from my place. I could hardly refuse, considering her distressed state and the fact she'd heard other noises, apart from the storm, which she feared to be a prowler. To make matters more awkward, she insisted on sleeping naked with me, while I lay there, in my flannelette pyjamas, wide awake, heart racing, listening to her snore, until sunrise. Yes, I was *that* niave back then, and yes, I *did* consider making a move on her, but that little "guardian angel voice" in my head kept telling me *this situation* was just too good to be true and to keep my hands off her. The kiss she gave me on the cheek, with a playful wink of her eye, as she returned home that morning, told me I'd blown a golden opportunity! It was an error of judgement that I would incredibly repeat, the following year, when a gorgeous, blond bombshell, who had just broken up with one of my mates, asked to stay over with me for consolation and company. In respect for my mate, I reluctantly kept a safe distance from her in my bed that night - which was another long, sleepless, tortuous eternity. Many years later, to add insult to injury, she confided that she also lay awake all *that* night, wondering why I didn't make a move on her, and assumed that I must've been gay! Life can be so cruel! - especially when you try to do what you consider to be *the right thing!* It's almost bizarre that, fifteen years later, my infants, knocking on my bedroom door in the night, after they'd had a bad dream, would be the inspiration for this song.

Can I Sleep In Your Bed Tonight

Sometimes you win sometimes you lose
Sometimes even beggars like me get to choose
Sometimes the wind will blow my way
Sometime I know I'm gonna hear that lady say

Can I sleep in your bed tonight?
My bed's too cold and your bed looks just right
I'll cuddle up to ya and you can hold me tight
Can I sleep in your bed tonight?

Sometimes the thunder shakes the night
That howlin' wind and lightn'n gives her such a fright
It wont be long 'till she comes knockin' on my door
Askin' me the question that I've been waitin' for

Can I sleep in your bed tonight?
My bed's too cold and your bed looks just right
I'll cuddle up to ya and you can hold me tight
Can I sleep in your bed tonight?

All those lonely nights that true love was denied
'Till the night we lay together
The day she was my bride.

Sometimes my wife and I retire
To rediscover the flame that set our hearts on fire
And just when things are gettin' hot
Our three year old walks in the room
And makes us stop.........(when she say's........)

Can I sleep in your bed tonight?
My bed's too cold and your bed looks just right
I'll cuddle up to ya and you can hold me tight
Can I sleep in your bed tonight?

Old Friends & New

Many of my old friends, from Maitland, often came to see me play at my Newcastle venues to support me on my new turf - and I was making new friends as well. Most of those *new friends* were made, one Saturday night, when I invited my audience at the Bel-Air Hotel that afternoon, to come back to my flat for a party. In the crowded mayhem, within my small apartment, I became friends with three distinct groups of people that night - who all remain friends to this day. Firstly, there was a group of people who had been following me from venue to venue, heckling me and singing along to my songs, who laughingly called themselves the Mormon No Knackers Choir [irreverently referring to the Mormon Tabernacle Choir!]. Their ring leaders were Paul and Eddie who, today, follow and support Paul's daughter, Jayde, around various venues as she performs her music, just as they had done for me when I was her age. The second, was a bunch of Kotara locals I called the Bel-Air Gang. They were a tight knit group of friends who became like family to me, especially the blokes who introduced me to trail bike riding and snow and water skiing - becoming the brothers I'd often wished for, as a child. Ringa and Gluey, in particular, were two of those new brothers that I would go on to share many adventures with, over the following years. The third group of friends I would come to know and share my musical career with, was indirectly introduced to me, that night, when I met Jus Gordon. He was a talented singer, pianist and guitarist, with a sharp wit, whose style of entertainment had definite influences from his family's vaudeville background. He was still employed as a tax accountant at I.T.P, and was interested in how I was managing - being a full time musician - after leaving my day job - as he wanted to do the same. I still remember my bemusement at his reluctance to go into a full time music career, considering his abundance of talent, and assured him I was doing great, so far, with no regrets. He had a regular solo gig at the Bel-Air at that time but was also in a band called The Orphans - comprising of Les Gully on drums, Jeff Dunn on lead guitar, Greg Dawson on bass and Pam Barnett on vocals. Gordon introduced me to these wonderful and talented people who I've been lucky enough to share the stage and recording studio with, on many occasions over the years, even up until recently. Les and Jeff played on my first studio recording of P.C.A. The Easy Way. Gordon and The Orphans were the first of the local musical family that I would become a part of, as I settled into my new life in Newcastle.

Life was good. I had set up my new, independent life in Newcastle. I still had the support and friendship from everyone I'd known - growing up in Maitland - and was making new friends every day, along my way.

To My Friends

*All of you through and through are my friends
and in this song my gratitude to you do I send
çause anytime I'm lonely I know that I can find
my peace of mind in your company it's so nice to see
you're friendship is the only cure for me*

*and that's why I must come out and tell you
without you here all around me I'd fall depressed and helpless too
you're the smile upon my face the beat of my heart
you've been there from the start
and I hope you'll be there to the end*

*Living our lives together we share the joy and pain
side by side forever in sunshine and in rain
now can't you see I'm trying to say your the sunrise of my day
my stars in the milky way and what ever you do
don't ever dare go away*

*Oh I'm so glad to have friends as good as you
Thankyou there's not enough I can do or say to repay you
Sing with me as you have sung a thousand times before
sing the song I wrote for you that tells you I am sure
that I have the best friends a man could ever need
and this my humble deed is only a token
of words never before spoken*

*Make me laugh let sorry pass use your magic power
you're the gift of life to me like sunlight to a flower
and though I cannot always be the friend to you that I should be
I am telling you right now you're forever on my mind
your always so damn kind
you're out to blow my mind*

*Of all the beautiful things that my eyes see
the most beautiful sight of all is to see my friends with me
listen to them singing loud and clear with me
watching them giving their friendship to me
that's what I love to see
and I'll give my friendship back to them for free*

*Oh I'm so glad to have friends as good as you
Thankyou there's not enough I can do or say to repay you*

Time to Party

The freedom of life as a full-time musician was wonderful - but a bit like a double edged sword. As I tried to create an atmosphere of *a party,* at all of my gigs - and because I was gigging nearly every night - every night *was* a party! To compound that, I often went out to parties - or night clubs - after nearly every gig, so, as my health started to suffer from my ill disciplined lifestyle, my conscience began to suggest curtailing my nocturnal festivities. I was learning that *"with freedom-comes responsibility"* but, as with many of life's other lessons, I was a slow learner! I prided myself in getting to know my audience, and if I got invited out after a gig, to party with them, I was too obliging and just couldn't say no. I often compared my lifestyle to that of a vampire - sleeping most of the day and coming to life at night. The only difference being, that I managed to get an hour or two at the beach in the afternoons - to keep a bit of colour in my complexion.

Wastin'

I've been dreamin', dreamin' 'bout my baby
Dreamin', dreamin' 'bout my baby
I've been sleepin' half the day
wastin' my life away

I've been sleepin' 'till past midday
Lyin' in bed I'm gonna sleep my life away
Dreamin' 'bout a better way
I've been wastin' my life away
wastin' my life away

I've been wastin' my life away
sittin' around just lettin' my mind decay
I've been dreamin' 'bout a better day
just wastin' my life away
wastin' my life away

I've gotta find a way to get up with the mornin' sun
gotta get to work gotta earn my pay
It's time for me to stop wastin' my life away

I've been dreamin', dreamin' 'bout my baby
lyin' in bed I'm gonna drive myself half crazy
sleepin', sleepin' half the day
Lord I've been wastin' my life away
wastin' my life away

Despite the battering I was giving my body every night, my general health was OK - except for a chronic sinus condition that I'd had since my early teens. Constantly sniffling, sneezing and blowing my nose, eventually lead to reoccurring throat infections that impacted on my singing. At a time when "smoking" was still allowed in pubs, it's really not surprising I suffered from respiratory problems, especially when most of the exhaust fans in the venues were often right behind the stage. As I was drawing in deep breaths to belt out my tunes, I was inadvertently smoking the audiences' second hand smoke as it travelled past me to the exhaust outlet! I wasn't a cigarette smoker - and never have been - but I was probably smoking a packet of them at every gig, without even knowing it! The smoke didn't bother me at the time, in fact the haze seemed to enhance the atmosphere, and I'd grown up accustomed to the smell, as both my parents had smoked in the house when I was a child.

My only vices, at the time, were beer, spirits and the occasional joint that might be passed onto me at parties. It wasn't uncommon for me to go straight from my Saturday afternoon gig at the Bel-Air hotel in Kotara, to set up my equipment in a backyard somewhere in Newcastle or Maitland, to play for someone's birthday - usually a 21st. The generosity of the people who employed me to do these gigs usually lead to me indulging in all the food, drinks and other substances that were on offer, and - with my recent "Drink Driving Offence" still fresh in my mind - I would stay the night there, sleeping in the back of my car with my equipment. They were great, fun nights, and although, sure, there might have been the occasional fight or gate crashers, I'm grateful to have experienced those times. Unlike today, where social media has made events, like that, highly risky! In 1981, the only way *word got around about a party* was by *word of mouth,* such as the time we cruised up and down the back streets of Waratah, looking for a party we'd heard mentioned at the public bar of the Delaney hotel in Cooks Hill!

The Typical Australian Backyard Party [circa 1981]

Tonight I'm going to a party not sure of the address
tonight I'm going to a party in a backyard just like all the rest
I'm looking for the cars parked up and down the street
coloured lights hanging on the clothes line
noise from a stereo, people going merryO
it shouldn't be all that hard to find

Tonight I'm going to a party, twenty first, I think
tonight I'm going to a party and I hope my breath don't stink
From eating little boys, party pies, sausage rolls and such
drinking beer from an eighteen gallon keg
probably drink gallons too much

Going to a typical Australian backyard party
Going to a typical Australian backyard party

Tonight I'm sitting at a party in a ten by twelve tent drinking with the men
talkin' 'bout cricket or karate
women in the kitchen like hens in a chook pen
Boys with the boys, girls with the girls
but they all get together by the end of the night
get the girl a drink a nod and a wink
looking for romance not a backyard fight

Tonight I went to a party, twenty first I think
and when I left that party
I knew I had way too much to drink
Drivin' home all alone 'cause I usually travel that way
policeman pulled me to the side of the road
and he booked me for P.C.A.

Going to a typical Australian backyard party
Going to a typical Australian backyard party

● Tony Johns . . . singing for show goers.

It's showtime for Tony

1980

A dark-haired, blue-eyed, 21 year old man is sitting at Maitland Show, singing to the people.

His tunes are appreciated, as the pile of coins in the basket in front of his microphone reveals.

The singer's name is Tony Johns and he lives in Maitland with his parents.

"Sometimes I think I am wasting my time," he says, "but all it takes is one person tapping his feet and whistling along, and it is all worth it."

Tony worked as a clerk for BHP "until I could pay for all my equipment." "Now I want to have a go at making a living out of my singing.

Tony started playing the guitar at the age of 18. He plays in local pubs and restaurants, and has recently found busking at the Newcastle markets profitable.

"Sometimes I can make $10 an hour," he says but would "really like to be able to make enough money to be able to busk around the whole of Australia."

"It's a good way to meet people and I enjoy it," he said.

Popular music

Tony's repertoire ranges from ballads and country westerns, to popular music.

"Things are beginning to get interesting for me," said Tony. "I'm now able to get out by myself and manage myself. It's great."

Hittin' the Road

The old adage of *"Find something that you love to do and you'll never work a day in your life"* certainly rang true for me in those first few years of my new career as a full time entertainer. I just couldn't get enough of it, sometimes playing seven days a week - with two shows on Saturdays. For a brief period I also taught guitar at my old primary school in East Maitland but I found it very tedious and tiring, and although the principal and students were sad to see me go, I resigned after just a few months. Teaching sapped the energy that I required for my gigs at night but the experience left me with total respect and admiration for anyone who adopted it as their profession.

Determined to make the most of the abundance of time on my hands I even tried my hand at busking during the day and was surprised at how lucrative it could be, especially the time I busked at the Maitland Show. The key to my success there, was in setting up right at the entrance to the main pavilion and using my public address system to be heard above the din of the fair. The local newspaper even ran a story on me, describing me as a modern day electronic troubadour, but I was more impressed with my earnings that week which, based on an hourly rate, were triple what I used to earn as a cost clerk at the BHP steelworks. I got to know a lot of the "show folk" that week and was impressed by their camaraderie and laid back, *"go where the wind blows"* outlook on life - so much so, that I seriously considered going on the road with them as part of the Shows' attractions. Upon hearing this, my parents, who were still coming to terms with me leaving my secure office job, couldn't hide their disdain for my consideration of such a lifestyle and pleaded with me to stay loyal to all the local pubs who were giving me so much work. I suspected they preferred their Son's job description to be "Musician" rather than "Carnie".

So, the Show left town, and I stayed, playing an average of six gigs a week for two years until it all started to seem too easy, not the gigs, but getting them.

I had set myself the challenge of replacing my employment as a clerk, with employment as a musician, and it had worked!

I had so much work now, that I rarely had two consecutive days off and hadn't had a holiday in over two years. The gigs, however, were still very challenging and that's what fuelled my enthusiasm. I still got nervous and excited before every gig and if, by the end of the night, I hadn't connected with my audience and made them laugh and sing along with me as if it was a party, I considered I had failed. With that, as my benchmark, just about all of my gigs around Newcastle and Maitland were successes, and I began to consider widening my field of operation.

It was time to go on tour.

Time to see if my style of entertainment would work on audiences in which I knew no one and they didn't know me. To set myself a new challenge. To up the stakes. To raise the bar. So I loaded my guitar and PA into my Valient Gallant station wagon and headed north, up the Pacific Highway. I had no set destination in mind. My plan was simply to find gigs in each new town I drove into. The challenge was in selling myself to each new publican that I approached, as much as winning over the new audience, when I had been given the gig. As well as negotiating a performance fee, I had to negotiate for accommodation and meals to avoid having to sleep in my car. My usual pitch to the manager was that if my first performance, at a cut rate, went well, they would supply a room with breakfast for the duration of my stay in that town, while I did other shows in the area and more shows at their venue.

My first port'ocall was only an hour and a half from Newcastle, at Forster and Tuncurry, where I snagged gigs at The Lakes and Oceans Hotel, commonly referred to as *The Shakes and Motions,* and the Belevue Hotel - which had the unusual distinction of having a swimming pool in it's beer garden! That swimming pool featured prominently in my gig there! I may have decided to leave Newcastle for a while but Newcastle wasn't quite ready to let me go, and as I set up my gear I noticed a lot of familiar faces sitting at tables around that pool. It seemed that word had got around about *The* first gig of my East Coast Tour, and a few car loads of my old supporters had made the trek north to see me off, including Bobby, my old flat mate, and The Mormon No Knackers Choir from Kotara, as well as others. The pub was packed that night, and with so many people dancing, singing and drinking around that pool, it was inevitable that many of them, and their drinks, ended up in the water. Some by choice. Most by being pushed. Although the overall mood was festive, there was a hint of animosity in the air, with the locals resenting the influx of so many Novacastrians onto their turf. Luckily, the antics in the pool kept the mood light, helping to avoid the tension developing into anything more sinister.

The night was a successful start to my sojourn, and I partied into the wee small hours with my supporters all crammed into the tiny motel room that the publican supplied to me as part of my performance fee. Sheepishly returning to the beer garden late the following morning for breakfast, it was hilarious to see the cleaning staff supervising a guy - dressed in a wet suit and scuba gear - diving to the bottom of the pool to retrieve the dozens of schooner glasses and broken glass that had drowned in the melee of the previous night.

Leaving the security of my mobile support crew, I inched my way further north to Taree where, although I scored an interview on the local radio station, I couldn't secure a gig. A highlight of my stay there, however, was seeing and meeting the members of a popular band, at that time, called Redgum, who were also touring the East Coast. It would be later that year, John Schumann would begin writing their number one hit, "A walk in the light green" or "I was Only 19" as it became known, which became a standard on *my* repertoire for years to come. I remember them saying *"I should have planned my trip and booked my gigs in advance"*, but I was enjoying the spontaneity of my journey....

so far! They wished me well in my quest, and although our paths never crossed again, I often saw their posters in towns that I passed through over the following weeks.

Shortly before I left Taree, to head further north, I met another Novocastrian, Steve Barrett, who was living in Old Bar, just out of town. He'd seen me perform in Newcastle, and also played a bit of guitar. He put me up for the night, and while we were jamming on the guitars, he showed me a song he'd been writing with a mate. It was a funny song - about making special biscuits - but it's musical structure was a bit messy, so Steve offered me the song to see if I could clean it up a bit. I suspect the boys may have been sampling some of the ingredients for these cookies while they wrote this song, which became a permanent fixture on my repertoire, and brought the house down where ever I played it, both here and abroad.

Tony takes on a minstrelling tour

A young man who says he can't even write music is doing very well at a musical career.

He is Tony Johns, 22, of Newcastle, who is in the Mid North Coast area to start off a minstrelling tour to Queensland.

Tony is a guitarist and singer, and has worked full time at a range of night spots and hotels in Newcastle for the past two years.

Brought up in Maitland, Tony has received no formal music training.

He just picked up a guitar and played by ear and "feel."

He claims he cannot write down music, or read it, but he does write his own songs about things that happen in his life.

Now Tony says inspiration for his song writing has dried up, so he's off in search of new experiences and places to sing about.

He writes mainly ballads, and hopes to make his first recording when he gets back from his trip.

The trip is totally unplanned.

All Tony will be doing is driving from town to town, and trying to get gigs in local hotels.

He will perform at the Lakes and Oceans Hotel tonight and at the Bellevue, Tuncurry, on Saturday night, and hopes to work during Easter at Port Macquarie.

He says if he can't get bookings in venues, he will simply take to the streets and busk to gain cash to keep him going.

Tony is accompanied on his trip by two guitars and his portable amplifying equipment.

THE MANNING RIVER TIMES, FRIDAY, APRIL 10, 1981 —

Marijuana Cookies

*I make marijuana cookies in the morning
eat'm at night before I go to bed
But if the old girl ever busts me
sure I'm gonna wind up dead*

*You see I get out the great big China mixin' bowl
stir it all up with a wooden spoon
a block of hash, put the oven on high
and they'll be right for the afternoon*

*Then I smoke that...tft tft tft tft tft
all through the mornin' woo I get out o' my head
but if the ol' girl ever bust me
sure I'm gonna wind up dead*

*for makin' those marijuana cookies in the mornin'
and every night 'fore I go to bed
But if the policemans ever bust me
sure I'm gonna wind up dead*

*and they're gonna throw me in a great big prison cell
put me behind big iron bars
and I won't know if it's day or night
because I won't see the stars*

*but I'll be dreamin' 'bout my
marijuana cookies in the mornin'
and every night 'fore I go to bed
But if the policemans ever bust me
sure I'm gonna wind up dead*

well we go pickin' magic mushies on the weekend
yee ha I get outta my tree
people think that I'm a fool and crazy
but that's the way that I'd rather be

When Suzie comes around to see me in the even'n
we play around on the big brass bed
but she really gets the shits when I send her to the kitchen
'cause I'd rather have a marijuana cookie instead
I'd rather have a marijuana cookie instead

makin' marijuana cookies in the morning
and every night 'fore I go to bed
But if the old girl ever bust me
sure I'm gonna wind up dead

for makin' those marijuana cookies in the morning
and every night 'fore I go to bed
But if the old girl ever bust me
I won't worry I'll be off my head
I won't worry I'll be off my head
I won't worry I'll be right off my tree
I won't worry I'll be off my head
yee ha

My next stop was at the Port Macquarie Hotel where I negotiated a weeks accommodation in return for a couple of discounted gigs, which I supplemented with a few lucrative days of busking in the main street. I'd visited Port Mac many times previously, for holidays, and as much as I loved walking along the rocky break wall - where visitors painted their names and pictures on the boulders - and swimming at it's many beautiful and secluded beaches, it still felt too close to home to be a challenge, so I headed north again.

Coffs Harbour had all it's entertainment pre booked, especially as it was the Easter Holidays, so I was very lucky to pick up a gig and two nights accommodation at the Hoey Moey Hotel. That was due to the generosity of the manager, Terry, who had previously employed me at the Bel Air Hotel in Newcastle, and was glad to help me out on my crusade. I performed to a very small audience that night, as most of the town's population was down at the Plantation Hotel watching Midnight Oil. Terry, once again, feeling sympathetic for me, let me pack up early and rush down to catch The *Oil's* last set. I can still feel the charged energy, and smell the sweat, in that hot crowded room, as Peter Garrett bellowed and contorted his body, as if in a convulsive fit, to "Run by Night", while steam emanated eerily from his moon-like, bald head. The absolute power of that performance and the total admiration of the audience, stunned me, and was a stark contrast to the experience, the following day, of passing Garrett on a sandy track as he calmly walked back from the beach with his surfboard tucked under his arm.

Although I never said a word to him [*starstruck for sure!*], that encounter, along with meeting Redgum a week earlier, held significance for me. It made me feel like I was a part of the *mobile entertainment scene* that was moving up and down the Pacific Highway along the East Coast of Australia. Regardless of how insignificant my contribution might be, it was turning out to be a fantastic learning experience for me. I was surviving from day to day, town to town, doing what I loved and, I was writing songs!

The next song I was to write was born of my stay in South Grafton where, along with the natural beauty of the land and the warmth of the people, my eyes and mind were opened to some of the more questionable aspects of Australian values. Within a day of arriving, I secured gigs and accommodation at the Marina Hotel, with my room and its balcony, overlooking the Clarence river and farmland. I also picked up work at the Blue Goose Hotel and Weiley's Hotel in Grafton. My stay there was idyllic. Sightseeing around the area, browsing the shops in town, writing songs on the balcony of my room, taking in the view then wandering down to the public bar to have a beer and chat with the locals. I even felt like Tom Sawyer in Huckleberry Finn the day I made a makeshift fishing rod with a tree branch and some string, and amazed myself by catching a mullet - from the jetty across the road from the pub - that the kitchen staff cooked up for my dinner that night. All my gigs went well, and even my original songs were well accepted, except for one old guy telling me to "*drop the yanky accent*" when singing my song about drunk driving [P.C.A. The Easy Way]. I agreed with him on his criticism but explained that I'd written the song based on Jimmy Buffet's style, and the accent was inevitable. He argued that it was a good *Australian* song and should be sung like Slim Dusty would sing it. I concede he was right, and conscientiously adopted a more "Strawn" accent in future performances of that tune. The theme of nationalism took a more sinister turn later that night, when some Aboriginal guys, who were playing pool in the lounge area, were told to finish up the game and leave because the pub was shutting early that night. After the publican had ushered them to the doors, which he promptly locked, they stayed around for quite some time out on the footpath, occasionally banging on the doors and yelling out abuse, and I couldn't help but empathise with them, as I sat at the bar drinking with all the other "white" locals, continuing to be served. I couldn't see what they had done to deserve this treatment, and assumed there might have been past incidents that may have triggered this course of action by the manager. It was my first experience of, what appeared to be, a *racially motivated refusal of service,* and I was surprised by my own naivety in such issues.

Closing Early

*I was drinking at a pub on the south side of town
when a group of aboriginals came around 'bout nine
two hours before closing time
from the corner of their eyes watched the locals at the bar
contempt in their stare said "who do they think they are to come our way"
then I heard the publican say*

*If there's gonna be trouble it's not gonna be in here
çause we're closin' all the doors so drink up 'cause that's your last beer
in my travels up the north coast that's the way I found it to be
'cause when the blacks came around they closed early*

*It was a strange night for me 'cause where I'm from
the aboriginals have long since gone with history
and not surprisingly
and now ignorance revealed in a man once assured
racial division was a problem abroad and not here
but now I've seen it and it's all too clear*

*I've seen there's gonna be trouble but it's not gonna be in here
I saw them closin' all the doors sayin' "drink up 'cause that's your last beer"
in my travels up the north coast that's the way I found it to be
when the blacks came around they closed early*

*I'd never seen it here before
but it's walkin' up our back steps and it's knockin' on our door
that closed early*

*And now ignorance revealed in a man once assured
racial division was a problem abroad and not here
but now I've seen it and it's all too clear*

*I've seen there's gonna be trouble but it's not gonna be in here
I've seen ém closin' all the doors sayin' "drink up 'cause that's your last beer"
In my travels up the north coast that's the way I found it to be
when the blacks came around they closed early
when the blacks came around they closed early*

*Closing early
closing early
closing early*

Circumstances were reversed fourteen years later, as *I* performed on the *footpath* in Peel street, at the Tamworth country music festival. Whilst promoting my latest album called "The Valley", inside the music store behind me, one of the finest indigenous musicians in the country was promoting *his* new album and signing autographs. That musician was Troy Cassar-Daley who, ironically, had lived in Grafton at the time of my stay there. I only became aware that *He* was inside that music shop when, a week later, I called Gina Mandello at Sony music, to try and get a record deal, and she declined my request, saying that all her energies where being directed at promoting Troy, and that I should've come into the store that day to meet him and her. Although I graciously conceded that *His* singing voice and guitar skills were far superior to mine, I heard remarkable similarities in our song writing styles, and, to this very day, I often imagine the honour I would feel to have him record the song I wrote for my father called "Tribute".

The racial incident that I encountered all those years ago in South Grafton opened my eyes to the plight of the indigenous people of this country, and I was to see more of it, a few years later, when I visited Wilcannia, where my old childhood friend, Ted, was teaching at the high school. He was well liked by the Koori students and he took me out to the settlements to meet some of the families, where we shared stories, songs and a few drinks at a special site, by the river under the gum trees, not often visited by whites. It was a special night that gave me a feeling of real connection with the original custodians of this land. The low point of the night was returning to town where we had to choose between the "whites" pub or the "Black's" pub, to go have a drink. I had naively thought that segregation of this type had only occurred in the "Deep South" of America in the 1960's or in the apartheid era in South Africa.

When I returned to Newcastle after my North Coast Trip, I was invited to a Koori folk music club by Bobby, my old flatmate, to perform my new song, and it was a big hit with them. Bobby's indigenous heritage was particularly displayed by his brother, Mini Heath, who was an accomplished artist, specialising in Aboriginal Themes. Some of his paintings adorned the walls of Parliament house and I proudly have his "Echidna" painting hanging on my bedroom wall.

Next stop, on the *"North Coast Tour"* was;

Ballina

I'll never forget the time I spent in paradise
in a place that for me was my sugar and spice
a town sleeping by the sea
with a countryside so heavenly
it's beaconing me back to Ballina

I'll never forget the people I met the friends I made
and my only regret was after I left
I wish I could 've stayed
They all made me feel so at home
and now as I wander here all alone
my mind goes back to them in Ballina

It was a lovely time of the year to be there
swimming in the crystal clear mountain streams
dried by the warm autumn air
or fishing off the bridge where the river meets the sea
and the waves rolling under that bridge would beckon me to stay
and never go away

The land was so green and the sky so blue
this magical place for me would be a heavenly dream if you
would come here and spend your time
to live with me
and I think you'd find
this is where our lives would unwind

I'll never forget the time I spent in Ballina

Happy to be back near the coastline, this part of my journey was like discovering Elysium. With lush green farmland and forests that rolled right down to the pristine beaches and coastline, and a mild climate, I was happy to settle here, and a chance meeting, with some acquaintances from home, made that possible. A surfer I'd met while playing at the Beach hotel, back in Merewether, and his girlfriend and sisters, were living near Ballina in a house that overlooked the ocean, and upon running into me at the Ballina hotel, where I was staying and performing, they insisted I come and stay with them. It was too good to be true. They were the most easy going, friendly people I could've ever hoped to hook up with - and the girls were gorgeous - so how could I not accept their offer. As an added bonus they even helped me acquire gigs at surrounding towns such as the Anglers Arms at Lennox Head and the Eltham Hotel in the magical Village of Eltham. The gigs there, out in the garden, with families, surfies and hippies, sitting on the grass around me, were as chilled as a gig can get - and felt to me like my own mini version of Woodstock. The theme of *"Yasgur's Farm"* continued when I was invited back to a property near there, where friends' of George lived in a type of communal set up - growing their own vege's and other recreational herbs! What a dreamlike day that was! - Jammin', drinking beer and smokin' weed - wandering the paddocks and swimming in the pond that even had it's own waterfall. Other days were spent fishing with George or going to the numerous, beautiful beaches nearby. As *I* didn't ride a surfboard, I had the enviable duty of swimming and sunbathing with the girls while George and his mates spent hours out on their boards, catching waves.

I remain forever grateful for the friendship and generosity that my friends showed me in Ballina and it was with a deal of reluctance and a heavy heart that I moved on, a few weeks later, to pursue new adventures on Queensland's Gold Coast.

Surfers Paradise- Life is a Cabaret

As I crossed the NSW/Queensland border at Tweed Heads and headed for Surfers Paradise I really felt like I was a long way from home and moving into unknown territory. I had pinned all my hopes of finding work in this big, vibrant and international city on one man whose name I'd carried in my wallet since leaving Newcastle. His name was Bobby Bugden, the former manager of South's Leagues club in Merewether, who had left Newcastle under dubious circumstances, to manage the well known, Tiki Resort, on Cavell Avenue, in the heart of Surfers'. I'd been told he looked after many Novocastrians who were seeking employment, and sure enough, as soon as I told him where I was from and what I did, he gave me a gig. I auditioned that night in the restaurant and stayed in a room in the resort. The following morning, while having breakfast by the pool, I met with him and his right hand man, to discuss the terms of my new position as *"Resident Artist"*. My role was to sing to the diners most nights of the week or when bus tours came through, as support act to the resident Maori show band - that included hula girls and fire eaters. For my services I received a nightly payment and meal, as well as accommodation across the road, in a high rise building, in the spare bedroom of his business partner's apartment. Although I was aware of his chequered history, I found Bobby Bugden to be more than obliging in the employment conditions he offered me, but there was an underlying sinister aura surrounding him to which I remained vigilant. I can best compare it to the gangster and mafia movies I'd seen - where the benevolent *"DON"* can be equally maleficent if you betray him. So, to that effect, I lived the high life in Surfers Paradise, gainfully employed for five weeks, boosting my bank account and preparing to venture further north.

The relentless performance schedule, along with the hectic night-life, soon took it's toll on my health, particularly my throat - which had become inflamed and sore - and so, on doctor's orders, I curtailed my nocturnal activities at the night clubs after work. More worrying for me was, while I was singing, I was occasionally experiencing difficulty in pronouncing vowels. I particularly recall struggling to sing the word, *"Cat's"*, in the Harry Chapin' song "Cat's in the Cradle", which was unusual, considering it was an easy song to sing - as far as vocal range is concerned. Never the less, I persevered and the problem abated. Little did I know, those same symptoms would re appear nearly two decades later - with devastating consequences to my career and personal life.

All the musicians that I'd met in my time in Surfer's Paradise had encouraged me to make the Whitsunday Islands my next destination - as gigs were abundant up there and the lifestyle was fantastic - so that's where I set my sights. To break up the long, thousand mile journey, I factored-in a couple of social visits along the way, to some old friends from Maitland who had moved to Queensland. Firstly, just up the road from Surfer's, I dropped in on Kim and Adrian and their new born son, Ricky, in Brisbane. They had been part of the *"Hunter River Hotel gang"* - that had lived in that crazy old apartment building in Melbourne Street, East Maitland - and had been the strongest supporters of my song writing. The next stopover was considerably further up the coast at Gladstone, to stay briefly with old high school friends, Gerard and Deb and their toddlers, Nicholas and Marianne. Gerard had been good friends with my school band members, Johnsie and Jinx, and was enthusiastic about my full-time musical career choice. I admired the bravery and determination of both couples in starting families at what I considered to be such a young age, and for relocating so far from their home town to pursue new lives and careers. As much as I appreciated the significance of their choice to become parents, for *Me* - and my new, free, bohemian lifestyle - it was incomprehensible. It would be nearly ten years before *I* made the nervous transition into parenthood.

As I drove out of Gladstone, past the Bulk Carriers tied up at the wharfs - waiting to be loaded with coal, alumina, cement or iron ore - I was reminded of the shipping activities I used to watch every day back home in Newcastle Harbour, and felt a pang of homesickness. That feeling soon dissipated, as I began to imagine the yachts and ferries moored in Airlie Beach and Shute Harbour, while I drove north with growing anticipation, up the Bruce Highway, aiming for Rockhampton as my next stop over. Rockhampton was more than accommodating, providing gigs and lodgings at The Ranch and Grosvenor hotels, which were advertised in the local Newspaper - along with a story and photo depicting my adventures from *The South*. The nearby coastal town of Yeppoon provided work and accommodation at the Pacific Hotel - where the kitchen staff also cooked up a feed of whiting that I'd caught while fishing off the rocks near Rosslyn Bay. It was while sitting on those rocks, that I watched, with envy, as the ferries came in and out of the Marina - en route to Great Keppel island with tourists - and wondered, which island, further north, would be my next conquest. As relaxing as it was to be sitting on those rocks, basking in the warm tropical winter sunlight, a tinge of trepidation ran through my mind about performing on those islands - to a predominantly "tourist" audience, similar to the audiences I had sung to back at Tiki Village on the Gold Coast. A transient audience. One, that I had little time to get to know - and who didn't *really* get to know *me* and *my songs* - unlike my loyal following back home. It was in that instant, I realised how tired I was of life on the road, and decided to head back to familiar territory. As I packed my bags that afternoon, I began writing *this* song - which I completed the following night in my motel room in the border town of Warwick. After three months of; not just surviving, but making a reasonable living, entertaining from town to town, state to state, I had proven to myself just how lucrative and liberating my new, independent, musical lifestyle really was. The Whitsunday Islands could wait for now. I just wanted to be home - and before sunset the following day, that's where I was.

Back in the Hunter Valley

*I was away from my friends and my home
Travelin this great land but feelin so alone
So I changed my mind and turned the car around
Drove a thousand miles back here to you
Back in this old town*

*Back in the Hunter Valley where my seeds are sewn
I told myself…your goin back home*

*Every day I was away I'd compare what i saw
With everything I knew back home
But the things at home always meant more
From Barrington Tops to Merewether Beach
The Hunter River runs on by
And even the stacks of the BHP would bring a tear to my eye*

*Back in the Hunter Valley where my seeds are sewn
I told myself…your goin back home*

*I wrote a letter to my friends, told them I was fine
Told them I was singing from town to town
And the audiences were kind
But i couldn't hide my homesickness
It just seemed to come right through
I'd write…the people up here are nice to me
But not as nice as you*

*You in the Hunter Valley where my seeds are sewn
I told myself…your goin home
Back to the Hunter Valley where my seeds are sewn
I told myself…my seeds have grown
And I'm tellin'you
It's good to be home*

That's Entertainment

The Power of The Press

I arrived home from my "East Coast Tour" on a Tuesday. By Friday, that week, I was back performing at the Belevue Hotel, and on Saturday at the Bel-Air Hotel. The following week, after being taken out to lunch by Donnie Graham, the manager of the Belevue Hotel, and Frank McDonald, the publican of the Cricketers Arms Hotel in Cooks Hill, I had residencies at four pubs, from Wednesday through to Saturday - which included every Friday night at Frank's pub for the next three years. My regular Wednesday night at the Beach Hotel was replaced by a long term residency at the Warners Bay Tavern. Every Thursday night I was at Donnie's, new, *Log Cabin Lounge,* and my regular Saturday afternoon at the Bel-Air also lasted another couple of years. All of these venues advertised heavily in the Newcastle Herald, The Post and The Star newspapers, so my name was getting plenty of publicity, but I owe much of my notoriety to a journalist named Leo Della Grotta who mentioned me favourably and often, in his "Steppin' Out" and "Out of the Mix" editorials. I still clearly remember calling Leo from the phone booth outside my new rental apartment in Berner street Merewether, telling him of my adventures up the coast and my plans for gigs and songwriting now that I was home, and hearing his enthusiasm and encouragement for me, saying he would run the story in that weeks' edition. The story did appear in the paper two days later, setting a precedent for more articles to be published about my career over the next decade. For the next two years I barely recall a week that my name or photo *wasn't* in a local newspaper - to the point where my *reputation* far exceeded my *musical talent*. These days, it's called "The Power of Celebrity", and although, in my case, it was extremely localised, it was invaluable in bolstering my confidence and audiences. It cemented my place in the Newcastle Music Scene for many years to come, and I'll be eternally grateful to Leo for initialising the *power of the press* behind me.

Life was too good to be true. My new career was not only making good money but it was making a *name* for myself - and who wouldn't agree that "it's nice to be known"? I was finally living near the beach in Merewether where I spent most days swimming and sun baking, recharging for the next gig that night. It was like a good dream;

Lost in My Dreams

*The darkness of my sleep is often broken by a light
a midnight sun illuminates the deepest hours of night
and so begins a story like a movie on a screen
I'm usually the star, and so begins my dream*

*In my midnight paradise is nothing that I can't achieve
a mockery of life of everything I believe
I've flown the sky, watched children die, many women have I loved
there's even been the times when I've talked with the Lord above*

*Another world, another time in a strange and misty space
living out my wildest fantasies
a time to reveal what my conscience won't erase
free to do as I please
here in my dreams*

*At times I'm in danger groping for my life
in the hands of a stranger at the end of a knife
but I know it's just a story like a movie on a screen
I'm usually the hero lost in my dreams*

*The darkness of my sleep is always woken by a light
the morning sun intimidates the dying hours of night
and so begins my day wearily it seems
I wish I could stay forever
lost in my dreams*

Steppin' Out
BY LEO DELLA-GROTTA

Tony is glad to be home

Tony Johns

TONY Johns is glad to be back in Newcastle after his three-month tour, but wouldn't swap the experience gained from the ambitious venture for anything.

The Maitland-born singer-songwriter headed north three months ago armed with little more than a car, a guitar and a desire to perform.

After winning large audiences here and in Maitland as a solo performer, Tony decided he needed to fuel up with new material and tackle totally unfamiliar audiences.

He left Newcastle at the end of April and the first stop was Taree, close to home but nevertheless a place were he was just another performer without a reputation. And the going was tough: certain work that he was assured he would find didn't eventuate.

Forster was better. Tony spent a week there entertaining locals interested in country and western music and heating up tourists.

One of his hotel appearances there was cut short after locals began throwing tourists into a small swimming pool. Fun-loving people up there, it seems.

Port Macquarie was a dead loss because Tony turned up right in the middle of the Easter weekend and all hotels had been booked solid.

Forced to busk because of limited funds, Tony at least did it in style. None of this shouting to be heard over the traffic din for him. He plugged his public address system into a chemist shop's power supply, sat on a speaker and gave a show that couldn't help but be heard.

'I had quite a crowd there at one stage,' laughed Tony. 'The chemist was happy.'

The amplified busking show put Tony back into the money and polished his morale to a brilliant shine, enough to encourage him to move on to Coffs Harbour.

He might as well have stayed in Port Macquarie. Coffs was band country: no soloists, thanks.

Three bookings within an hour of reaching Grafton put the smile back and he stayed the week.

Former Newcastle publican Mr Bobby Bugden took Tony under his wing when the lad wandered into Surfers Paradise.

Bob employed Tony at the Tiki Village resort for a month, working him as a dinner musician cum immediate floorshow whenever a busload of tourists dropped in for the night.

'I had to condition myself to blend in like a piece of the furniture in my dinner music role and then suddenly burst into the Don Lane super host at the drop of a hat.'

'Thanks to Bobby I feel that I can add more to my performances.'

Those valuable three months have hopefully given the 22-year-old what he needs to handle the tougher Sydney audiences which he plans to tackle soon.

Three-in-one or all alone

● Probably Newcastle's favourite singer guitarists, Jus Gordon, Tony Johns and Jim Overend have a go at playing the same guitar in the Log Cabin lounge at the Bellevue.

WELCOME TO "DEE GEES"
BELLEVUE TAVERN
BANK CORNER, HUNTER ST. NEWCASTLE WEST.

The power of the publicity I was receiving had a significant effect on the size of the crowds coming to my gigs, particularly my regular Friday nights at the Cricketers Arms Tavern where the main bar would be filled to capacity and people were forced to congregate out on the footpath and eventually spilling onto the intersection of Bruce and Bull streets. The need for the police to come and control the crowds - and keep them off the road - attracted further press which, in turn, attracted even more people to the venue. I was mentioned in one newspaper story that included a photo of the chaotic scene - showing the crowds drinking on the footpaths outside the pub. I recently googled that photo and, on close inspection, to my absolute surprise, I spotted my old flat mate, Bobby, standing right in the middle of the shot, holding his glass of bourbon and coke. Even more amazing, was seeing my Bose 802 speakers - through the windows on the ledge above the doors. Due to the cramped conditions in the bar, that was the only place available to put them. As for me - I had to sit on a corner bench with my mixer beside me on a window sill because the only available floor space was barely enough to place my microphone stand!

Drinkers prepare for cycle pubcrawl

POLICE found 30 cyclists at the Cricketers Arms Tavern in Cooks Hill having a trial run on Friday night of a cycle pubcrawl in readiness for the introduction of random breath-testing this week.

The police were called to the hotel after nearby residents complained that about 200 people had gathered on the footpath outside the hotel.

One man said that they were standing outside because there was no room inside the hotel. A top Newcastle singer/songwriter was performing that night.

A police spokesman said yesterday that three paddy wagons and six policemen went to the hotel but found that the people inside and outside were behaving in an orderly manner and were not excessively noisy.

However, a number of people who told the police that they had decided to cycle to hotels around town as a way of beating breath-testing were asked to move their bikes because they were obstructing the footpath.

The policeman said that cycling was not an answer to random breath-testing. People could be charged with cycling under the influence of alcohol.

'It's no good having a lot of drunken cyclists run over by drunken motorists,' he said.

A nearby resident of the Cricketers Arms Tavern said on Friday night that some people on the footpath outside the hotel were annoying and frightening residents.

The resident said she was worried about what would happen as the crowd began to go home. Her husband had driven their new car out of the area because they were worried that it might have been damaged by patrons as they were leaving the hotel.

The police spokesman said yesterday that the licensee of the Cricketers Arms Tavern, Mr F. McDonald, was appealing against a Newcastle Licensing Court judgement made last month. Pending the appeal, the existing licensing conditions would apply.

Under the court judgement Mr McDonald was ordered to reduce the trading hours from midnight to 11pm. He was ordered to employ two security guards on Friday and Saturday nights to supervise the conduct of patrons on the footpath, to ensure that patrons drank liquor inside the hotel and not on the footpath, and to ensure that patrons, when leaving the premises, maintained the neighbourhood's quiet and good order.

The hotel was ordered to close its doors on nights it provided entertainment.

The crowd on the footpath outside the Cricketers Arms Tavern at 10.30 on Friday night.

Feelin' Festive!

In October that year [1981] a music festival was held, near Stroud, on a property that is now called Riverwood Downs. It was an opportunity for music lovers in our region to experience what the Sunbury Pop Festivals - held in Victoria in the early 1970's - must've been like, and, to a much lesser extent, The Woodstock Festival in America, back in the sixties. It's easy to recall one of the longest nights of my life - as I packed up my equipment from my gig at the Cricketers Arms - and began the hour and a half drive to Stroud at midnight. Upon arriving at Stroud at 1.30am I joined a traffic cue, of other festival goers, that stretched from the outskirts of Stroud for, the whole, ten miles to Monkeria, where the event was being held. I watched my petrol gauge drop - from three quarters full to near empty - over the next six hours, as my car crawled along the dusty gravel road with all the others, in first gear. Alone in my car, I kept myself awake, twirling the dial on my car radio/cassette player, trying to find a decent station because all my music cassettes were being chewed up from the constant vibration of the corrugated country backroad. The passengers in the cars in front and behind me kept me amused with their antics while they drank beers and surfed on the roofs and bonnets of their friends' cars. I watched the sun rise with bleary eyes as I finally drove through the gates of the property, handing my entry fee to the guys marshalling the cars to their parking or camping sites - looking just as weary as I felt.

After a short cat nap in the back of my wagon I made my way down to the main stage area, staggering through the, almost, thirty thousand bodies curled up in sleeping bags on the ground or slumped listlessly on the tail gates of panel vans. I eventually teamed up with my two mad muso mates, Jus Gordon and Greg Davidson - or "Rocky", as we affectionately called the crazy Irish folk singer. In between watching the bands on stage, we amused ourselves, and our fellow festival goers, by singing folk songs - in three part harmony - with an acoustic guitar, wandering, minstrel style - weaving our way through the masses gathered in the paddocks - accepting beers and joints [as tips], on our merry way. Understandably, my memory of the headlining acts are vague, apart from thinking that Rodriguez seemed more stoned than just about any one there, and Billy Thorpe was so loud I thought the stage would collapse. He'd been recording a new album in America, using a lot of new electric sound effects, and his first onslaught of ear bleeding feedback sounded as though a spaceship was landing on top of us! The crowd were indifferent to his new material and only warmed to him when he started playing songs from his earlier years in The Aztecs. I was particularly proud to see my old "Tenambit Tiger" football mate, Mick Hawke, perform with his band - "Total Fire Band" - and receive overwhelming adulation from the crowd. Other headlining bands included; Split Enz, Midnight Oil, Redgum, Goldrush, Matt Finish, Broderick Smith, Kevin Borich, Men at Work, Mi-sex and Swanea - which made for a smorgasbord of music, in a weekend of peace and good vibes, out in one of my favourite places - the Barrington countryside.

The "Tanelorn Trio" Me, Greg Davidson (Rocky) and Gordon Mclean (Jus'Gordon)

Campin' in the Barringtons

*If you're feelin' blue you don't know what to do
I think it's time to make you an offer
to come a way for a day or two
Campin' in the Barrington mountains
just me and you*

*I've got all the gear
all the food the wine and beer
and I could think of nothin' finer
than to be alone in the hills with you
campin'in the Barrington mountains
just me and you*

*ah we could drift away on an Autumn afternoon
lyin' by a mountain stream singin' it's happy tune
then in the dark of night cuddled up by a fire
thinkin' 'bout love, the stars above
and the moon that gets us high*

*well, If you're feelin' blue you don't know what to do
I think it's time to make you an offer
to come a way for a day or two
Campin' in the Barrington mountains
just me and you*

This song, although written in the early 1980's, wasn't recorded until the early 1990's for my album called "*The Valley*", and was used to promote another music festival, held regularly, near Gloucester. It was called "*Poley's Place-Country Music Hoedown*" and, although much smaller than Tanelorn and very much country music oriented, it was just as popular with it's patrons - and still is, to this very day. Poley Everett was a well known country music singer/songwriter in the region, and along with his wife, Rosemary and their farmhand, Steve, they would invite campers and country musicians onto their property, near Barrington, to soak up the clean country air while listening to their favourite country music. Professional and amateur musicians entertained the campers from morning to midnight standing on the ramshackle stage constructed from rough sawn timber and corrugated iron. I was extremely grateful to Poley for his support of my new album, as it introduced me to a whole new audience - who only new me for my original songs and became loyal supporters. After performing a one hour set of my new songs, I sold more albums, backstage, than I had in the previous six months.

There was a very special magic in the air around that Gloucester region which kept drawing me back for camping trips with my friends - and years later, with my kids - but one visit in particular had a profound effect on me. I was catching up with my old childhood neighbour and friend, Ted, who had been posted to teach at Gloucester High School. It was a reunion of a small group of old Maitland friends, and we spent the weekend at Ted's house in Barrington. I was enjoying the time-off, from gigs, as my voice was worrying me again - like it had in Queensland - and I was hoping that, this time, relaxing with mates would help it repair. Late one afternoon, just on dusk, I went for a walk in the paddocks at the back of Ted's house to soak up the calming rural atmosphere - while the others prepared for dinner and the night's partying. While walking through the knee high grass - that dairy cattle were grazing on, all around me - admiring the glowing haze of the sun sinking behind the misty blue mountain range, hearing the gentle breeze rustling the nearby gum trees, I suddenly felt an overwhelming sense of absolute calm and contentment that stopped me in my tracks and enveloped me like a warm blanket. It was the most sublime experience I had ever encountered and I stood, motionless, for five minutes, absorbing it's soothing effect. It was an epiphany - and the first thought to enter my mind was... "everything's going to be alright". Although my days of being a practising Catholic were long gone, I am convinced that whatever God is, *it* paid me a visit that afternoon! - and I've spent the rest of my life hoping to experience it again.

Looking For The Light

In the darkness of the night I'm searching for a light
in the darkness of my mind
stumbling doubts and fears are blind

I'm looking for the light
the light that shines inside
looking for the light
the light that shines inside

As the sun begins to rise I open up my eyes
but what is there to see
when there's no dawn in me

I'm looking for the light
the light that shines inside
looking for the light
the light that shines inside

At the sunset of my pain the questions still remain
always will and ever be
the light within and all of me

I'm looking for the light
the light that shines inside
looking for the light
the light that shines inside

The soothing influence, of what I can best describe as a revelation, that I experienced that afternoon, stayed with me for many years, and whenever my personal or professional life encountered problems, I would recall that event, to calm down and centre myself. My voice problem eventually dissipated, particularly after spending a few weeks in Perth with Helen, my old duo partner, doing a few gigs while visiting her brother, and generally relaxing and sightseeing. I returned home from that holiday with a more tempered, but focused, attitude to my life and career - and that's when it all went to another level.

From Dirt Tracks to Rock City

1982 was another good year for me. I was averaging five gigs a week and earning good money. I even managed to win a few local song-writing and entertainment awards, the most rewarding being the *Rawworths Rock Awards,* in which I shared first place with a local band called "Skates" as well as picking up the "Peoples Choice Award" sponsored by the Post newspaper. I was more relaxed about my career path knowing my place in the entertainment scene was well established, and *that* confidence fuelled my song writing.

My confidence also grew in socialising, and I began to make many new friends around Newcastle and the surrounding towns from all the Hotels and clubs in which I was performing. One group of people that were regulars at my Saturday afternoon gig at the Bel Air Hotel in Kotara eventually became like family to me - as I began to spend more time with them, out of work hours. I called them the *Bel Air Gang.* They'd been regulars at the pub since well before their legal drinking age of eighteen and even boasted about the protection and immunity offered by their surrogate mother, Maureen - the legendary, long serving barmaid of the pub who adopted each customer, myself included, offering friendship and worldly advice when the need arose. More than half of the thirty blokes and girls had grown up around the suburb of Kotara and all shared a common sense of humour and a zest for fun, music and sport. Some of the blokes had nicknames that were as unique and humerus as their personalities.

Guys like "Salty McNulty"[RIP], former bass player with Newcastle Rock band "Air Lord", who was as intelligent as he was funny, who jumped on stage with me at every opportunity to sing the classic Fielding and Dyer sea shanty called "The Whale". Continuing the maritime theme, next was "Capt'n" Pete Pickard,[RIP] a skilled engineer who built a fifty foot yacht in his folks backyard. Then there was "Stanoola",[RIP] a giant of a man with a heart to match, who invented his own hilarious language by combining parts of Aboriginal and English words during his time spent working in the Kimberlys. He often reminded us of this, by saying in his best Aboriginal impersonation..."I been t' Meegathara!". And so it went, with others such as; "Gluey", "Ringa", "Pretzil" "Germully", "Mungo", "Mirri" and "Spring". Names that sounded like acts in a circus which, along with their incredibly caring, tolerant but sassy girlfriends, turned any occasion into a mad cap party.

My first foray into their adventurous lives took me to Perisher Valley - to try my hand at snow skiing - where we hired a lodge for the weekend. They managed to teach me the basics of snowploughing on my skis but the majority of the time was spent in the lodge, around the open fire place, playing drinking games with beer and schnapps. I initiated myself into the Gang late one night by running around the lodge wearing nothing but my black and white Pumkin Pickers Scarf, much to their amusement and approval. The next sporting activity they invited me to participate in was water skiing where, on the Williams river at Raymond Terrace, they helped me master skiing on one ski. My chief instructor on that occasion was Gluey - an insanely good bare foot skier - who often limped out of the river with bruised, blistered and bleeding feet after hours of enjoying his passion. Gluey and I went on to share many other adventures, including parachuting at Luskyntre and travelling through Europe - highlighted by an impromptu visit to Berlin and Check Point Charlie back when *The Wall* still existed.

In these lyrics, I tried to capture the thrill and exhilaration I felt - while getting propelled along the water - behind Gluey's speed boat, called *"The Compressor"*.

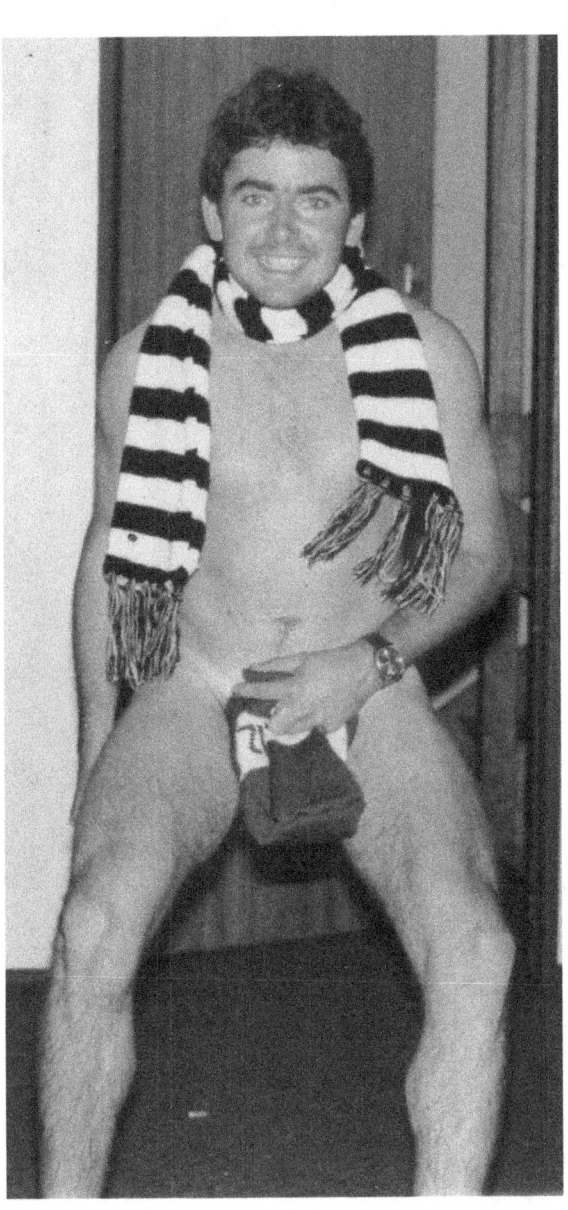

Rollin' in rock riches

THAT'S a $1000 smile they're wearing... and each earned his share of the bonanza with a 20-minute show of talent in the biggest rock music gig of the year.

Soloist Tony Johns, bottom left, and rock band Skates, clockwise from left, Grant Waring, Peter Wholohan, Peter Teague and John Nicholas, tied for the major prizemoney in a music-packed grand final to the POST-sponsored 1982 Raworth's Rock Awards at Cardiff Workers Club.

The spectacular concert, featuring acts by Rock, Heavy Rock, Concept, Country Rock, Solo/Duo and Original Composition category winners, drew a capacity audience of rock fans, many of whom had followed the winners' successes through seven weeks of eliminations at different live music venues throughout the district.

The climactic night was also a triumph for soloist Jacqui Lawson, who carried off the $300 second prizemoney.

Tony Johns was voted $250 Popular Choice favourite in a poll of POST readers, while concept band D-Flex received the $150 Encouragement Award.

All grand finalists had qualified for $500 best-of-category awards before the play-off.

POST reader Kathryn McIlwraith of Roxburgh St, Stockton, won our $100 voters' bonus for the Popular Choice poll.

Walking on Water

I can walk on water longer than I oughta, longer than you
I can slide on the water, glide along the water right behind you

I can race on the water, make pace on the water longer than you
I can slip on the water, skip along the water right behind you

Racing along with the boat I can fly with the spray and the wind in my hair
Sun on my face and the rope in my hand feeling I haven't a care
Man, I'm alive out there

I can walk on water longer than I oughta, longer than you
I can slide on the water, glide along the water right behind you

I also enjoyed water-skiing trips with old Maitland friends at a camping area called "Shalimar" on the Wallamba river near Tuncurry. On one occasion, I skied behind an old school mate's boat that was simply named "Pig" - partly because it had plenty of grunt and partly from his nickname of "Porker". That night around the camp-fire, after too many beers, I attempted to throw my old nylon string guitar on the smouldering embers to reignite the flames, but thankfully my mates stopped me and the old "*gat*" lived on to be part of many more sing-a-longs. My passion for skiing waned a few years later when another mate, who had just bought a very high powered speed boat, put me in a turn on the river near Clarencetown, that propelled me, at full speed, straight through the high reeds growing near the river bank. The resulting cuts and scratches, to my legs, groin and scrotum, brought home the meaning of "*death by a thousand cuts*" and caste doubts in my mind that I would ever father children!

The biggest thrill about hangin' out with the Bel air gang was going trail bike riding with them at a camping area near Wollombi called "*Hungry Creek*". The element of "*finally having a bunch of big brothers to do crazy stuff with*" really kicked in here - as they showed me how to ride a motor bike and do minor mechanical repairs. They even helped me buy my own *Yamaha I.T.175cc* trail bike, which, to be honest, I never *could* fully control, and, almost resulted in my demise. I tried to jump a creek on one occasion – *daredevil, Steve McQueen, style* - only to slam into the earthen bank on the far side and catapult over the handle bars, landing in a paddock thirty feet away. I couldn't feel my fingers afterwards and was unable to play guitar for two weeks - before a chiropractor finally realigned my neck and backbone. A stern lecture from my *other* "*musical*" big brother [*Tinno*], convinced me to curtail my motor bike activities for the sake of my burgeoning musical career. He was happy to see me take his advice, opting, instead, to sing the praises of "*biking*" - in *this* song, which he also helped me record.

Attempting repairs to my Yamaha IT 175 with little help from Bobby (straw hat) and the Hungry Creek gang

Hungry Creek

It was the long weekend I was goin' 'round the bend, felt the need to get away
took a trip with friends to the Watagans, the mountains up Wollombi way
we were there four days now my heart's full of praise
for the heaven and the hell we raised

well we set up camp in the dark and the damp, our first night I recall
sittin' by a fire wishin' we were drier as the rain began to fall
but when the mornin' bought the sun my head went numb
as a thousand bikes roared as one

Hungry Creek's no place for the meek, the weak or the faint of heart
it's a motorcross land, throttle in your hand, revin' it from morn' to dark
if you wanna let off some heat
ride it off at Hungry Creek

Well for ten hours a day the bikes revved away, only stoppin' when the tanks ran dry
and if ya didn't get scarred, bruised or jarred, you were bound to get mud in your eye
then at night spinnin" yarns, sittin' by a fire, tall tales like the flames grew higher

we were talkin' 'bout
Hungry Creek's no place for the meek, the weak or the faint of heart
it's a motorcross land, throttle in your hand, revin' it from morn' to dark
if you wanna let off some heat
ride it off at Hungry Creek

I learnt to ride on a CR one twenty five, never dreamed I'd be
ridin' through creeks, in mud or up mountain peaks, next year I'll be
ridin' on my own Yamaha I.T.

Doctor Jurd's Jungle Juice eased our aches and pains
drinkin' Tooth's and Toohey while Gluey Paluwe
Lit up the bong again
and again and again and again

Well when we packed up camp and turned for home I couldn't say that I was sad
"cause I'd done everything I'd come to do and smellin' like an oily rag
I got home, had a shower, a good night's sleep
and a home cooked meal to eat

and I've been to
Hungry Creek's no place for the meek, the weak or the faint of heart
it's a motorcross land, throttle in your hand, revin' it from morn' to dark
if you wanna let off some heat
ride it off at Hungry Creek
if ya gotta let off some heat
let it off at Hungry Creek
if ya think your oil's got a leak
plug it up at Hungry Creek
If ya pretty little lady's on heat
ride her up at Hungry Creek
yeah
If ya wanna let off some heat
get it up, rev it up, take it up, break it up
Ride it up at Hungry Creek

The first time I sang this song to *The Gang*, all eagerly gathered at the Bel Air hotel one Saturday afternoon, I had arranged a special stunt, with one of the boys, to add a bit of theatrics to it's debut. "Ringa" - my closest friend in the Gang, who eventually was "best Man" at my wedding - rode his *Yamaha 250cc* trail bike into the lounge area where I was *just* singing the last chorus. He then pulled up in front of the stage - where I dropped my guitar and jumped on the back of the bike - then proceeded to exit the pub, throttling so hard that the bike went up on it's back wheel - causing the tyres to chew out junks of carpet that splayed across the room being filled with choking exhaust smoke and deafening engine noise - and disappeared down a concrete storm drain at the rear of the pub's car park. He dropped me off so I could clamber out of the drain and return to my stage through the pub's side door while he then continued to ride a further half mile down the drain to avoid detection from the publican who was furious at our antics. I successfully pleaded ignorance to any prior knowledge of the stunt, or rider, to the boss, and, however hard and long he investigated, he never found out who the *helmuted, "Evel Knievel" culprit* was that day. The incident became part of The Pubs' folk law, but sadly, today, the only remnant of that crazy gig is the concrete drain that runs at the back of, what is now, a McDonalds Restaurant.

Welcome to the House of Fun

The British band called "Madness", released "Welcome to the house of Fun" in 1982 - a title who's relevance to me was most apt at that time!

The fun I was having by expanding my social network also encouraged me to give up my solitary lifestyle - residing in one bedroom apartments - and move into a *house-share arrangement* with a group of blokes best described as rogues and larrikins. In fact, when I recall our madcap antics in that old "federation style" house in Windsor street, Merewether, I always think of the John Bellushi movie called "Animal House"! Myself and Bobby were the permanent residents with our own bedrooms while the sun room and sofa in the lounge room accommodated a rotating array of tenants including; Ringa [from the Bel-air gang], Chris [the mad helicopter pilot], Mick [the Casanova] and Cookie [the John Belushi of the house]. Any vestiges of my moral Catholic upbringing, that may have survived up to this point, were certainly extinguished while residing at this address - but it was fantastic fodder for my song writing! I even ended a relationship with a sweet girl called Wendy because the temptations of the sordid activities within that house were bound to eventually lure me into infidelity - and she was much too innocent to have ever survived a visit to that *den of wolves*! When we all went out on the town for a drink and to "chase some skirt" we were like a *nineteen eighties version* of the Bob Hudson, Newcastle Song - trawling the Newcastle pubs and clubs, narrowly avoiding fights with rival suitors in the hope of snagging

the Maitland area – a bold statement, meant as a compliment rather than a demand, loudly announced with cheeky irreverence, that simply said.. "Show us ya Mota!". As I began to construct a song around that phrase, all the boys chipped in with suggestions for lines, particularly Mick, who guided me through various engine parts and car maintenance procedures. It became our "Team Song" and a huge hit with punters at all my gigs. It also, to this very day, became the advertising slogan for a large car dealership in Cardiff, west of Newcastle, which caused me suspicion because I'd met people from the advertising agency at my gigs where I played that song. They changed the tune and only used the main catch phrase, so I had little recall to pursue royalties, but I'll always be left pondering that I may have inspired that campaign.

a little romance. The occasions that we managed to bring our catch of women back home usually resulted in noisy all-night orgies that resulted in visits from the police who had been alerted by our disgruntled neighbours. Just as in Hudson's hit song, where "Normie" would approach the girls with his infamous catch cry of "G'day.... do ya do it?", my mates had a similar greeting call - which I'm certain had emanated from

Show Us Ya Mota

Once upon a road I was carrying a load when I came across a girl in distress
seems she'd burn't out her clutch
I said it wouldn't take much for me to fix her up without any mess
so I pumped up my jack, laid on my back,
with a turn of my spanner and a blow from my hammer
when the job was done I pulled out my head
winked at her and said

Show us ya mota, show us ya mota
lift ya bonnet up and let me look it over
show us ya mota, show us ya mota
start it up and take me for a ride, oh yeah
start it up and take me for a ride

Now I've seen all kinds of mota's I've had my share of quotas
four cylinders are sweet and tender
but when I saw her big V8 I said "well shut the gate"
and proceeded with my tool to mend her
first I tuned her carburettor, got her muffler soundin' better
cleaned her dirty points, grease nipples and joints
when the brakes where bled, dipstick in my hand, I said...

Show us ya mota, show us ya mota
lift ya bonnet up and let me look it over
show us ya mota, show us ya mota
start it up and take me for a ride, oh yeah
start it up and take me for a ride

*Now if ya timings' out of whack, your heads' about to crack
your piston's need a re bore, your clutch went through the floor
it's time you had a tune up, just watch ya speedo zoom up
if ya get the right mechanic there"ll be no more need to panic*

*No more need to cry when your petrol runs dry
I've got gallons of juice for you
just let your tyres scream, flash on your high beam
and I'll be there like a doctor for you
I'll strip ya mota down 'till I'm sure I've found
the screw that's out of place
I'll put a smile back on your face
[alternate line] just sit on me face
I'm better than the N.R.M.A. And this is what I'll say*

*Show us ya mota, show us ya mota
lift ya bonnet up and let me look it over
show us ya mota, show us ya mota
start it up and take me for a ride,oh yeah
start it up and take me for a ride
["let me tell ya Sol...oils ain't oils"]
start it up, kick it over
show us ya mota.*

The most convincing evidence that my song *had* inspired the car dealership commercial was it's replication of my exclamation of the words "Oh Yeah" - in the chorus - with which they substituted the words "All Right ". Sure, it sounds like sour grapes on my behalf, and it's impossible to claim the rights on a phrase that was in common use around Newcastle at that time, but knowing that my song *probably* inspired the jingle - without receiving recognition or royalties - played on my mind. The *upside* was that the *jingle* served to spread the popularity of *my song,* as most punters believed it *had* inspired the advertising campaign anyway.

Practical jokes were a daily obstacle course - in the House on Windsor Street - that we *all* had to navigate, sometimes with dire consequences. Like the night they locked me in the back shed at 2am, where I stored my trail bike. I was furious, as I was *"on a sure thing"* with a girl I'd brought home, and they were trying to move in on her. To break out of the shed I jumped on my motor bike, kick started it and attempted to break down the door by riding, at full throttle, into it. The door didn't give, and I was flung into the handle bars, gasping for fresh air as the exhaust fumes filled the small shed to a near toxic level. Along with the annoyed neighbours, the boys heard the frantic revving of the bike and released me just before I passed out from carbon monoxide poisoning. It wasn't uncommon to come home from a gig to find my bed sheets messed up and stained because one of the boys had *"got lucky"* and needed somewhere to consummate his romantic conquest. Even though I eventually started to lock my door whenever I went out, one of the lads was so desperate to find a love nest that he broke in through my window and hauled his nymphet up into the room, exiting the same way after they'd completed their courtship. *Their* intrusion annoyed and amused me, but I *was* appeased when he offered to wash my sheets for me as penance. That window was also accessed by another intruder who I suspected lived across the road in a house with a dubious bunch of blokes suspected of being drug dealers. Although he stole a small amount of cash and some personal items, I fiercely resented the feeling of being violated by his act of thievery. I had restructured my life to independently support myself - and was extremely proud and protective of my possessions and achievements.

I've Been Robbed

*You just can't trust anyone
not even your friends, that's where it ends
you've got to carry a gun
to protect what is yours, lock all your doors
lock them up tight or they'll come in the night
and take it away, they'll steal all your pay
listen to me when I say*

*I've been robbed
I've been robbed*

*You work so hard for it all
you're breaking your back to get what you lack
sick of feelin' so small
so you strive and you wait and plan your escape
the flaw in your plan is the evil in man
who will take what you need to furnish his greed
pity the man as he sobbed*

*I've been robbed-call the police
I've been robbed-give me my peace
I've been robbed-when will it cease
I've been robbed*

*All those years I made my way, paid for my own fair
If you can't afford your own don't think that I don't care
But does that give you the right
to take what I have worked for, for all my life*

The location of our house was ideal for a bunch of bachelors as it was flanked by South's Leagues Club at one end of the street and The Burwood Inn Hotel at the other - where counter lunches and bistro meals were our main source of sustenance. The Burwood was our favourite haunt - where we would often sit on the cracked and uneven footpath, outside the bar, in the afternoon, planning the night's adventures in town. Although being situated in a trendy beachside suburb, the pub had the feel of a classic old Australian country hotel where people of all walks of life could share a yarn while enjoying an ale. I recall sitting at the bar one day, chatting to "Larry", the local truck driver, who was describing the hazards involved in delivering "Port'a'loos", while on the other side of me was a retired Barrister espousing the shortfalls of Bob Hawke's leadership of the new labour government. The publicans, Barry and Debbie, became like part of our family - and treated me like a celebrity when my P.C.A. Song appeared on the pubs' jukebox. It was an eerie twist of fate how their baby daughter - who used to run around the bar, barefoot and in nappies - years later, would become my supervisor - as a traffic controller in a road maintenance gang - after my music career had come to an abrupt end.

It was no surprise that the usual topic of conversation - among my, *young, testosterone-filled,* house mates - was about women - and it was an endless source of amusement discussing their various *"chatting up "* techniques. Bobby and Mick were the *smooth talkers* of the group - and had the confidence and finesse of a couple of snake charmers. Mick, on one occasion, even managed to get the phone number of an attractive police woman who was involved in apprehending him when he was found, sleeping naked, on our neighbours front verandah, after thinking he was back home from a boozy night out. Bobby trumped that effort by chatting up a telemarketer who was trying to sell him window blinds - and she and her cheeky girlfriends became regular visitors to our fraternity. Ringa was renowned to have a particularly large part of anatomy - that often managed to [excuse the pun] *"come up!"* in conversation - helping to spark the women's curiosity. Cookie and Chris adopted a more direct approach - with a dialogue that might involve a question like..."would you like to come home and have sex with me?" - which, after having a drink or hand slap thrown in their face, they would move onto the next victim until the odds moved in their favour or they simply gave up and drowned their sorrows. I was astounded at how Chris's *helicopter-pilot uniform* often made *that question* less offensive to some of the girls that he approached. He certainly impressed my date, one time, when he picked us up at the dock area - that is now the site of Darling Harbour - and took us on a joy flight over Sydney Harbour - that included a very illegal manoeuvre of flying over *and* under the Harbour Bridge! Admittedly, *playing the field,* for me, was made easier if the girl I was *chatting up* had seen me performing on stage that night. She already new a bit about me and, whether she was interested or not, I didn't have to sell myself too hard - but that didn't necessarily immune me from the odd *face slap* or *drink in my face* either!

Essentially, the residents of that house in Windsor street - the equivalent of what could be considered a male bordello - were aspiring playboys and heart-breakers who unwittingly managed to leave a trail of bitter and dejected women in their wake. One of those women saddened and inspired me to write *this* song - about her determination to pursue one of my house mates, despite knowing his dubious reputation.

Chasing Love

*I know you now I know what you're about
I've wasted too much time I'm getting out
you only looked toward the night ahead
I saw you in my life and not just in your bed*

*I should've known that we'd never last
when will I learn the lessons of my past?
But still I follow you around on bended knees
come crawling back to you begging you to please...*

*Give me a break
it's my mistake
to reach out for and try to rise above
chasing love*

*And the way you treat me when you don't want me around
must you defeat me to defend your sacred ground?
The fool who fell for you is lying at your feet
I've lost my pride the victory is yours so sweet*

*Give me a break
it's my mistake
to reach out for and try to rise above
chasing love*

*And the way you treat me when you don't want me around
must you defeat me to defend your sacred ground?
But still I follow you around on bended knees
come crawling back to you begging you to please..*

*Give me a break
it's my mistake
to reach out for and try to rise above
chasing love*

As low as my moral standards may have dropped while living in this house of sin and seduction, there was one particular *affair* - that took place between one of the guys and a married woman - that played on my ethical conscience and inspired me to write a song about it. I held the sanctity of marriage in high regard, especially where children were involved – which, doubtless, explained my utter dismay and total disillusionment when my own marriage failed, decades later.

Love on the Line

*Every morning at six he waits by the phone while her husband is waving goodbye
but she can't make the call until she's alone, the child in her arms starts to cry
and she'll phone just to say "how are you today?,don't be too late for work again"
and she'll call back at nine and again at lunchtime
their voices relieving the pain*

*As they Love on the line, talking out their time
a time alone to embrace
a love meant to be
some other time, some other place*

*She's a mother of four and she doesn't know how
she could ever be caught in this mess
To be married so long and faithful 'till now
still loving her husband no less
and he knows who she talks to for hours each day
when he calls her the phone is engaged
but he lets it go on, wondering where he went wrong
slamming the phone down enraged*

*As they Love on the line, talking out their time
a time alone to embrace
a love meant to be
some other time, some other place*

*Both of them know this affair is so wrong
the children will suffer the cost
that's what they've been told by their friends for so long
but without her he knows he'd be lost
so he stays home alone and he waits by the phone
how long will it take 'till he knows
that he's wasting his life on another man's wife
reliving her youth as it goes*

*As they Love on the line, talking out their time
a time alone to embrace
a love meant to be
some other time, some other place*

Apart from *that* sordid affair, most of our life in Winsdor Street revolved around fun and games. Bobby's past experience in being a green keeper lead to him designing a mini golf course in the backyard - complete with a Tee-off near the back door and a finely manicured green up in the back corner, with a proper cup and flag. My short chipping game improved out of sight as we had daily "*hole in one*" competitions. We practised our long range shots by hitting the balls at the two story brick wall of the apartments behind our back fence - hoping the balls would ricochet back into our yard. They usually didn't! - and I wonder how many golf balls must've ended up on roofs, and in yards, all over Merewether! We also held regular poker game nights early in the week when the nightclubs were a bit quiet. I often played the pokies at lunchtime, with my mate, Bazza, up at South's Leagues club - and usually won at least enough to pay for my lunch in the bistro. Saturdays were regularly spent down at the Burwood Inn, having a punt, and then there were the games we played with the neighbours; like when Bobby would play his Culture Club album at full volume to stir up the gay guy next door who was always screaming his lungs out to his Barbara Streisand records. Another colourful neighbour was our friend who lived in the apartments up the back - who was a madame at one of the brothels in town. She often had young trainees staying with her until they could afford their own apartments - and more than once, the boys and I jumped the fence to see if we could score a freebie!

Yes, it was all *fun and games,* and we were living life-*hard and fast*. There were bound to be *casualties* at such a fast pace - if not physical, then certainly emotional ones - and I had a suspicion that all the bluff and bravado around me was possibly masking deeper fears.

Musical Chairs

Love is a game of musical chairs, do you remember the rules?
We all sit down when the music stops, and laugh at the fools
the ones who are left standing alone, they always miss out
it's cruel for a game but larger than life
and we learn what loosing's about

We play musical chairs
so many hearts with no home
we play musical chairs
and when the music stops
we're alone

Love is the search of a lonely heart, only few ever find
for me and you how could it be wrong
I must be loosing my mind
'cause you feel so good and you look so right
just to give it a try
but no sooner for us to be saying hello
and now we're saying goodbye

We play musical chairs
so many hearts with no home
we play musical chairs
and when the music stops
we're alone

Love is a game like musical chairs
and if you miss out
it's cruel for a game but larger than life
and you learn what loosing's about

Handing Over the Reigns

By this time, it had been almost three years since I had left my full time office job to support myself as an entertainer - and I was convinced that I had made the right career choice. I was enjoying my *work*, [if you could call it that!] and earning great money. I traded in my old *Valiant "Gallant"* on the latest *Mitsubishi "Sigma"* station wagon and paid it off completely in less than a year! I covered my rent *easily* each week and still managed to dine out and frequent night clubs - up to six nights a week. I'd applied myself diligently to my new occupation and I suppose my choice to live in the *"Funhouse"* was my way of letting off steam. I knew, however, it was time to reign in the *party animal* and refocus on developing my musical career. That decision was validated one afternoon while jogging along the shore - between Merewether and Bar Beach - when I met another jogger, who's name was Peter Anderson. Pete was the proprietor of a musical booking agency called "Rock City Promotions" which he had recently established, and was running it with a small staff, in the garage at the end of the driveway of his mother's house in Hamilton. He was also the "frontman" for a popular local band called *"Atlantis"*. He had a flare for *"old style"* showmanship and I vividly remember him strutting the stage of the Rosebuds Soccer club in his coat tails and top hat while belting out *"Hotel California"* and *"Stairway to Heaven"*. He'd seen me perform, and suggested I join his agency which could promote me on a larger scale - and help me with recording my original songs in his new premises, that included a recording studio, at 21 Tudor street, Hamilton. Although I knew I could easily keep finding gigs for myself, it was the allure of getting into a recording studio that sealed the deal for me on Pete's offer. I had quite a swag of original songs in my repertoire at this stage and was beginning to wonder if I could take things to the next level by aiming for radio airplay. Although I had the resounding support of friends and punters, my biggest obstacle was my own lack of confidence;

New promotional poster under Rock City management

What's The Next Step

You've stood by me
you've watched me change
but through it all you've still remained
what can I say
how can I convey
my thanks to you for being here today

I'm trying to give you more than I'm capable of
and miracles are far and few between
the blood in this stone is seeping away
it's drying on the ground
when will it be found?

What's the next step?
where do I go from here?
Do I search for my future
or is my moment near?
I have something to give you
willing to receive
You've followed me this far
and still, I can't believe in myself

Signing up with Rock City Promotions helped to allay the doubts I had about my performing and song-writing abilities as I was promoted to a whole new level. Pete and his staff worked on sharpening my image with striking changes to my appearance - including; professionally painting my Maton acoustic guitar a glossy bright red colour to match my new red boots, and a custom designed leather patchwork vest. The new image was captured on huge posters and promo shots that appeared in the press regularly - due to Pete's extensive accounts with local media. This, in turn, led to me performing in larger venues as support act to Headliners such as Roy Orbison. On that occasion I performed a few of my own songs but also had the immense pleasure to sing in a duet with a beautiful and talented local songstress whose name was Marguerite Ashford. We mesmerised the packed auditorium of the Newcastle Workers Club with a heartfelt rendition of the Neil Diamond and Barbara Streisand hit, "You Don't Bring Me Flowers" - played with only our acoustic guitar accompaniment. That night was the highlight of many support gigs - that included; The Hollies, Max Merrit, Ross Ryan, Tom T Hall and Wendy Mathews - but the biggest thrill was fronting my own *Band*.

The "Tony Johns' Band" was created to promote my "P.C.A. The Easy Way" song which was recorded at Studio 21 and released on a single in June 1983. Mark Tinson produced and engineered the recording - with Greg Dawson on bass guitar, Jeff Dunn on electric guitar and Less Gully on drums. The band that promoted the single at various venues around Newcastle and the Hunter Valley - including The Ambassador night club and Maitland Leagues Club - featured Tinno on bass, Dennis Butler on lead guitar and Phil Screen on drums. It was a great Band, and I was ecstatic to be on stage with musicians I had looked up to since my teenage years in my high school rock band. We hired a big PA and road crew - and the *sound* was *fat*. Our repertoire was a mixture of my originals and covers, including Ian Hunter's "Once Bitten Twice Shy", but my *favourite*, was a fictional story I'd written – about; *just enjoying singing the blues;*

My version of The Monkeys ("speak, see&hear no evil" a jibe at my-Gibbons-surname) Dennis Butler, Phil Screen & Mark Tinson

Tony Johns to release debut single

"JUNE 1983"

Former Maitland musician, Tony Johns, will release his debut single on Tuesday night. The single is none other than the lad's all time great original PCA (The Easy Way).

Newcastle firm, Rock City Promotions, has organised the single's release, which will be held at The Ambassador Restaurant in Newcastle.

Tony's new single is like Tony himself—witty, spirited and a little tongue-in-cheek—the qualities that have made him the good time performer he is.

The single is a more than truthful account of the kind of personal experience most other people would rather forget, but Tony's unique talent has produced one of those truly accessible songs . . . . the kind that leaves you chuckling to yourself.

PCA (The Easy Way) was produced by Heroes guitarist, Mark Tinson, at Studio 21 in Newcastle with support from Greg Dawson on bass guitar, Jeff Dunn on electric guitar and Les Gully on drums.

Every good soloist deserves a good backing band, so to promote the single, Tony has formed his own band called The Tony Johns Band. During June and July the band will work a limited number of venues around Newcastle coinciding with the release of the single.

● PICTURE: Tony Johns and The Tony Johns Band. From left to right: Tony Johns, Dennis Butler, Phil Screen and Mark Tinson.

The band is: Mark Tinson (bass guitar and vocals). Mark, who also grew up in Maitland, is a founding member of Newcastle band, Heroes, and is currently playing guitar with top Australian band, Swanee.

Phil Screen (drums). Phil, who also is a founding member of Heroes, ends a year-long retirement having been conscripted into the Tony Johns Band as a drummer and non-vocalist.

Dennis Butler (electric guitar and vocals). A seasoned session musician and former lead guitarist—song writer—sometimes vocalist with the now defunct Newcastle group Atlantis.

Tony and the band are currently working on a album of original songs which will be released towards the end of the year. Much of this material will be previewed in the band's repertoire. After the June-July dates with the band Tony will return to solo work.

Sing my Blues Away

When I was a child before I was wearin' shoes
I had learnt to live with and sing the blues
my mother was a dyin' drunk and daddy just a no good skunk
so I had to learn to live by my own rules

So I sang my blues, sang my blues away
yeah I sang my blues sang my blues away
gonna sing my blues until my dyin' day

well we lived in a tin shack with a floor of clay
and that's the way that it was 'till we packed up and moved away
I'd earn our bread by choppin' wood
and prayed like I knew I should
but I stayed right there just to pass the time of day

and I sang my blues, sang my blues away
yeah I sang my blues sang my blues away
gonna sing my blues until my dyin' day

Now when mumma passed away Daddy went insane
I'd sit down and sing
just to try and ease the pain
now here I am thinkin' of my wasted years
drowned in endless tears
but I'll stay right here and never ever break the chain

until then, I'm gonna sing my blues, sing my blues away
I'm gonna sing my blues sing my blues away
gonna sing my blues until my dyin' day

That promotional tour, during June, July and August of 1983, gave me exposure in newspapers and on radio and TV, and the subsequent airplay saw my song, PCA the Easy Way, make it to the top twenty of the local charts. It wasn't uncommon, at the time, for record companies to employ people to buy a single at record shops - that conducted the Top Forty surveys - in order to ensure it got on the charts. That prompted *me* to enlist my *Housemates* to go and buy *my* single - to achieve the same purpose. Sure, not the most ethical move, but I *was* up against Michael Jackson's- "Beat it", The Police's- "Every breath You Take" and Bonnie Tyler's- "Total Eclipse of the Heart", so I figured *"a little help"* was justified. Despite the mediocre quality of the recording, my song did receive reasonable airplay on the local AM band radio stations - 2NX and 2KO - and well known presenter, Matt Tapp, told me it was a pity the recording wasn't done on a bigger budget - as it didn't do the song justice. I was just happy to have one of my songs on the airwaves - and hearing it come on the radio at my bedside, late one night, took me back to my childhood - lying in bed, listening to my crystal radio set and wanting to be one of those singers coming through the ear piece.

After receiving airplay - and selling a few singles! - it was amazing to experience the crowd reaction at gigs when I performed the song. To have people actually singing along with me - to my own song - was like riding a wave. The gigs became effortless - as I let the audience take over - and it was the biggest adrenaline rush I had ever felt. It was like jumping off those bridges and cliffs when I was younger, only this time I didn't hit the water. I flew. It gave me a small taste of what successful recording artists must feel when their audience knows all of their songs - and it made me hungry for more. It compelled me to keep on writing - with the aim of recording as much of my material as I could afford to finance. I didn't have enough good, original, songs to merit recording an album at this stage, and the ones I had were too varied in style and theme to all appear on the one record. Other acts, in the "Rock City" stable, were busy putting albums together, and I watched on, from the corner of the studio control room, taking it all in and dreaming of my turn, one day, to do the same. Bands like DV8 and Vegemite Reggae were busy self promoting their new material, and later on, the guys from those bands, such as Greg Bryce, Tony Heaney, Kim Pink, Jason Nelson and Martin McLauglin, sat-in on sessions for my new material. It was a supportive environment - as we all strived to make our mark on the music scene. Some made a bigger impact then others - which couldn't be exemplified more succinctly when I recall walking out of Ando's office as four young guys brushed past me to talk to Pete about the plans for their band called "Aspect". They were eventually signed to a major record label as The Screaming Jets.

The biggest lesson I learnt from the promotional campaign for my single was that "fame comes at a cost". I was prepared to pay commission to Pete for his agencies work but I wasn't prepared for the costs associated with recording, musicians, roadies, truck and PA hire, photographers and printing - and when they were all deducted from our concert takings, there was very little left for me! It made me realise the value of my previous, "one man show", existence - so I opted to scale back to that format, to re establish the income to which I'd grown accustomed. I was more comfortable doing the solo shows. As well as being more profitable, they allowed me that, one-on-one, banter with the audience that I'd grown accustomed to in my earlier years.

The *Agency* kept the "*solo*" work pouring in for me, increasing my fee and even booking me into Sydney venues to widen my audience. I was on rotation at some of *those* venues with artists such as John Williamson and Pat Drummond - making me feel like I was working my way up the ladder. Some of the Newcastle Hotel managers resented having to negotiate with my agency, over the phone, instead of directly with me as we had done previously. One in particular was Barbara Morely, who had employed me at the Casbah Tavern in Hunter street and later at the Cricketers Arms Hotel. Her and husband, Dave, or Big Dog as he was affectionately known, had supported my earlier career, and even got my first spot on radio, singing one of my songs to advertise the Casbah. She argued it was unnecessary to involve a *middle man* in our small scale dealings and, although I empathised with her, I justified *it* as part of the process to try and take my career to the next level. Sadly, it became a common practise in the industry in the 1990's and 2000's - as more booking agencies rose to prominence - and performers became just another name on a revolving calender of acts that all conformed to a bland format on the entertainment menu. I prided myself in wanting to stand out - and develop my uniqueness - and although the pubs were full of musicians and singers far more skilled than me, they all seemed *the same*.

Average Song

*Just an average song tellin' you about my average day
with no excitement and working for an average pay
I'm thinking very slowly with nothin' to stoke my flame
I'm feelin' kinda lowly 'cause every day is the same*

*Just an average song tellin' you about my average day
no change in the weather so there's really nothin' new to say
I think I need a break I think I need to get away
to where it's all happening
and people will listen to what I say*

*Average ways, fine sunny days, nothin' hard or complicated
I'm not complainin', just simply sayin'
I'm bored with the way my life is situated
I've got to make a move
if only just to prove that I'm strong
and I'm sure better things will come along*

*Just an average song tellin' you about my average day
with average words and music arranged in the same old way*

That year [1983] was inspiring for me. Being part of Pete's agency really made me feel like I was a *professional entertainer* - and having my songs played and recorded by stalwarts of the local music scene validated my *song-writing* path. At the ripe old age of 24 I felt that *time* was getting away on me and I needed to step up the pace if I was to achieve all I could from my profession. That was until I saw, on the TV news, a 61 year old man, named Cliff Young, win the Sydney to Melbourne Marathon. A remarkable achievement for an untrained athlete and farmer who simply relied on will power and stamina. With no formal training in music or singing, and fuelled only by my passion to entertain, I felt a strong affinity with that man.

You're Never Too Old

When I feel my life is slipping through my hands
as if my time is running out
like an hour glass loosing sand
I think about an old man I saw running down a road
I realise that my time will come
'cause you're never too old

Your're never too old
Your're never too old

Got to do this, got to do that
don't let it get to late
get it while you're young
'cause time doesn't wait
Just think about that old man running down the road
I realise that my time will come
'cause you're never too old

Your're never too old
Your're never too old

I'm gonna run down the road with him
run in the race and win
run down the road, carry the load
let the race begin

Writing *that* song had a calming effect, and centred me. It made me realise I'd lost touch with my true self. The modest, fun loving me. I'd begun to take myself too seriously, caught up in the hype that the Agency manufactured. Don't get me wrong, that was Pete's Job and he did it extremely well and that's what twenty percent of my wages was paying for. But it was giving me an overblown sense of self importance that wasn't part of my true nature. I particularly noticed *it* the morning I berated one of Pete's staff for accidentally double booking one of my gigs. I remember yelling into the phone at him, like a prima donna, saying.. "you're fucking hopeless!" and "what am I paying all that commission for?!". I still feel ashamed when I recall that conversation with Chris Varley, who, incidentally, is still involved in the booking agency business.

Things settled down after that incident as I resumed my regular, four to five night, schedule of solo gigs, most of which I'd established prior to joining the Agency - making the twenty percent commission a continued matter of contention. Most of *it's* value for me was in access to the recording studio where I could demo my original songs or sit in on sessions to play harmonica or acoustic guitar. That experience was invaluable as I became accustomed to studio techniques and had the pleasure to work with so many talented musicians. The resident engineers in the studio were Colin Tegg, Mark Tinson and Dean Tollhurst - all of whom helped nurture my song-writing and supervised my projects over subsequent years.

 Back in my high school years I had read the George Orwell novel, Ninety Eighty Four - which had a profound effect on me. Whether it was the terrifying image of a rat in a cage attached to my face, gnawing at my nose, or simply my long held distrust of social institutions, but a sense of nervous anticipation grew in me as that year [1984] proceeded. I was restless. As much as I'd appreciated and enjoyed the efforts of Pete's agency to bolster my profile, I felt like I'd become part of one of *those* institutions of which I was so wary. I'd been given a glimpse of what "*going for the big-time*" involved - and wasn't sure if I had the talent or stamina to pursue it. I was in my "*comfort zone*" playing my songs in the local pubs and - knowing how productive it had been for me over the past three years - I was content to remain there, for now. Walking into the office, one day, to find my old family friend and mentor, Mark Tinson, sitting at a desk, taking phone calls and booking acts, made my heart sink. To see this incredibly talented and intelligent musician, who'd achieved national success with his bands - A Rabbit and Heroes - entrenched in menial, nine to five clerical duties, served as a sobering reminder of the fickle and insidious nature of this *entertainment industry* - that could send me back to the "salt mines" of my old office job at a whim.

Just like Orwell's novel, the *future* suddenly didn't look all that promising and, like a child with it's comforter, I just wanted to return to my small pub gigs - enjoying those nights with my songs and audience.

Taking a break from it all, my next move,

although not my wisest, was to board the Fairstar - on a South Pacific cruise for fourteen days - with a wild bunch of blokes from Maitland who called themselves "The Vege's". Their *tag*, relating to the vegetative state that they were constantly in - due to massive alcohol consumption! This cruise was the ideal getaway for *these* boys as it was designed for the eighteen to thirty five year old market and could best be described as a *floating orgy* of booze and sex. I was a willing participant of the fun and games on board and rarely woke up in my own cabin, partly due to the generous hospitality of the girls I met, but mostly because I was too drunk to find my cabin. I do, however, recall one night, being swung over the back railing of the ship by two guys who knew me from the Cricketers Arms. As each of them held me by the wrists and ankles I squealed with drunken delight as I looked down at the churning wake, far below me, wondering, without a hint of concern, what it would feel like if the boys let go. I was lucky to survive that encounter and even luckier to survive the ones, of a more personal nature, with some of the female passengers, but at this stage of my life, taking risks was *par for the course*. That didn't, however, immune me to feelings of regret!

Shouldn't've Done What I Did

I shouldn't've done what I did
I shouldn't've done what I did
treatin' that girl like a kid
I shouldn't've done what I did

I shouldn't've said what I said
I shouldn't've said what I said
I should've gone straight home to bed
I shouldn't've said what I said

Every time I hit the wine
trouble seems to tag along
she's wearin' a dress but I couldn't care less
'cause she's sayin' that I'm doin' her wrong
but I never did nothin' wrong
I never did

I shouldn't've stayed so late
I shouldn't've stayed so late
I shouldn't've taken the bait
I shouldn't've stayed so late

Never gonna do it again
never gonna do it again
If I do I'm gonna flip my lid
no, I shouldn't've done what I did

After a week of "*drying out*" from the cruise, I returned to my regular gig schedule for three months - before flying out of Sydney with my mate, Gluey, to embark on a, two month, *Contiki,* bus tour of Europe.

That *escape* marked the beginning of a new and wonderful phase in my life and career - that was expressed in the most productive and creative period of my song-writing. As I said my goodbyes to family and friends, the most difficult goodbye was to Kirsty, a girl I'd just started seeing in the previous weeks. Like me, she had Scottish heritage, and even her surname was eerily similar to my Grandmothers' maiden name. Although I visited her Grandmother - while travelling around northern England – Kirsty and I didn't reconnect when I returned home. Our affair was one, of many, that would suffer the consequences of my new found love of travel and adventure.

Time to Say Goodbye

I dont know just why I'm going
but I'll try and tell you why
I feel a need within me growing
and as a tear comes to my eye

It's time to say goodbye

You see I have an urge to travel
to see what makes the world go 'round
to watch life's mysteries unravel
and though I don't know where I'm bound

It's time to say goodbye

I don't know how long I'll be there
and I don't know if I'll stay
and though it seems to you I don't care
I'll think of you while I'm away

I don't know just why I'm going
though I tried to tell you why
But there's no comfort in knowing
and as we both begin to cry

It's time to say goodbye

Europe & London 1984-1985

Bound for Europe

Maitland-born singer guitarist, Tony Johns, is bound for Europe.

Tony decided last week that he needs and deserves a break. He has been playing at Maitland, Cessnock and Newcastle venues for many years and feels the holiday will give him the chance to take it easy in a new environment.

Good friends and fellow musicians Jus Gordon, Tony Tynan and Anne Orrett are in Europe so Europe seemed the obvious choice.

Born in Maitland in 1958, Tony paid his dues in the usual garage bands and a clerical job. By 1980, he had perfected the folk, ballads and blues combination that kept him heavily booked on the local pub and club scene.

Tony will be leaving in August and between now and then will work hard on recording more of his own material as a follow-up to PCA The Easy Way.

■ *Tony Johns with all the essentials ... guitar, esky and a change of clothes.*

Goin' Back To Europe

When I was young and the world was an opened book
in my hand and the teacher said take a look
look where you came from
'cross the see, many miles to another land
back to where history and it all began
he took me on a journey
As I read the book each page became a door
it was strange to feel I'd passed through them before
so on I read and found it hard to stop
'cause I was goin' back
goin' back to Europe

Rushing years of my youth 'till my life was mine
slowing down when the books were so far behind
asking no more questions
'till one day when I found I had reached an end
I left my past and my home with a friend
who took me 'round the world
far above the clouds we sailed toward my dream
to be in those school book pictures I had seen
I couldn't wait any more, my time was up
I was goin' back
goin' back to Europe

I had to go and you set me free
you knew how much it meant to me
was it a question of reincarnation
or just a vivid imagination

Another country another steeple
wishing I could talk to the people
wishing they could talk to me
all the hours joining towns on an open road
feeling tired, feeling worn, and the feelings showed
sleeping where I made my bed
passport stamps and postcards show my trail
souvenirs and snapshots tell my tale
of endless queues and stairs I've had enough
but I'll be goin' back
goin' back to Europe

Apart from my visit to Fiji on the Fairstar cruise and a two week holiday in New Zealand after leaving high school, I was as green as a traveller could be when it came to wandering the world. Gluey and I were like the 1984 version of *The Adventures of Barry Mackenzie* movie from 1972. Two, true blue, antipodean tourists wearing our *Aussie flag* sweat shirts and thongs, lugging our *Aussie flagged* backpacks loaded with enough jars of Vegemite to last a year. En route to London we stopped over in Hong Kong and blew a week of our spending budget on a steak meal - thinking it was a bargain but later realising it was priced according to it's weight in grams! We made the same mistake in Nice - buying a kilo of prawns and some beers, to have, while enjoying the scenery, sitting on a jetty in the French Riviera. We weren't quite ready for Europe and Europe wasn't quite ready for us! The language barrier was always going to be a problem, especially with our broad, strawn slang that even the Pom's had difficulty interpreting! I regretted not completing my French language studies at high school the day we got lost on the Paris Metro and I declared we were going 'round in circles because every train station we stopped at had the same name - of "Sortie" - only to find out later, that "Sortie" meant Exit!

Upon boarding our Contiki tour bus in London, we quickly became friends with the thirty other like minded Aussies and Kiwis on board who had come to share the trip of a life time. There were numerous communication issues on that 61 day bus tour—that took us to 14 foreign speaking countries—but the most compelling language barrier that intrigued me was with the two deaf and mute girls who had courageously signed up as passengers with us. They were friendly and bubbly characters who became a special and much loved part of our crew, who tried, in vain, to give us lessons in sign language that usually ended in tears of laughter —as we failed hopelessly to get it right. Despite this, we got to know them and they got to know us, and they left a special mark on my soul that had significance for me in years to come— when I struggled to deal with a voice disorder that would impact severely on my personal and professional life. It was only *then* that I realised the true extent of their courage and tenacity - to travel the world with *no* hearing or speech - as I pathetically bemoaned my *dysfunctional* but *usable* vocal ability.

Contiki tour group of GE149 in Florence.

Doin' it tough! ...sailing the Greek islands

Talking with Her Hands
Dedicated to Marie & Cathie

*She smiles with her eyes
she sees through your disguise
she'll hear you with a stare
you'll wish that you weren't there*

*She'll lead you with a smile
caress you with her style
her confidence will loom above your fear
protected by the right
to lead her silent fight
with her hands she'll draw you ever near*

Talking, talking with her hands

*Search for words to say
conversation is her play
your lips talk to her eyes
her hands will hypnotise*

*you'll come to know her well
but you'll never break her spell
her silent would has magic you can't hold
her energy, her charm
will never do you harm
but be careful as she lets it all unfold*

Talking,talking with her hands

*She'll lead you with her smile
caress you with her style
she's glad to know you want her to belong
content in silent bliss
sadder still than this
she'll never hear the music of this song*

Talking, talking with her hands

I had packed my *Maton* acoustic guitar for the trip - in the hope of scoring some pub gigs in London when the bus tour was over. It spent most of the tour packed away in a storage locker under the bus and it's hard case was eventually covered in stickers from each country we visited. I couldn't resist buying a genuine Spanish flamenco style guitar, in Barcelona, which served as a party starter for sing-alongs on the long bus journeys between cities and at camp-sites where we would party with other bus tour passengers. The following excerpt—from my promotional bio - was inspired by one of those continental camp-site gatherings;

...As I remember, it was in the bar of a camping ground on the outskirts of Paris, late one warm European summer's night in 1984. I was standing on a table bashing out an old Bob Dylan favourite with a classical guitar I'd picked up for a good price in Barcelona. There were nearly 200 people in the bar that night, travellers from all over the world. I counted 14 different nationalities including my Aussie companions. It was a party atmosphere-a united nations sing-a-long I called it-and although half those people didn't speak English, my music and songs held everyone together in a common bond of fun and friendship for over 3 hours. That night was a revelation in my life and a pinnacle in my musical career.

When the camping ground's 2am curfew saved me from a certain bout of laryngitis, I took the hat they'd passed around for me and sprayed it's contents across the bar. I ordered a beer for myself and my mate, whose hat it was. The dumbfounded barman looked up from the mess of coins and notes and said; "you could do this for a living!" I raised my glass to him, nodded my head and said; "I do!"...I still do.

                       Tony Johns. November 1990.
              [For Bookings; phone (049)477710]

I could rightly claim to have sung my way all over Europe on that party bus and probably missed half of the tourist attractions—due to sleeping off hangovers in my coach seat or on the floor in the isle. After the first fifty castles and church steeples, I figured.. "seen one, seen them all!" and allowed myself time to recuperate for the mischief at the next stopover. There weren't many dry nights of the sixty on the road and no shortage of willing partying participants in our group of revellers. One particularly colourful character in our group was Glenda, who often shared the entertainment duties with me, flaunting her outrages, vaudeville style of showmanship. Her signature act was singing "Rubber Ducky" - utilising her buxom physique, as a stage prop, to tease and delight the audience. I became involved in her routine, at times sitting on her shoulders, playing the guitar while she sang.

Despite the hectic party schedule, I did, however, manage to take in all the historic aspects of Europe that had fascinated me since my childhood—particularly the ancient Greek and Roman architecture and culture. Our Contiki tour guide, Trish, had an extensive knowledge of European history, and would spend, what seemed like, hours each morning on the bus's microphone telling us about the Ottoman Empire or the Hapsburg Family -

while we tried to feign interest as we nursed our hangovers from the previous nights stopover. The week that we left the bus to sail around the Greek islands on a yacht was a major highlight and the beginning of my life-long passion for yachting, that continues to this day.

Gluey provided a fair share of comic relief throughout our journey, most notably, when he asked the Italian water ski instructors, on the island of Corfu, to give him a go at it. Proudly strutting their well oiled and tanned bodies around in their briefs, the Italian guys had been showing off their skills in the sport to our female companions, when Gluey - dressed in stubbies and T-shirt - jumped into the water behind the ski boat, grabbed the rope, and gave the signal to the driver to accelerate as fast as he could. The Italians looked on in disbelief when he didn't put on the skis and hurtled along, behind the boat, on his back, eventually popping up onto his bare feet. With their thunder well and truly stolen, they acknowledged his skill, but were glad to see him leave - so they could retain their dignity and monopoly on impressing their foreign female admirers. On another occasion, when exploring a cave, on the Amalfi coast, we came to the bottom of a stone well, and to surprise the rest of our group back at the shoreline - Gluey and I decided to scale it's, twenty metre high, walls. To make it even more interesting, we swapped bathing costumes with two of the girls in our group. After emerging from the top of the well - Gluey in a tight one-piece swimsuit and me in a tiny bikini - we scratched our bodies to pieces while making our way back down to the beach - through prickly scrub and bushes – and were greeted by howls of laughter from our companions - and the two girls [topless] dressed in our board shorts.

The tour took on a particularly special complexion when I was lucky enough to become romantically involved with one of the female passengers on-board. Corrine was an exceptionally attractive young woman from Perth, and her thick, jet black, wavy hair, olive complexion and long shapely legs, gave her the appearance of being a *"local"* in some of the Eastern European Countries. With *my* Scottish heritage and *her* Yugoslavian ancestry, we both shared a common belief that our *crusades abroad* were like a kind of homecoming - and *this* served to strengthen our bond. We shared many magical moments on that tour - that would've otherwise been unremarkable had we not teamed up. The hauntingly surreal image of lying together on the deck of a yacht - moored at an ancient Greek island port, under the glow of a million stars, on a warm summers night - and seeing a *mystical-looking* fox scurry along the wharf as a Mediterranean sea fog drifted in, will float in my memory forever! The only glitch in our holiday romance was when I became a participant in an erotic stage act at an Amsterdam Strip Club - where one of the strippers performed a mesmerising feat of making a banana disappear into her vagina. Male members of the audience were invited to take a bite of the banana as it slowly re emerged - and I was invited to eat the *last* segment. As I knelt down to devour the fruit, one of the other strippers kicked me from behind - sending my face ploughing into the Divas' fanny! Always the consummate professional, and primed with the complimentary Jack Daniels, I rose to my feet to face the hysterical audience - and victoriously devoured the small portion of banana that had lodged itself between my lips. The next morning, at breakfast, I was served a banana with my cornflakes, and sternly told by Corrine to.. *disinfect my face and mouth, or she would never kiss me again*!

We continued our relationship after the Contiki Tour - living and working with other expatriates in London and travelling together to Ireland and Portugal - before she returned home to Western Australia a few months later. We parted on amicable but platonic terms, knowing that our personal and professional lives were set on different courses that probably wouldn't intersect again.

What We Left Behind

Seems so long ago that we both smiled in each others arms
and saw the world hand in hand
so many miles we shared in love, the days and nights were free
but our journey's road has reached it's end
and you don't know what it's doing to me

I've been inside this room before
and laid awake all night
asking where did we go wrong
and trying to make it right

It won't be the same when we get home
we'll be so many miles apart with our own lives to live
I've no regrets, just sweet memories of a holiday romance
but for the pain it's causing now
were we wrong in taking the chance

I've been inside this room before
and laid awake all night
asking where did we go wrong
and trying to make it right

Both of us know it's time
both of us cry
One of us knew all along
but I'm tired of saying goodbye

I'll never forget you, so don't be cold
I'll keep you warm inside my soul
just think about the friend you made who couldn't make up his mind
Have faith in what must lie ahead
and cherish what we left behind

I've been inside this room before
and laid awake all night
asking where did we go wrong
and trying to make it right

Upon returning to London, after the Contiki tour, a group of us began searching for reasonably priced accommodation, and - as fate would determine that we keep in line with the Barry McKenzie theme - we ended up living on Hogarth Road in Earls Court - where almost ten thousand other Aussie and Kiwi ex pat's traditionally resided. As our travel budgets tightened we managed to squeeze as many fellow countrymen as possible into that one bedroom flat, to keep our shares of rent to a minimum. The *record* number of tenants, sleeping over at one point, was fourteen, with one guy even sleeping in the bath tub! To ensure *some* degree of privacy, I claimed the broom closet, located beneath the building's stairwell, as a bedroom for me and Corrine. To sleep, we shared one pillow located in the centre of the floor space, and our bodies faced opposite directions, with *my* toes touching the steeply angled ceiling at one end. It was tight, but provided some degree of privacy from the bedlam and congestion out in the rest of the apartment - although the stomping of other tenants feet on the steps directly above our heads was unnerving at times. My small stature made it a cosy place for me to relax - reading a book or playing guitar - and it affectionately became known as the Catacomb - in honour of one of my favourite tourist sites back in Rome.

Late for a gig...wheel clamp on my Renault in Hogarth Road, Earl's Court, London

In the Catacomb

Inside our house as quiet as a mouse
I sleep in restful solitude
inside my room it's more like a tomb
that is why it's called the catacomb

In the catacomb, in the catacomb
in my room under the stairs all alone and no one cares
in the catacomb, in the catacomb
as happy as a lark just sleeping in the dark
it used to be the room where the cleaner stored the broom
where the big cockroaches loomed and the dirty laundry strewn
there's only room for me in my den of iniquity
squished up in my room called the catacomb

With a torch for a light that isn't very bright
in my skinny fold up bed I lye so straight
my suitcase on the floor is holding back the door
for if it shuts I'm sure I'll suffocate

In the catacomb, in the catacomb
in my room under the stairs all alone and no one cares
in the catacomb, in the catacomb
as happy as a lark just lying in the dark
it used to be the room where the cleaner stored the broom
where the big cockroaches loomed and the dirty laundry strewn
there's only room for me - all of my five foot three
squished up in my room called the catacomb

In the catacomb, in the catacomb
in my room under the stairs all alone and no one cares
in the catacomb, in the catacomb
as happy as a lark just wanking in the dark
it used to be the room where the cleaner stored the broom
where the big cockroaches loomed and the dirty laundry strewn
there's no room to swing a cat
but who the hell wants to do that?
I just wanna get you in the catacomb
locked up in my room called the catacomb
think what we could do in the catacomb
it's a lovely kanggaroo in the catacomb
squished up in my room called the catacomb
catacomb.

Helmut's Pub, Hopfgarten

Shortly after settling into our new digs in London, Gluey and I jumped on another Contiki tour bus to return to Austria for a two week skiing holiday in a small Tyrolean village called Hopfgarten. A friend of mine from Maitland was working at a pub *there,* and suggested I bring my guitar in, to possibly pick up a gig. Anne introduced me to her boyfriend, Helmut, the publican, and upon hearing a set of my music at an Apre's ski session, he offered me work in his pub for the rest of the season.

Returning to London from the ski holiday, I hastily purchased a small PA system and an old Renault hatchback to get me back to Hopfgarten as soon as possible. Finding a used car in the London classifieds took a while because all I could see was "Used Motors for sale" - until Jus Gordon, who had been living there for a year, laughed and told me; "that's what the Pom's call used cars!"...it gave my "Show us ya Mota "song a whole new perspective...and I began to pronounce the word "*mota*" in a cockney accent - like the British comedian, Alexei Sayle did, in his 1982 hit song... "Ullo John, got a new motor ". For fear of having no idea what I'd do if the car broke down, I drove, non stop, for almost twenty four hours, from London to Hopfgarten - via the midnight car ferry from Dover to Ostend in Belgium - sharing an overnight cabin on the ferry, with three European truck drivers who didn't speak a word of English. My only navigational aid on that exhilarating but stressful rally was a folding road map that *my route* had been highlighted, in red pen, by the Contiki bus driver who had taken me on the skiing holiday a few weeks earlier.

My relief was palpable as I triumphantly drove up the ancient cobbled lane to Helmut's Pub early the next evening and, as exhausted as I was, Helmut, Anne and the welcoming locals plied me with schnapps and even managed to talk me into singing a few songs with the guitar - before I passed out and was carried to my room in the cellar of that enchanting eight hundred year old building. That historic building became my home and office for the next three winter seasons and although my grasp of the German language never improved, my connection with the warm, loving and friendly locals flourished.

It was one of the most magical times of my life - living a carefree lifestyle of skiing all day and singing and socialising at night with happy holiday makers from all over the world in the fairytale-like scenery of the Tyrolean alps. My contentment was reflected in my song writing and the gig was the perfect platform to trial my new material - especially to the European audiences who were *so* accepting of my songs. The truth of *"music being the universal language"* was never made more clear to me in that crowded little bar that introduced a world of new friends to me - every night.

Along with most of the other tourists, I learnt to ski in the local Ski School and was also given private tuition by Helmut - who had trained with the Austrian Olympic ski team in his youth. His employment deal with me included free accommodation, meals, drinks, skiing equipment and apparel, as well as a season pass on all the ski lifts in the area - so he felt the need to protect his investment by ensuring I could ski safely and not injure myself. When he thought I had reached a competent level he challenged me to a race, from the top of the local mountain, [*Hohe Salve*], down to the front door of his pub in the village. To give me a fair advantage he handicapped himself by taking off one of his skis and holding it over his shoulder. As we began our descent he disappeared from my view within seconds and when I eventually stumbled into the bar, he was already finishing his first beer and ordering another - for which he made me pay!

I ventured, on my skis, to the other side of the mountain one day, to the village of Soll, and while having a beer in the local pub, I heard an English duet performing a song about ski lessons. I saw the song as a perfect tool to engage *my* audience and shamelessly plagiarised it - to become one of the most popular and polarising songs in my winter wonderland repertoire;

Team Helmut's Pub (Helmut, Me and Bernie-Helmut's brother)

The Eight Days of Ski Lessons

[Sung to the tune of The 12 Days of Xmas]

On the first day of ski lessons my instructor said to me;
put zee weight on zee down hill ski
on the second day of ski lessons my instructor said to me;
bend zee knees, put zee weight on zee down hill ski
on the third day of ski lessons my instructor said to me;
don't lean back, bend zee knees,put zee weight on zee down hill ski
on the fourth day of ski lessons my instructor said to me;
snow oh oh plough!
don't lean back, bend zee knees,put zee weight on zee down hill ski
on the fifth day of ski lessons my instructor said to me;
schuss down the mountain!
Snow oh oh plough!
don't lean back, bend zee knees,put zee weight on zee down hill ski
on the sixth day of ski lessons my instructor said to me,
Look out for the tree!
schuss down the mountain!
Snow oh oh plough!
don't lean back, bend zee knees,put zee weight on zee down hill ski
on the seventh day of ski lessons my instructor said to me
Have you got insurance?
Look out for the tree!
schuss down the mountain!
Snow oh oh plough!
don't lean back, bend zee knees,put zee weight on zee down hill ski
on the eigth day of ski lessons my instructor said to me,
may I sign your plaster? And he wrote on the plaster;
You should have got insurance!
Look out for the tree!
Schuss down the mountain
Snow oh oh plough!
don't lean back, bend zee knees
put zee weight on zee down hill ski

The Ski Lesson song facilitated an instant bond to every tourist and ski instructor who came into the pub - and was a permanent fixture in my Apre's ski and evening sessions repertoire, six nights a week, for the whole season. The next song I wrote became an even *bigger* hit with the locals and tourists, and surprisingly, even with punters back home. Meant as a *tongue-in-cheek* dig at the constant ringing of the bells in the church across the road from Helmut's Pub, it also became a *standard* in my growing repertoire of original songs. Many disgruntled mornings were spent in my basement room of the pub, nursing a hangover, with my head buried under my pillow, trying to drown out the noise and vibration of those bells!

The Curse of the Austrian Bellringer

When I lived in a town in Austria I was lucky I lived in a pub
my room was right next to the cellar and the publican gave me free grub
but one morning while lying in my room with a hangover giving me hell
some ratbag in the church right next door
began to start ringing the bell

It went ding dong bing bong over and over it played
rang tang gang bang for twenty five hours a day
crash boom into my room driving me right off my gong
if I ever catch up with that bellringing bastard
I'll hang him and cut off his dong dong dong

And so these bells would ring each hour intent on taking their toll
that bellringer driving me bonkers thereby achieving his goal
of reminding me when to be praying
when I knew I'd rather be laying
and when it kept up, all that banging of balls
I said, "Helmut, I won't be staying!"

"cause it goes ding dong bing bong over and over it played
rang tang gang bang for twenty five hours a day
crash bash it flared up my rash driving me right off my gong
if I ever catch up with that bellringing bastard
I'll hang him and cut off his dong
yes if I ever catch up with that bellringing bastard
I'll hang him and cut off his dong dong dong
dong dong dong, dong dong

Solving a Problem like Maria

The picturesque city of Salzburg was only a ninety minute drive from Hopfgarten and I visited it's scenic surrounds and historic castle on several occasions, seeing where scenes from the Sound of Music movie where filmed. A particular scene comes to mind, as I write this chapter, where the nun's are singing about the dilemma of Julie Andrews' character, Maria. I too, sang a song that I wrote about meeting someone whose name was also Maria - who was just as perplexing. Before I tell you about Maria, allow me to draw a very long bow, and refer to an event in the life of one of the greatest entertainers of all time, Elvis Presley.

The only thing I had in common with "*The King*" was that I sang a few of his songs and we both made a living from music, up until now that is! You see, back in 1959, when I was barely two years old, Elvis, who was serving time with the US army based in Germany, controversially, became infatuated with a fourteen year old school girl named Priscilla. They had a bizarre courtship that was governed by her parents insistence that he marry her when she finished high school and that they live separately until the wedding, which eventuated in 1967. It was a controversial affair that never sat well with my, somewhat vague, moral compass, which is why I was so conflicted when fourteen year old Maria, from Hopfgarten, walked past me on stage, staring mesmerisingly at me with her gorgeous, large brown eyes, and placed a guilt ridden spell on me. She was a stunning 5'4" beauty with waist length black hair and a figure that belied her young age, who spoke little English, but used her beckoning eyes and cheeky smile to do all her bargaining. It wasn't easy summoning the will power to stay detached from her charms but I did allow myself the pleasure of skiing with her on occasions. As with most of the locals, her skiing ability was exceptional, having grown up on the slopes, and unlike Helmut's ski lessons, I'm sure I improved much faster as I tried to keep up with the shapely figure in the tightly fitting ski suite gliding just out of my reach in front of me. Stranger still, was that her mother would often come to the pub at night to watch me perform - as if weighing up the prospects of *me* being a reasonable suitor for her daughter. The night I was invited to their house to meet the whole family was even more surreal! Like a scene from the little red riding hood fairytale, the small, cottage-like dwelling, was nestled in an isolated lane on the outskirts of the village, flanked by the pine tree forest at the base of the mountain. It was a wooden structure, painted in pastel colours, with flower planter boxes on the window sills and lace curtains dressing the windows. The *only* things missing, were Grandma and the big bad wolf! It was literally like a doll house, and, even with my small stature, I was forced to duck my head when I walked through the tiny doorways. The father was polite but not as friendly toward me as the mother or Maria's older sister, who was equally as stunning in looks and figure. The visit was short and pleasantly uncomfortable as I could barely communicate with any of them, other

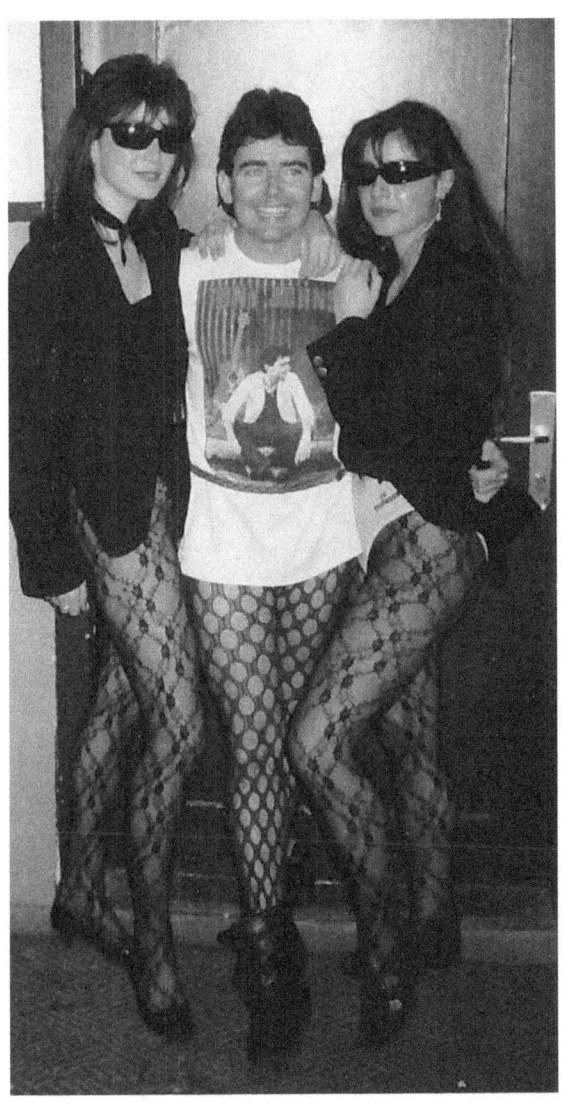

"Legs 11" (Manuella, Me & Maria)

still was and that I didn't want to be involved in bringing her innocent childhood to an end. That decision was put to the test - each subsequent season that I returned - as I watched her mature into a beautiful young woman, but my final visit - when I brought my Australian fiance' back with me and introduced her to Maria, who had recently turned eighteen - was the last time I saw her.

It was on a cool, clear, sunny April morning - appropriately, *April Fools Day!* - while packing my bags to return to London, that this song was written for Maria.

than in smiles, but I think I realised on that evening that my destiny wasn't to play the role of the woodcutter in an alpine pantomime. Walking past Maria's bedroom and seeing her carved, four post, wooden bed - draped in pink lace curtains and covered with a mountain of fluffy toys - made me realise just how young she

April [Fool]

Any time I be with you
you're near me
any time I talk to you
you hear me

April, oh April

Every time I dream of you
you wake me
every thing I feel for you
you make me

April
Oh April

I know it's wrong to want to be with you
too young to understand the things I do
My heart will sing the same old lovers tune
but nothing like the song I sing for you

Anywhere I go from here
you'll be near me
'though far away I'll find the love
you give me

April, oh April
April, oh April

Burning the candle at both ends

Whether it was the clean, fresh, mountain air or that I was pickled with Schnapps, but it was amazing how I kept up my performing schedule - singing for two hours at the Apre's Ski sessions from 4pm to 6pm and then from 8pm to 11pm at night, six days a week - for the whole winter season. Equally as gruelling was my nocturnal social life after each gig - which included visits to the night club/discos located in the basements of the buildings just across the street from Helmut's Pub. They were called Chin Chin's and Offenlauch. The first, being geared more for the tourists, and the second, being a popular haunt of the locals. I tried to patronise each of them equally, often determined by my willingness to attempt to practise my Deutsch speaking capabilities at the locals' bar, which was ironic, as even my English speaking skills were questionable at that, inebriated, stage of the evening!

As if possessed by the spirit of a schnapps sucking vampire, my *late night lusting* continued, even after the nightclubs shut their dungeon doors, and, just like a bat, that's when I ascended to the rafters, back in Helmut's building. It was up there, in the roof space, that an Aussie guy, we called Stubbo - who worked in the kitchen of the pub - had converted the attic into a cosy apartment that, also, regularly, became our last *port o' call* on those long, alcohol fuelled, alpine evenings. It was known as "Stubbo's Bar".

Stubbo and I shared common interests in music, humour and getting into *"trouble!"* [our code word for *"getting stoned"*]. We also shared a road trip across Europe - when we were commissioned to deliver a ski tour company vehicle back to London at the end of one of the winter seasons in Austria. Taking advantage of our free ride back to England we detoured through Germany and Holland visiting the many friends we had made who had stayed in Hopfgarten on their skiing holidays. To amuse ourselves during the long hours between towns and countries we would commentate on the passing scenery - imitating the voices of Mike and Mal Leyland who created the iconic Australian TV show called Ask The Leyland Brothers[1976-1980]. Each time we crossed a border I would adopt my broadest Australian accent[strawn] and ask..."where are we Mal?" and, in an equally broad drawl, Stubbo would excitedly, reply..."Well Mike...we're in another Country!". It became our "catch-phrase" and we *still* use it [almost 40 years on] as our standard greeting! Our last stop-over, before boarding the car ferry at Brugge to cross the channel back to Dover, was in Amsterdam - where we couldn't resist sampling and purchasing some of the elicit substances on offer at one of the city's notorious cafes. Driving out of town, the following morning, we personified the lyrics of the Men At Work song - *"Downunder"*..."Travelling *in a fried-out Kombi, On a hippie trail, head full of zombie"* as we blissfully cruised along the motorway that lead to *Brussels*. After smoking a joint of our *special Dutch tobacco* we found ourselves driving on an isolated, two lane, country back-road. It was then, that Stubbo, in his best *ever* Leyland brother impression, calmly asked me..."do you think we're back in Australia Mike?". Slightly puzzled, I replied [in character]..."no Mal, why do you ask?" to which he casually replied..."well, it's just that, in Holland they drive on the right hand side of the road – and you've been driving on the left hand side for the last five kilometres!" Paranoia began to set in after *that* potential disaster, and, with the Belgian border approaching, we began considering ditching our bag of weed. Now, adpoting Cheech and Chong persona's, we momentarily considered smoking the whole bag, but, flustered and panicking, I threw the bag out the window, into a field, as the border crossing came into sight. We soon regretted *that* decision as we drove straight through the rudimentary, provincial, station with it's tiny wooden office and flimsy boom-gate – that was opened! – and not a guard to be seen!

Back in "Stubbo's Bar"; Our industrious host – the blonde-haired surfer from Maroubra and ultimate *"Mr Nice Guy"* - always kept a good, cold, supply of beer out on his window sill, that, incidentally, looked straight across to the belfry of the church that housed those infamous bells! He'd buy the beer from the local supermarket and simply ask for donations, in a jar, to cover the costs of maintenance to his abode as well as funding his ski pass for the season. His small, select, group of clientele usually included other Aussies, Kiwi's and South African's - who were working in the village for the season - as well as some European tourists and locals with whom we'd all become close friends. One wall of the apartment was dedicated to the signatures and musings of every visitor - and signing *it* was a compulsory condition of entry. Just viewing that wall, with all it's cartoon-like drawings, signatures and anecdotes written in a dozen different languages, was entertaining in itself! Donations of hash and weed were encouraged, and placed into a bowl in the middle of the typical Tyrolean bench style table, built into the corner of the room, that we would all sit around -rolling joints, playing cards, telling side splitting yarns, singing songs and laughing and generally disturbing the peace of that quaint little town - until almost sunrise. Some of those nights were the most enjoyable of my whole time in Hopfgarten but I'm reluctant to use the word *"memorable"* - as little else comes to mind of what we actually did up there... in Stubbo's Bar!

Stubbo's Bar

Well goodnight everybody it's time to go
sleep tight I hope you enjoyed the show
well you can come here again
but ya won't know where to go

It's upstairs way up among the clouds
ain't got no cares away from all the crowds
but ya better hang on to your head
you could loose your mind for hours

You just sign on the wall
put your money in the jar
smokin' with a beer
you're in Stubbo's Bar

Stubbo is everybody's friend
and you know you can depend
on the time of your life
that you wish would never end

You just sign on the wall
put your money in the jar
smokin' with a beer
you're in Stubbo's Bar

Well goodnight it's nearly dawn
hold tight the steps are worn
you be sure and tell your friends
that the welcome is always warm

You just sign on the wall
put your money in the jar
smokin' with a beer
you're in Stubbo's Bar

Stumbling down the worn steps of that ancient building, to my room below, without incurring injury, was an achievement, but even more remarkable, was that I was able to get up and be back skiing on the mountain before midday the following day - repeating the whole process for the *next* twenty four hours! It seems I was living by the words of an old Tyrolean saying..."*it's a hard life in the mountains!*"

We *all* worked and played hard - itinerant employees and locals, alike - cashing in on the tourists dollars while there was still plenty of snow on the mountain. As the season drew to it's close, and the snow, as well as the numbers of tourists, began to thin, we all drew a collective sigh of relief and relaxed. A group of Aussies, who had rented a whole apartment building called House Hoffer, decided to celebrate the end of the winter season with a champagne breakfast - held in the street, outside their building, one sunny spring morning. They were an eclectic bunch, who had worked in the village for the season as bar attendants, cleaners, kitchen staff, tour guides, bus drivers, ski instructors and musicians - and others, who had simply scrounged their way through the winter, as ski bums. One of the organisers of the event was an ex footballer from the eastern suburbs of Sydney who was simply known as *TB*. He was the *unofficial* landlord and rent collector of House Hoffer, and along with the other colourful tenants, such as; *Jeffro, Fly, Ewan, John Oliver, Marie* and *Mum*, they arranged tables and chairs out on the lane in front of the building and supplied the mixture of orange juice and cheap, sparkling, Austrian wine - to anyone passing by who was game enough to sit down and join in on the festivities. *My invitation* involved TB barging into my cellar bedroom, at the pub, and dragging me out of bed and up the street - still in my pyjamas and still half pissed from the previous night! In fact - being nine o'clock in the morning - I'd only been asleep for two hours, before I, reluctantly, began to pour that toxic breakfast juice down my throat! More lethal was the concoction of hash and weed that the seasoned tour guide, we called *Fly*, was rolling into joints, to smoke with our *spritzers*. He had collected his *mind altering mixture* of narcotics during the year - while travelling across North Africa, Europe and Turkey - and reverently referred to it, as... "*The Bitch*". If I remember anything at all, of that crazy morning, the most vivid image is of Fly's maniacal chuckle and the menacing glint in his eye as he invited me to... "*Come and meet the Bitch!*"

Champagne "Breakfast with the Bitch" Instigators; Fly, Euan, TB & Stubbo

Breakfast With The Bitch

Five a.m.-Scarred and scratched-I dribbled into bed
two hours later, you know I hate her
poundin' in my head
I'm an engineer in the kitchen
when my hand starts to itch
that's çause I'm waitin', anticipatin'
breakfast with the bitch

Breakfast with the bitch
breakfast with the bitch
breakfast with the bitch

TB sleezin' out the back çause he's a stud
he pulled a dud, sowed a stitch
havin' breakfast with the bitch
now where's Mum? Eatin'chips
that's how she gets her kicks
Ewan I stubbed out the Fly's eye
Oliver died in a ditch
havin' breakfast with the bitch

Breakfast with the Bitch
Breakfast with the Bitch
Breakfast with the bitch
Cancel the day
I've got no more to say than this
I'm havin'
breakfast with the bitch

I think I'm in trouble
yes I'm in trouble
I know I'm in trouble

That event was certainly not my finest hour, and my performance, later that night in the Pub, was even worse! - and the first occasion that Helmut actually asked me to stop playing and go to bed, to sleep it off! The line in the song - about *"eatin' chips"* - was a veiled reference to the lady who operated a small cafe just down the road from where we held our street party. Her shop had a servery window, facing onto the street, that we would stop and lean on, to eat her speciality dish of hot chips. It was probably the closest thing to a *Macdonalds Drive Through,* for it's day, except you walked through.

The other unique aspect of her business was that she would often entice you to share a special alcoholic beveridge with her [*"on the house!"*], that was a strange tasting mixture of brandy and coke - called a "Rochelle". A visit to the *Chip Lady*'s shop could be a very risky move - especially when the Rochelles were flowing freely! - and the glint in her eye told me that, maybe, the *chips* weren't the *only* hot item on the menu! Unlike many of the other residents of the village, who passed by our rowdy gathering - casting glares of disapproval at these foreigners behaving badly in their town - the *Chip Lady* joined our party, offering her Rochelles to any of the boys who were keen to flirt with her. Although she was quite attractive, the only impediment to her amorous endeavours was the lingering odour of stale cooking oil that emanated from her - being a consequence of the endless hours, locked in that tiny shop, frying chips!

Returning to the Motherland

When the winter season officially closed I said my good byes to all the wonderful locals I had got to know and who all insisted I return the next winter. This was assured when Helmut offered me the job for the next season, and ensured my acceptance of the deal by offering to pay my air fare from Australia. Agreeing to the deal, I loaded the Renault hatchback with my guitar and PA equipment, and, along with Gluey - who had returned for the final weeks of the season - as navigator - we headed back to London. On our way back, while being honked at and overtaken by the endless procession of speeding BMW's and Merc's on the German auotobahn, we saw a sign - saying.."Berlin -500kms" - and we both nonchalantly looked at each other and said..."do you want to go to Berlin for the night?" As we both nodded in agreement to the proposition, I instantly swerved onto the *off-ramp - [called "Ausfahrt"-an amusing and appropriate term for two Aussie tourists, travellin' by the seat of their pants!]*. It was just before midnight that we began to rue our decision - as the West German border guard leaned over to look into the back of our car, at the border crossing, near Berlin. We hadn't realised that the musical equipment we were carrying could be considered as taxable foreign goods that could be confiscated if we didn't pay the excise, but, being late - and the, *tired looking,* guard seeming unimpressed by our frail looking Renault - we were waved through, after the mandatory frowning glance at our Australian Passports. Adhering to the *Barry Mackenzie principal,* we found a bar in an outer suburb of Berlin, and while celebrating our nervous border crossing - with a beer - we managed to sort out accommodation at a nearby hostel and arrange a sightseeing tour of the town - with a friendly local taxi driver who was keen to practise his English speaking skills with us. He picked us up at the hostel the following day and drove us all around Berlin in his Taxi, filling us in on all the history, as best he could, with his limited vocabulary. The highlight, was dropping us at Check Point Charlie, at The Wall, to cross over into East Berlin for a few interesting Hours. The following day - after a five hundred kilometre detour, and *only* twenty four hours in Berlin! - we resumed our journey back to London - and our abode in Earles Court - where *I* resumed gigging around town and *Gluey* picked up electrical contracting work.

Gradually, over the next few months, Gluey and the rest of the expat's who had shared our travels throughout Europe and accommodation in Hogarth Road, flew back home - and as I drove one of the last flatmates to Heathrow Airport I realised that a fantastic period in my life - of travelling adventures and friendships - was drawing to a close.

My trusty Renault at a castle near Hopfgarten (above) and the Berlin Wall with Gluey (below)

My Hendon, London, car collection-Left hand drive VW and Renault with wheel bearing repairs under-way.

They've All Gone Home

I heard you were leaving
I'm here to say goodbye
You're the last one to leave
I'm the last to cry

We all went on a journey
that now seems like a dream

When we met we were too shy to even share a smile
In the end we were sharing all we owned
Now they've all gone home

So many friends I made
travelling half way 'round the world
London can be so cold when you're all alone
and they've all gone home

I heard 'bout the reunion
they all said how they envied me
wish they could see me remembering, alone
but they've all gone home

They've all gone home

Hendon NW4

My next address in London was in the northern suburb of Hendon, to a spacious two story house on Green Lane. It was being rented by a bunch of muso mates of mine from Newcastle, including; Jus Gordon, Steve Werrin, Doug Gillespie, Jeff Dunn, and [sound engineer] Col Tegg - as well as their friends, who rented space in the house as a stop-over between jaunts around England and Europe. As I recall the fun and mayhem I experienced living at this address, I'm reminded of the TV sitcom, popular at that time, called "*The Young One's*" - whose cast of socially dysfunctional misfits had much in common with me and my flatmates! Every day and night - living in that house - was a constant challenge to see who could survive the endless assault of practical jokes and pranks, that, in most cases, were masterminded by Steve Werrin - or "*Wezza*" as we all called him.

One of the first victims to come to mind, was, ironically, a friend of Weza's who we called *Sudsie-The Butcher*[relating to his profession back home in Newcastle]. Sudsie had begun to think the house may be haunted, telling us he had seen ghostly figures walking up the stairs. Weza capitalised on Sudsie's concerned disposition, and rewired the electrical circuits in the house so he could make the lights go on and off whenever Sudsie walked into a room. This had the desired effect of unsettling him even more but had ramifications for Corrine and myself as we shared a room with him and often lost sleep, listening to him having nightmares and grinding his teeth throughout the night.

Sudsie was furious when he found out he'd been the victim of this prank, and vented his anger by dragging Jeff Dunn's mattress out into the yard and setting it on fire. The mattress burning incident related to festering issues between him and Jeff, but, unfortunately for me, had no impact on Weza's mischievous antics, as I was the next target.

Weza's technical skills with electronics were next focussed on the public phone box just up the road from our house. By modifying the hand piece of an old *corded* phone handset with alligator clips - and attaching them to wires at the back of the public phone - he had made it possible for all of us to call our families, back in Oz, for free! This was before mobile phones, so *that* rigged phone box was like *gold* to us. To avoid detection from Telecom authorities, we would take turns, late at night, to use Wezás invention - but on the night that Corrine and I walked up to the phone box to call our respective families, something strange occurred. As we were about to enter the booth, the phone inside it began to ring. I still can't explain why, but I instinctively stepped inside and lifted the receiver and said.. "Hello?". Answering back to me was a stern, posh, English accented male voice, saying…"This is British Telecom and we've been monitoring this phone box for illegal activity regarding unauthorised use by Australian tourists calling home…is that what you're planning to do right now?" Corrine saw the colour drain from my face as I slammed the phone back onto it's hook, grabbed her by the hand and ran out of that booth and back to the house as fast as my legs would take the two of us. I explained the grave situation to her, in broken sentences, as I gasped for breath, while we ran, but stopped abruptly when we reached the front gate - to find all our house mates standing at the front doorway, howling with laughter and imitating the stern British accent, saying..."this is British Telecom... what are you doing in this phone booth?". It was *Weza* who had called the phone booth from our home phone, and impersonated the Telecom Officer. He had watched us from the house, with binoculars, the whole time, and couldn't believe his luck in pulling off the prank - when I played right into his hands and naively answered the phone when he called it. With thoughts of *being deported* for the crime, still rushing through my head, I reluctantly accepted that I'd been pranked - "*big time*" - and have been constantly reminded of *it*, by members of that household, to this very day. Lionel Richie's massive hit song, at that time, called "Hello?...is it me you're looking for?" was also a painful trigger to remind me of that humiliating event - for many years to come!

Hendon, at that time, had a large Jewish population. Seeing groups of men with bushy grey beards, dressed in elaborately-hooded, long black robes, strolling past our house, was a constant reminder that... "*I wasn't in Tenambit anymore!*" Many of the houses had the *Star of David* displayed above their doorways - as did ours - which, to me, seemed almost sacrilegious - being inhabited by all of us Godless misfits and rogues. I was assured, however, that we weren't the only heathens in the neighbourhood when I was told that a sign, advertising the latest Hollywood movie at the local cinema, had been altered, from..."Who Shot Roger Rabbit?"..to..."Who Shot Roger Rabbi?". Another ethnic issue at the time, was the number of "*Bombings*" and *Bomb hoaxes* being reported in England - most notably, a bomb threat against the Queen by the IRA. An unfortunate coincidence, that same week, was that two of our, newer, house quests - fresh off the plane from home and full of "*warm Pommie piss*" - decided to do a bomb threat of their own, against a local nightclub that had refused them entry - due to their inebriated condition! Being unable, or incapable, of finding the nightclubs' phone number in the local telephone book, Bill and Dougie made the fatal error of calling the local police station - to report their *fictitious bomb* at the club - in their *best, mock Irish accents!* The *call* was obviously traced to our address, and, within 15 minutes, Green Lane was full of Police cars - and detectives were knocking on *our* front door. Luckily, some of the *sober* members of our household, who had been informed of the hoax, conceived an alibi, that..."we'd just hosted a large party- and that numerous people had used our home phone to call cabs - and that it could've been any *one* of those people that made the hoax call". They even embellished the story by adding, that..."there was a variety of nationalities at the party - some of whom were Irish!". To make the story even more credible, the boys, hurriedly, messed up the house with empty beer cans and bottles of wine - items, that were always in vast quantities and easily accessible, at the side of the house where the trash bins resided. To our amazement, the police officers accepted the story and left us with a warning..."to be more vigilant about *who* uses our phone!". It was ironic that Weza came home late that night and thought *we* were pranking *him* - with the story of surviving our, bomb-hoax related, *police raid* - but the two, suited, detectives, watching our house from an unmarked police car, parked in our street for a week after the event, eventually convinced him of *it's* validity.

Finding a parking space anywhere in London was always challenging and at one point I found myself the owner of two vehicles that required garaging - while I carried out mechanical repairs. The first car was my trusty Renault that had taken me to Austria and back - as well as right around England, Scotland and Ireland. The other was a bright yellow, left hand drive, VW hatchback with Dutch number plates, that I'd bought for fifty quid from Tony Hinton, the mischievous Governor of the King's Head Pub at Putney Bridge. It had been owned by numerous expat's and had survived countless treks to and from Austria, mainly to the Top Deck Ski tours headquarters, near Kitzbhule, called Club Habitat. My father had taught me to do grease and oil changes on my first car but that was about the extent of my mechanical ability, until now, but with guidance from Gluey, Sudsy, Teggie and a very tolerant mechanic from Chelsea, I managed to replace wheel bearings and brake lines in both cars. Both procedures weren't without incident however. The first,

being to neglect replacing the *inner* - as well as the *outer* - wheel bearings, and driving the Renault all the way from Hendon to Chelsea with the wheels wobbling so much that I could barely steer it. The mechanic at Chelsea was amazed that the car survived the journey and after loaning me some of his tools to complete the job, shook his head in disbelief as I drove back to Hendon - with my wobbly wheels - to complete the repair. My next mistake was forgetting to bleed the lines after replacing the brake fluid. This became painfully obvious as I drove through central London - surrounded in traffic by expensive Mercedes Benz's and Roles Royces - with a brake pedal that simply fell to the floor of the car when my foot touched it, meaning my only option to stop or slow down was by changing down gears and pulling on the hand brake! Being uninsured, caused my heart to palpitate as I rolled slowly toward the rear end of the luxury cars in front of me in the erratic London peak hour traffic.

I learnt some invaluable lessons lying under those two cars parked, in pieces, on the front lawn of 27 Green lane, which, due to our tenancy, was beginning to look more like a property in one of the working class suburbs of western Sydney. The biggest lesson I was to learn, however, was to *never* sell your old cars to a mate - which was made clear to me after selling the Renault to Jus Gordon before I flew back to Australia. I did warn him that some of my mechanical repair work may have been somewhat below par but that the car was running well and the only issue, requiring constant monitoring, was an unusual glass container located near the engine that had to be refilled with water, daily, to maintain a safe engine temperature. The long distance phone call I received back home from a disgruntled Gordon, telling me that he and Jeff Dunn had to abandon the car on the side of the M2 motorway while enroute to a gig in Bath - because the engine overheated and seized - confirmed that my instructions weren't followed! It has been a humorous point of conjecture between the two of us ever since!

Another car that was also parked in the yard of our Hendon mansion was a sad looking Ford Cortina station wagon owned by Weza. He paid very little for it - as it was unregistered - and we often used it to transport us and our equipment to gigs in London - such as The Walkabout Club, Deckers and The Kings Head Pub. Late one cold rainy night, returning from one of those gigs, a passing police van slowed down to check us out - and our worst fears were realised when they did a U turn and began to follow us. Assuming that they must have seen the car was unregistered, Weza immediately turned off the main road and accelerated away, down a series of suburban back streets. All our hearts were racing as the car slid around corners on the greasy wet road but we were relieved when the distance between *us* and *the police* widened. Although about a block behind us, the patrol car continued it's pursuit, so, eventually, as we approached an intersection, Weza suggested he would park the car around the next corner and we should all jump out and hide in the front yards of nearby houses. Dousing the headlights and skidding the car to the curb, parking tightly between two other cars, Weza - and the rest of us - fled from the Cortina - scurrying over nearby bushes and fences like commandos on a clandestine mission. We must've all breathed a collective sigh of relief as the somewhat cumbersome paddy wagon ambled around the corner and sped off, up the street - past our *fugitive* car, parked in the shadows. After remaining in our hiding spots to ensure the police were well out of range, we then triumphantly returned to our car to resume our journey home, all the while celebrating our escape, with nervous relief. Our celebrations were short lived however, when, within five minutes, another police vehicle - this time, a patrol car - performed a U turn to also follow us. We assumed that the officers, involved in the initial car chase, had broadcast our car's description to other patrol cars in the area. His confidence boosted from the previous pursuit, Weza pushed the accelerator to the floor in another attempt to out run the cops but the faster patrol car was right on our tail within seconds, and he had no option but to pull over to face the music. Weza's quick thinking and creative comedic mind went into gear as the patrol-men interrogated him about his attempt to outrun them and the lack of registration on his vehicle. In his broadest - and dumbest sounding - Aussie accent he admitted to speeding up when they came up behind him because he thought they were trying to get to an emergency and he didn't want to slow them down and that he couldn't stop until he found a parking spot. Regarding his car's registration, he assured them that... "the Geeza who sold me the car had said that the rego was good for six months - and that was how things worked in England, just like back in Austraya mate!" The two patrol-men almost laughed at his feeble excuses and, rolling their eyes, turned to me and Jeff - sitting in the back seat doing our best to look and sound just as typically antipodean and naïve - taking a line from a Kevin Bloody Wilson song, saying in unison, …"yeah mate, that's what he really said', bloody oath!". Growing weary of trying to explain the British laws of vehicle registration to this bunch of ignorant Aussie tourists, the cops, to our utter amazement and relief, simply ended up giving us a warning and telling us to leave our car parked where it was until we arranged the proper registration. We still pushed our luck by asking for a lift home because it was raining and we didn't want our guitars to get wet but they'd had enough of us by then and simply drove off, shaking their heads at our impertinence. Even after surviving two brushes with the law - and walking the three kilometres home, in the rain - we pushed our luck even further by returning to retrieve our parked car at about three am because we were concerned about all our amplifiers locked inside of it. On that final leg of our adventurous evening we narrowly missed being spotted by, *yet,* another patrol car, as we crossed the motorway not far from our house! Incredibly, a few weeks later - having still not registered the Cortina - I was with Weza as he, once again, adopted the dumb Aussie persona and talked his way out of another infringement from a Bobby!

Having established myself as a *one man band* for the previous five years, it was a wonderful experience to live and work with so many other musicians in that exotic location.

We *all* had regular work throughout London - utilising a network of local booking agents and tour companies such as Contiki and Top Deck - and it was rare for all of us to be in the house at night because of the amount of work we had. It was like a *household cooperative* of musicians. An agent would call our home phone, some afternoons - requesting a soloist or duo or trio - and we'd all call *dibs* on which gig suited us, or team up to meet the venues requirements. The Sunday afternoon Thames River Cruise that I performed on with Jeff Dunn really epitomised my crazy musical life in London as I recall the conflicting images of sailing past the majestic British Houses of Parliament buildings while singing Kehsan to a rebellious mob of sloshed Aussies and Kiwis - some of whom stripped off and jumped into the river! It was like the *convicts* had returned to take their revenge for being deported in the first place! Another *stand out* gig, this time with me being the sloshed one, was attempting to sing Eric Bogles, "The Band Played Waltzing Matilda" to a thousand, equally sloshed, Aussies and Kiwis, on Anzac Day, at the Empire theatre in Leicester Square. I made the mistake of mingling with the audience before my performance on that occasion and the spirit [or should I say "Spirits"] of the event overwhelmed me! Luckily, Jus Gordon, was with me on stage to salvage the remains of the song that I had wrecked! He was also with me at a gig in Brixton - at an *early opener* pub one Sunday morning - when I risked life and limb singing another Eric Bogle tune called "I Hate Wogs" - to an unimpressed audience of, predominantly, black shift workers. Thinking the song would

Me & Jeff Dunn performing on Thames River cruise, London

be a hit with the local Londoners - who had little regard for European foreigners - I was informed, by Gordon, that the word - "wogs" - was a derogative term - used to describe African migrants - and the fact that the ones in the bar that morning probably couldn't understand my broad Aussie accent, was the only reason I was still alive!

Of all the gigs that I performed in and around London, the one that captured the essence of my desire to be self sufficient and independent was when I went busking in Charring Cross tube station - purely for the fun of it. Listening to my voice bouncing off the tiled walls of that long, windy tunnel, deep beneath that iconic and vibrant city, made me feel like a part of it's soul. Like a local. And after only one hour I'd collected enough coins in my guitar case, from the passing procession, to go and buy a beer and lunch at a nearby pub. It was an experiment that proved to me I could survive anywhere in the world with just my voice and guitar.

Leo Sayer wrote a song about busking in London called "I'm a One Man Band" and I fondly remember driving down Ladbroke Grove - which is mentioned in the song - humming the tune, a regular in my repertoire, and realising it's significance to me.

It was painfully ironic, years later, that I would meet Leo at the Hunter Valley Gardens, near Cessnock, while attempting to perform an instrumental gig with just my guitar and harmonica - after I'd contracted a voice disorder that made it difficult for me to sing. He was the patron of an art exhibition being held there, and, either out of a sense of camaraderie or sympathy, he was the only person who talked to me in the whole three hours that I played that afternoon. He complimented my playing and quizzed me about my Guitar Loop pedal, but I sensed he was mainly offering me moral support when he commented on how hard it is to perform at those sort of events where no one is really listening to the musician. The lyrics - of his hit song -..."I'm a one-man-band, nobody knows nor understands...." gaining even more significance with our chat! The high esteem I all ready held for him was doubled after *that* brief encounter!

One of my last memories of living in that crazy, muso-infested, household in North London was of all of us sitting in the lounge room, one Saturday afternoon, watching the Live Aid Concert on television. We all appreciated the enormity of such a ground breaking event and as we added our commentary on each of the acts' performances - many of whom had inspired us to enter show business - I sensed a feeling of frustration that we were watching a historical event that was occurring just a few kilometres down the road from our house, at Wembley Stadium! I remember thinking that if I walked out into the backyard I would just about be able to hear Freddy's voice wafting across the roof tops, singing..."We will, we will rock you!"

Satisfied that I'd proved I could earn my musical living in one of the largest cities in the world, I was keen to return home to the comfort of my local gigs around Newcastle and Maitland and showcase some of my new original material. I was also returning with a new piece of equipment that had become a part of my arsenal in London. It was a drum machine. No bigger than a small box of chocolates but with the capability of adding more power to my performance if the audience wanted to dance to my songs. Frowned upon by purists colleagues in the industry, the drum machine and later, the sequencer, became valuable song-writing and recording tools for me when composing. My decision to adopt this equipment was justified when I read that Phil Collins even used the *same* drum machine when he recorded "In The Air Tonight".

My companion on the *home-bound* Quantas flight was Peter Tapp, an entrepreneur from Newcastle who had been staying at our house in Hendon. It was, coincidently, Peter's Father, Matt Tapp, who had helped launch my career by playing my first single, P.C.A. on his radio programme at 2KO. Peter's *advice* was just as valuable - as I headed back to enter the next stage of my musical journey - it was to..."lie on the floor - under my seat - in order to get some *good* sleep on the long, twenty hour flight!"

Sept-Dec 1985 Back in Newcastle

The Boy's Back

I clearly remember the look of relief on my parents face when they drove down from Maitland to pick me up at Sydney airport. I wound down the windows to smell the *Australian bush* as we drove home on the freeway, that, when I was a child, had been cut through the sandstone hills overlooking the magnificent Hawkesbury river gorges near Brooklyn. "The road to know where" as it's political opponents had labelled it - back in the nineteen sixties - arguing that it was a waste of tax payers money and that it would never be fully utilised! A road that, today, is so congested, can turn into a car park for hours if even a minor accident occurs! A road that I got to know intimately over the next ten years - while commuting between my gigs and homes in Sydney and Newcastle.

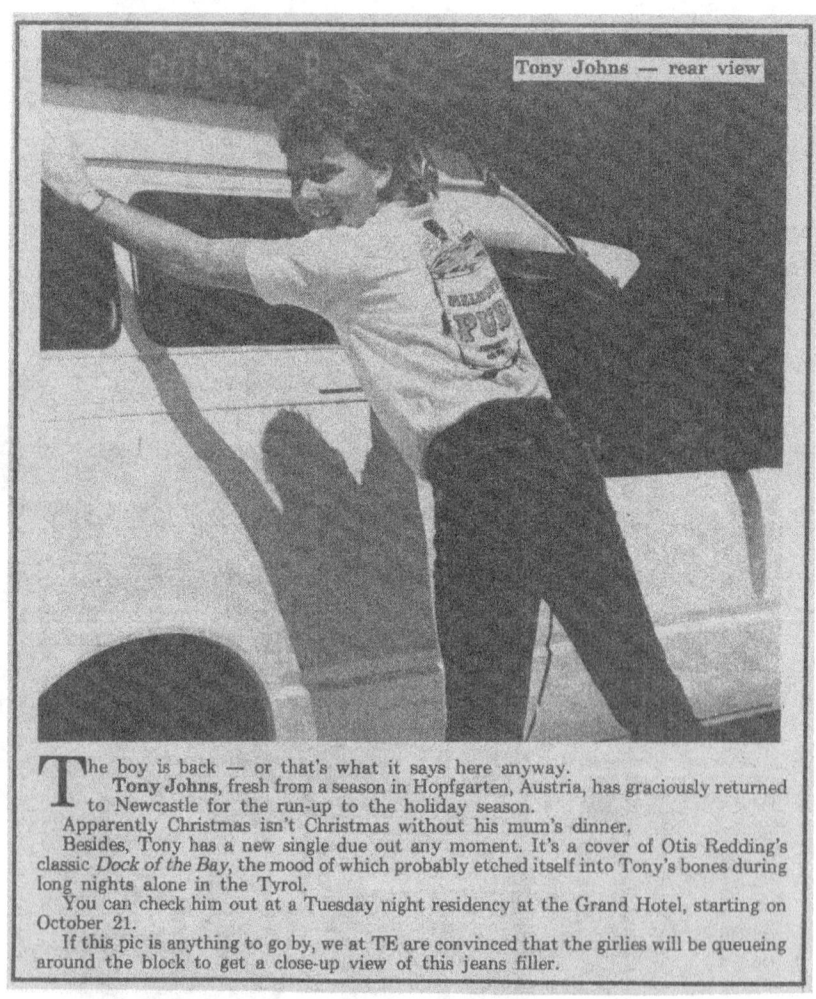

Tony Johns — rear view

The boy is back — or that's what it says here anyway.
Tony Johns, fresh from a season in Hopfgarten, Austria, has graciously returned to Newcastle for the run-up to the holiday season.
Apparently Christmas isn't Christmas without his mum's dinner.
Besides, Tony has a new single due out any moment. It's a cover of Otis Redding's classic *Dock of the Bay*, the mood of which probably etched itself into Tony's bones during long nights alone in the Tyrol.
You can check him out at a Tuesday night residency at the Grand Hotel, starting on October 21.
If this pic is anything to go by, we at TE are convinced that the girlies will be queueing around the block to get a close-up view of this jeans filler.

I Know This Road

I know this road,
I know the way,
'cause I drive this road every night and day
I know this road
every lane, every centre line
I own this road
this road is mine

I know this road and this road knows me
and it takes it toll
no free way is free
I know this road, every speed limit sign
I own this road
this road is mine

So I drive to the city from a little country town
just two hours on this road
is all it takes to be back where I love

I know this road and it drives me 'round the bend
I built my life a highway
but just turned down a dead end
I know this road, I drive it all the time
I own this road
this road is mine

My senses feasted on the aroma and vista, and I was intoxicated with excitement and the comfort of being Home. After being abroad for twelve months - reconnecting with my ancestry - I also felt a strange sense of being a foreigner in this country - as if I was returning for the second time - and part of me was experiencing the same awe and apprehension the early settlers had felt when *first* arriving in this vast, rugged land. That uneasy feeling - of not really *belonging, here* or *overseas* - has lingered within me ever since - and although I wrote this song describing an experience in Fanny's nightclub on Wharf Road in Newcastle, I believe it's implications originate from much deeper within my consciousness.

Clique

I've been watching you for sometime now
I've even tried to hear you talk through the noise of the crowd
All the time I stare at you you never notice me
Doin' something wrong, lack of personality, maybe

You see the problem here is not knowing where to start
which line to use, which words to choose
I wish I had the heart
But every time I get the chance I freeze in my shoes
I don't understand myself, I've got nothin' to loose

So I hang around and let my confidence run down
I'd love to ask your friends "what is the trick?"
How do I join your clique?

Let me join, let me, let me join your clique
who've I gotta see to pay my membership?
It seems so exclusive, do you think I have a chance?
Or to you am I just a fool
Tryin' to get into your pants

And I feel like I'm pryin' but I won't stop tryin'
to penetrate the wall that seems so thick
that surrounds your clique

Let me join, let me, let me join your clique

I've been watching you, I watch you every night
sitting in the circle of the boys who did it right
Is it what they wear?
Is it how they make you smile?
I just need a chance to be alone with you a while

But I can't lure you away
safe inside the group you stay
The blood that holds you there is much to thick
I wanna join your clique

Let me join, let me, let me join your clique

I'd no sooner stepped off the plane and arrived back in Newcastle, and Peter Anderson and the team at Rock City Promotions had launched an advertising campaign called "The Boy's Back" - announcing my return - highlighted by a resident gig at the recently refurbished Newcastle Hotel, in Scott street, every Saturday night. The bar manager, Johnno, was a mate of mine so I had *free range* to entertain in a similar style to what I'd been doing in Helmut's Pub back in Austria - which included promoting drinking games and constantly engaging in banter with the customers while singing all the silly dity's in my repertoire, like... "The Ski instructor Song" and Kevin Bloody Wilson classics, such as... "Do you Fuck on First Dates"!

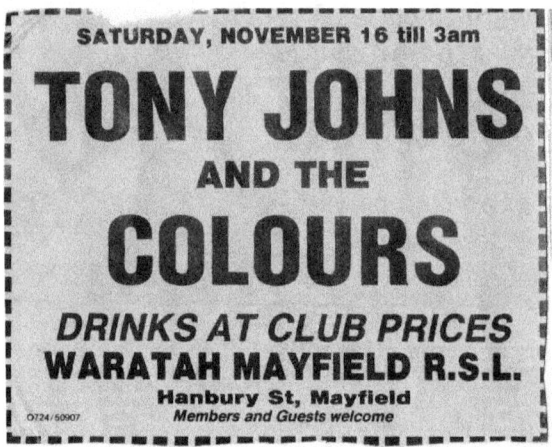

I was only home for four months - after which, I planned to return to Austria for the next winter ski season in Hopgarten - so my attitude to gigs and life in general was fairly "*GungHo*"! I was on a high, knowing that the world was completely at my disposal. Where ever I chose to be, I had gigs lined up and my life was fun and exciting. I felt invincible, which, on some occasions, led me to taking some fairly risky and foolish chances. The first of those poor decisions - after moving into my new, one bedroom flat, back in Mitchell street, Merewether - was to offer to store and distribute a large garbage bag full of marijuana for a group of my mates who had bought it from friends up the coast. It was only a few days later - when I walked into the small apartment, after a warm day, swimming up at Dixon Park beach,and the pungent odour of the Pot nearly knocked me over when I opened the front door - that I realised my error. The stench was so strong that I feared even a policeman walking past on the footpath would smell my stash and surely bust me. So to remedy my predicament I hurriedly set about distributing the contraband to my friends living around the area. Fearing that I may be pulled over by a patrol car - if I *drove* around town to make the deliveries - I decided to divy the goods into plastic sandwich bags and place them in a backpack which I slung over my shoulders while I rode my push bike all over town, making house calls. Rather than despising myself as a drug dealer, I considered my service to be that of a *middle man* for my friends - and it had the added bonus of ensuring I never had to pay for weed, for my personal use. I didn't consider myself to be a big *pot smoker,* but the night I ordered a taxi to take me to the Jolly Roger Night club, late one Saturday night - after priming myself up on half a joint - and the driver glared at me with disdain while he rolled down his window to avoid the stench on my clothes and breath - gave me cause to question the extent of my vice.

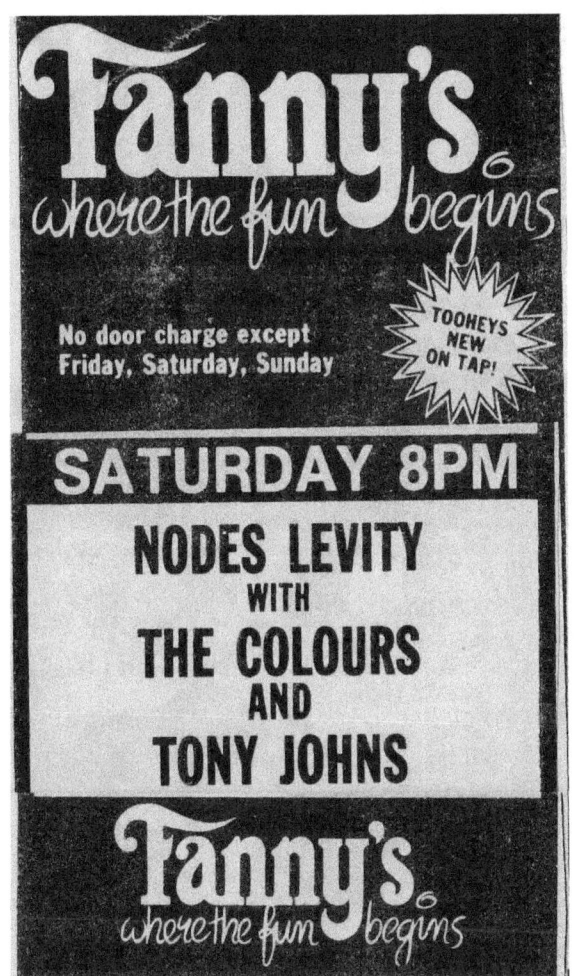

My other solo gigs – that year - included residencies at The Delany hotel on Friday nights, The Castle Nightclub on Tuesday nights, The Stag and Hunter hotel on Wednesday nights, and alternating Thursday nights at the Belair hotel in Kotara and the Imperial Hotel in Maitland. The musical *highlight*, however, at this time, was to perform a series of shows with my mates in their new band called "The Colours". As well as being great fun, I considered it a great honour and privilege to perform with the wealth of talent that Tony Heads, Dave Carter, Mick Punch and Craig Lancaster possessed. As well as giving me exposure in some of the larger venues - such as Fanny's Nightclub and the Cambridge Hotel - it also allowed me to showcase some of my new original material - such as this one, which I wrote as a result of a punter complaining to me that.. "too many of my original songs were sad and depressing!"

Happy Chap

I'm smiling I'm a happy chap
I'm smiling and I'm glad I'm back
it's about time to sit down and have a chat

I'm laughing I'm in the clear
I'm laughing and I love it here
so don't tell me that I've changed
I've got myself in top gear

I still remember what you said
"sing a song sing a happy song"
it's always been there in my head
the sad song is dead

I'm laughing I'm in the clear
I'm laughing and I love it here
so don't tell me that I've changed
I've got myself in top gear

I still remember what you said
"sing a song sing a happy song"
it's always been there in my head
the sad song is dead

I'm screaming I'm hysterical
I'm reeling on a merry go round
Hey look what I found
I picked it up off the ground
I pulled it out of my hat
what do you think about that?
I'm a happy chap

Without doubt, I certainly *was* a *very* happy chap at *that* time. I was revelling in being back with friends and playing to familiar faces at my resident gigs. My *time* in Helmut's Pub - playing two sessions a day for six days a week - had conditioned me to handle my busy schedule - which also included going out to nightclubs and parties after most gigs. My busiest week saw me perform eight gigs - three of which were all on the Tuesday when the Melbourne Cup was held. That day started at the Belair Hotel - where I compared and judged a fashion parade - which, by the time the "swim wear" models came on, convinced me I had definitely chosen the best career path! From there, I drove over to the Delany Hotel for a three hour gig, then finished the night singing down at the Castle Nightclub until two AM.

As much as I wanted to take advantage of the warm Australian weather and beach - before returning to the Austrian winter - I struggled to drag myself out of bed, before midday, on most days ;

I Can't Wake Up

*I can't wake up in the morning
I'm too tired to raise my head
I can't wake up in the morning
I prefer to stay in bed*

*Call me lazy, call me crazy
but I'm happy where I lie
come and join me don't annoy me
I could lay here 'till I die*

*And I sleep as the day goes by
I'm asleep so don't ask me why
I can't get to my feet however hard I try*

*And I sleep far beneath closed eyes
and I sleep as the morning flys
I can't get to my feet however hard I try*

*I can't wake up in the morning
I'm too tired to raise my head
I can't wake up in the morning
I prefer to stay in bed*

On the days that I *did* manage to get out of bed before midday I would go down to the recording studio at Rock City Promotions [Studio 21] in Hamilton to lay down tracks for my next single *and* the album I was going to take back to Austria to sell in Helmut's Pub.

The single was *my* interpretation of the Ottis' Reading classic, "Sittin' On the Dock of the Bay", which was produced and engineered by Col Tegg and featured the hauntingly beautiful fretless bass skills of my old school band mate, Giles Smith. I started the project with Col before returning to Austria and he surprised me with the finished product when I came home in September the following year. My only regret was that I wasn't in the studio with Giles when he contributed his magic. It would've been our first collaboration since our school days. Col had recruited some of Newcastle's finest musos to complete the song - including Tony Heany, from Vegemite Reggae, who's skilful effects on keyboards were outstanding. We released the single in December 1986 and although it received very little airplay on local radio, I was very happy with, and proud of the end result. The fact that Joe Cocker *and* Renee Geyer also released their versions of the same song - at that same time - didn't help my cause either, but it did boost my profile, regardless.

The *album project,* that I was hurriedly putting together, was a collection of my own songs that I'd written and performed while in Europe during the previous year - which I planned to sell to tourist, over there, in the coming season, on audio cassette. As well as producing and engineering, Dean Tolhurst provided an array of keyboard enhancements [including the church bell sounds for the *Bellringer Song*!] for the songs, that were mostly accompanied by my acoustic guitar and drum machine. The album's title was *"Goin' Back to Europe"* - it was an eclectic mix of my ditty's and ballads that I primarily threw together as a means of having some merchandise to sell in order to finance my travels abroad. Although it was not my finest musical creation, the lessons I learnt from all those [free] hours in the studio were invaluable. To *poke fun* at my *sub par* effort I even credited the project under my old nickname of *"Funky Gibbon* Productions". My plan was to take a master tape of the album to Austria and have it mass produced into cassette tapes - over there. My craziest memory is of the last day of recording, before I flew back to Austria, and hounding Col to hurry up preparing the master tape, while a taxi waited outside the studio to take me to Newcastle station for the train to Sydney - and onto Kingsford Smith Airport.

TONY JOHNS — GOIN' BACK TO EUROPE

SIDE A:
GOIN' BACK TO EUROPE — SHOW US YA MOTA — DOIN' TIME* — BACK IN THE HUNTER VALLEY* — CURSE OF THE AUSTRIAN BELLRINGER — TALKING WITH HER HANDS

SIDE B:
WHAT WE LEFT BEHIND — P.C.A. THE EASY WAY* — IN THE CATACOMB — SING MY BLUES AWAY* — THE BALLAD OF WALLABY TED — THEY'VE ALL GONE HOME

ALL SONGS WRITTEN BY T. JOHNS. RECORDED AT STUDIO 21, NEWCASTLE, AUSTRALIA. PRODUCED AND ENGINEERED BY D. TOLHURST EXCEPT (*) M. TINSON.
COPYRIGHT © 1985 FUNKY GIBBON PRODUCTIONS

1986 Austria & Greece

Back in Europe - January 1986

Helmut greeted me at Munich airport on a cold morning, early in January, 1986, to drive me back to Hopfgarten. The transition of leaving Newcastle's summer, dressed in board shorts and singlet and stepping off the plane in, a snow covered, Germany, wearing an overcoat, scarf and beanie, always amazed and confounded me - and played havoc with my sinuses. I'd had sinus and hay-fever problems since my high school years, and, unfortunately, my lifestyle and occupation – spent, mostly, in crowded bars filled with dense cigarette smoke - didn't help to alleviate my condition.

From the airport we drove to a very modern and clean industrial estate where Helmut had arranged a meeting with an A&R executive - at a cassette and record manufacturing company - to have the Master Tape of my new album mass produced. It was a strange meeting, with Helmut as my interpreter, as I explained to the executive that I wanted several hundred cassette copies of my master tape - to sell as merchandise while performing in Hopfgarten for the winter ski season. He seemed to be very interested in my career and played the tape while we talked, complimenting me on my songs, and even suggesting to Helmut [in Deutsch] the possibility of signing me to their label. That proposition excited me, but I later realised he was probably just keeping the vibe of the meeting positive to keep his new foreign client keen to do business. I also suspected that Helmut may have embellished the conversation to impress me with his managerial and promotional skills - as my new, *European,* manager. Either way, I was impressed and flattered at the chance to break into the German Country Music Market, but doubted it would eventuate. After negotiating costs and printing requirements for the labels, I ordered 400 cassette tapes that we agreed would be ready for us to pick up in one week's time. I had calculated that if I sold all my cassettes that season, I could pocket an extra $2000 - on top of what Helmut was paying me. What I hadn't factored into my calculations was the possibility of paying excise tax, on the goods, when we crossed the Austrian border the following week, after picking them up from the factory. Helmut saved me from paying that tax - when he was questioned by the Border guard about the boxes of cassettes in his car boot - by saying I was a musician, and the cassettes were my personal music library for research. It was only a miracle that the guard didn't open the boxes, where he would've found the cassettes to be all the same! - with *my* photo on the front of each one!

This wasn't the only time that Helmut had used his charm and finesse to talk his way out of a tricky situation - involving me working for him. Later that season, when Licensing police dropped into his pub and enquired about my authority, as a foreigner, to be performing there, he casually said I was just a tourist who was passing through town and had jumped on stage

to sing a few songs. He was a loveable rogue but a very shrewd businessman, and I'm sure he was *greasing a few palms* around town to ensure my tenure at his pub avoided any bureaucratic complications or costs. There was little [other] Live Music entertainment in the town that season so I was a major draw card for his pub and he did all he could to nurture and protect his prime investment - Me!

I'd be lying to say I didn't enjoy the *celebrity status* that being the only entertainer in the village awarded me! A big fish in a little bowl! A far cry from trying to make a name for myself back in Newcastle and Sydney, and much more fun! It was an entertainers *dream gig*. No driving, no lugging equipment. Just walking downstairs, from my room, to the bar, and plugging my guitar into the house PA system. Playing to a happy and excitable audience who had come from all over the world to be in this charming village for a winter skiing holiday. An audience that didn't tire of my repertoire as they only stayed long enough to get familiar with my songs - before having to return home - often taking my cassette album with them as a memento of the crazy fun nights in Helmuts' crowded and chaotic little bar. Week after week, as one group of holiday makers said their good byes to Hopfgarten, another bus load would arrive to take their place at the bar and the snug alcove wooden tables - yelling "Prost!" with Schnapps glasses held high and singing along with whatever song I was belting out at them.

As exciting as it was to be entertaining people from all over the world, the most memorable nights were when - on the lulls between departing and newly arriving tour groups - the Hopfgarten *locals* would come in to Helmut's Pub to reclaim their watering hole. These occasions had a more intimate atmosphere and I got to know and became friends with many of them. People like Charlie Biembacher who was a ski instructor and physiotherapist at a nearby hospital - who invited me to perform in the rehab ward of the hospital where he worked. His thoughtful and caring nature sort to utilise the therapeutic value of my music for his patients and it turned out to be one of the most rewarding moments in my time abroad. There were countless other locals that I considered friends such as;.. Gerty, the buxom jolly waitress who worked at Ghastoff Riggi, the restaurant near the summit of the local mountain-*Hohe Salve*; Margit, the elderly lady who ran the wine bar beneath Helmut's Pub, who was like my second mum; Rheinhart, who was a railway track maintenance worker that often interpreted for me while I tried to have conversations with other locals; George,

the manager of the Aufenloch disco-across the street from Helmut's, who also helped me bring a batch of cassette albums across the border from Germany; and two guys, both called Franz, who always requested my song about the Hunter Valley. I mustn't forget to mention Marco, who was an officer in the Austrian Army. He would take me sightseeing to Zalsburg or Innsbruck or Kitzbhul, on my day off, with his girlfriend who happened to be the sister of Maria, the young girl for whom I wrote the song.. *"April"*. There were many more - beautiful, warm and kind hearted souls - who adopted me as there own, inviting me into their hearts and homes and making me feel as if part of me had always lived there - and I regret not being able to list all of their names.

Behind the bar was no less hectic, with Helmut and Anne struggling to dispense the illicit refreshments that helped make the audience so malleable for me. On nights when the crowd spilled out into the foyer and pool room and down the winding stone stairway to the front door, Anne would ask her friend, Trish, and her brother, Paul, [or *Punk*, as we called him] to help out behind the bar - along with Helmut's brother, Bernie, and his friend, Hans Peter. The sight of so many people behind that tiny bar, jostling with each other to take orders and serve drinks, often spilling much of the goods over each other, was added amusement for the customers who's loud laughter and singing fuelled the cacophony of merriment.

Despite all the fun and frivolity, the Schnapps and beer, the late nights spent partying and the exhilarating days spent skiing in the clean crisp air of the Tyrolean Alps, I never lost sight of the fact that *this* was my *occupation*. My living. The best job in the world, as far as I was concerned! For *that* reason, I cherished every moment I spent there. I was riding a wave that I knew would eventually run out of energy - so I simply enjoyed the ride. I continued to develop my song writing - often stopping on a ski slope to pen some lyrics - and even though many of the songs I wrote, while viewing those stunning alpine vistas, never made it into a recording studio, they were, never the less, part of my life's musical journey. Songs, such as this one - written on top of, and dedicated to, mount *Hohe Salve* and the charming Austrian beauty who I'd met at my gig, the previous night, but who, unfortunately, lived in the village of Soll, on the other side of the mountain.

Right: Helmut & Anne in costume for the Fasching Festival

Over The Hill

I saw her late that evening
her eyes were like glue
the crowd had got me weaving
but I finally made it through
We made easy conversation
we both had time to kill
but when I asked her destination
She said I live over the hill

I've got to go
over
over the hill

I said walk with me to my place
she said you've got a nice room
but I couldn't keep a straight face
when she said "I've got to go soon"

I've got to go
over
over the hill

She really drove me crazy
but I knew I had to stay
and it's not that I was lazy
I just couldn't get away
'cause the valley was my prison
and that mountain was her guard
I've got to make her listen
then she'll know why it's so hard

For me to go
over
over the hill
I've got to go
over
over the hill

At a time, well before mobile phones, the process of making new acquaintances - or *"Networking"*, as it is now called - and keeping in touch with them, was usually achieved by writing addresses and home phone numbers on drink coasters or in pocket sized note books. While researching this book I found two of my old pocket calender notebooks from that time. One; was a, 1985, Collins pocket notebook that had maps of the London Tube Lines and English motorways on the inside sleeves. The other; was a complimentary, 1986, Allianz notebook that I received when I opened up a savings account - to deposit my wages and cassette sales - at the local bank in Hopfgarten. In these books, I recorded where, and when, I played gigs and what I earned from them, as well as keeping a tally of my album cassette sales. Dispersed throughout the pages were names and addresses of people I'd met at these gigs. Names, that as I read them, clearly evoke images of their smiling faces and the wonderful moments we shared - over thirty five years ago! Names, such as; Brikit and Ellie, from Zwaagdyk in Holland, who's family pub I visited when driving back to England from Austria - and who recently reconnected with me through the magic of Facebook!; Mike and Jack, from Seattle, in America, who constantly imitated my broad Aussie accent; Andy Blaickner, [one of Helmut's brothers], in Myconos, Greece; Sloane Services,Chelsea - the Renault Mechanic who helped me repair my car in London; Marianne, from Ulvenhout, in Holland, who also, recently reconnected with me on Facebook; David, from Beijing in China; The flamboyant Marie, from Bachus Marsh in Victoria, Australia - who I still have contact with; The crazy Danes, Lars and Einar, from Roskilde, Denmark - who taught me to ski with no fear; Karen, from Thunder Bay, Ontario, Canada, who always requested *The Rodeo Song* – which, she claimed, was the unofficial Canadian National Anthem; Francesca and Juan, who I stayed with in Lagos, Portugal; and so on, and so on. Dozens of names and addresses of people from all over the world - who insisted I stay with them, if I was ever in their nick of the woods. If I'd taken them up on *all* their offers, I'd *still* be circling the globe today - living out of a suitcase! Those tiny notebooks were like *international phone-books* that I carried around in the back

Jeff Dunn, Les&Pam Gully, Jus Gordon and Me performing in the snow for the Teddy Bear's Picnic near Kirchberg, Austria

pocket of my jeans for the three years that I lived the life of a nomadic musician.

One name, that caught my eye while flicking through the faded, dog eared, pages, was that of a Greek guy, called Vayios, who was working as a chef in one of the restaurants in Hopfgarten that season. He often came into Helmut's pub, after his shift, for a drink and to watch me perform. He convinced me to travel to the Greek island of Rhodes - at the end of that winter season - where he guaranteed to secure me employment as the resident entertainer at his friends new resort. It was an easy decision - to spend the following summer there - as the Greek Islands were one of my favourite destinations that I visited, two years earlier, on my Contiki Tour, and I was thrilled to be returning there, to live and perform.

The rest of the winter season passed quickly as I fulfilled my gruelling schedule of two shows a day for six days a week. The Apre's Ski session, from 4.30pm to 6pm, often saw me perform, still clad, in my skiing attire - complete with ski boots, jump suite and beany. This was because I often skied straight from the mountain slopes, right down to the front door of Helmut's pub, arriving just in time to step onto the stage and start singing. Dressed this way, gave me the opportunity to advertise the local store that had supplied all of my ski apparel - for free - in return for promoting *them* at my gig. I also had a "*free drink*" arrangement with one of the local disco nightclubs - if I announced I was going there after the pub closed.

Lots of *dealing* was done between businesses

in the local area. Helmut even loaned *me* out, to the Contiki Ghastoff, *[Schoneck]*, to play to their guests, if, in return, their guests were encouraged to visit the pub for a night out. He also brokered a deal with The *Londoner Pub,* in Kitzbhul, for me to perform *there,* one night, but *that* backfired when I suffered a severe bout of performance anxiety - due to the over-hype of the gig and the new surrounds. I'd grown *so* comfortable, playing in the one place for so long, that the *new venue* threw me off balance. Luckily, I was accompanied to the gig by a visiting musician, from Newcastle, *[Les Gully]*, and between he and *"Oddball"* - the Londoner bar manager, also an expat *Novacastrian,* who primed me with enough *Yagermeisters* to cure a leper - I loosened up and eventually won the audience over.

Word spread back home about my resident gig at Helmut's pub - and there was barely a week go by without an old Maitland friend or Newcastle musician walking through the door - next to my *soapbox-sized* stage - while I was singing - and saying.. "g'day *Dozza!..*bet you didn't expect to see me here?!" - but it became *so* common place, that, eventually, I *did* expect to see someone from home, every week! Some of the best nights were when musician mates, such as Jus Gordon, Steve Werrin and Les and Pam Gully would visit and perform with me. Even my agent and manager from Rock City Promotions, Peter Anderson, came over for a holiday and wowed the audience with his vocal performance of *Stairway To Heaven* - one night, with me and Weza. Unfortunately, he collapsed later, from an overdose of Schnapps - supplied by his adoring fans - and was, luckily, revived when Weza threw him under a freezing cold shower! Not to point fingers, but it was usually *me* who collapsed from alcoholic overload whenever Jus Gordon performed with me - and *he* was often left to complete the show alone!

Of all the mad antics we got up to on that stage, the *stand-out* has to be when Weza and I performed a whole set of songs wearing nothing but ski socks and scarfs. Butt naked. The term, *"Unplugged"*, hadn't been coined at that time, but it's an apt description! Weza was renowned,

Me and Steve Werrin[Weza] after bearing it all!

Me, Peter Anderson & Weza

back home, for such stunts, but I was a novice - and a very modest and blushing one at that! Let me assure you, I have no illusions about my diminutive stature - and I guarantee some parts of my anatomy were exceedingly diminished on that occasion! - so I strategically positioned my guitar to hide my shame. To counter my embarrassment, Weza, on the other hand, openly promoted his manliness by hitching his bass guitar high up above his waist - to give the audience the best possible view of *what he had to offer*. The looks of utter astonishment of the customers - walking through the door, next to the stage - as his *bits* almost brushed their cheeks, were priceless, and are etched into the canvass of my funniest memories.

You Only Want Me For My Body

You only want me for my body
you only want what's in my clothes
you only want me for my body
from my head down to my toes

You only want me for my body
you only want me to be teased
you only want me for my body
I think you must be easily pleased

But I have intelligence, there's a brain inside my head
there's more to me than style or elegance
and how I perform in bed
there's more to me than my immaculate masculine composition
my muscular physic with every organ in position
and what about my modesty?
There's so much more to me...but

You only want me for my body
you only want what's in my clothes
you only want me for my body
from my head down to my toes

I am financial I have investments far and wide
and I'm a wizard in the kitchen
[ön the table Mable"]
I'd make you a happy bride
But every chance you get you take me in the bedroom and pervert me
molest me, kick me, scratch me, lick me,
then simply desert me
I wake up in the morning alone and groan
["oh my bloody back!"]

You only want me for my body
you only want what's in my clothes
you only want me for my body
from my head down to my toes

You only want me for my body
you only want a gigolo
you only want me for my body
but why my body?
I don't know!

And even though it disappoints me cause you only seem to use me
at times when I'm alone and sad it's nice to know you'll chose me
it's nice to know there's someone there

who only wants me for my body
who only wants what's in my clothes
you only want me for my body
but why my body? God only knows!

You only want me for my body
well tonight you're in luck
you only want me for my body
you only want me for a …....uhh

you only want me for my
body body body body
body body body body
body body body body
body body body body
body body body body
from my head down to my toes
from my head down to my toes
from my head down to my toes
from my head down to my toes
my toes,my toes,toes,toes

(top)Maitland blokes-Ernie and Dory, (bottom) Me and Helmut

Guest singers; Top left-Austrian celebrity, Top right-Dutch vocalist, Brigit, Bottom left-local guitar virtuoso, Zep; Bottom right-Maitland blokes?, Punk and Me

Rhodes, Greece

Eventually, after three months - ascending the slopes in chair lifts then skiing back down - stepping onto the stage in Helmut's Pub and raising my voice in song as the crowd raised their glasses and downed the grog - climbing the stairs to Stubbo's Bar in the attic then stumbling back down to my room - the snow began to thin and the Winter season drew to a close. Now, thoughts of Summer, swimming, sunbaking and Souvlaki, filled my mind and I headed south to Greece, and the island of Rhodes, to seek out Vayios, to take up his job offer of singing in his friends' resort.

I was fortunate enough to hitch a ride to Athens with a Contiki Rep, called Louise, whose job involved inspecting the company's camp-sites and hotels. Another Aussie girl, called Keryn, who had also been working in Hopfgarten, tagged along for the ride which involved a brief stopover in Venice, at the Contiki Camp-site. A rowdy night was spent in the bar there, which was run by a couple of blokes from Newcastle, who, to my amazement, had worked with my father at the Floating Dock in Newcastle Harbour. I enjoyed their stories about the antics my dad got up to in his job as *"Leading-Hand, Painter and Docker"*, and swelled with pride when they described the high esteem that all the workers there held for him. Equally surprising was hearing them talk of the admiration he showed for me in my musical career - as he often boasted to them of his son's achievements. He had rarely shown much enthusiasm when I'd tell him how much my singing career was earning for me and at what venues I was performing - but he obviously *was* listening and would relay it to his work mates. Final confirmation of his acceptance of my career path was made clear to me when I was cleaning out his car - shortly after he died - and found two musical cassettes. The first; in the glove box, was a Johnny Cash album. The other; still in the cassette player, was *my* album, *"The Valley"*!

The following morning, slightly hungover, we resumed our journey, on the hazardous and unnerving Italian Motorway, towards Brindisi. We quickly sobered up as the frantic pace of the traffic slowed down and we passed the body of a motor cyclist, lying at the end of a smeared trail of blood, in the middle of the road, convulsing in *Death Spasms*. The morbid sight sickened the three of us, and, as onlookers tried to comfort the accident victim until an ambulance arrived, we drove on in silence, contemplating *our* lives - so far away from our homes and families.

It made me realize just how risky it was for me to be venturing to a foreign country purely on the word of a man who was virtually a stranger. Just *another* person I'd met in Helmut's Bar. To add to my concerns at that time, the *Chernobyl Nuclear Disaster* made the headlines and fears were being expressed of n*uclear fallout* becoming a health risk where I was heading. There were particular concerns that local produce might be contaminated and we were advised to wash all our fruit and vegetables.

Another disaster occurred earlier that year which particularly caught my attention and sparked my imagination. It was the *Challenger Space Shuttle* explosion in which all seven crew died, one of whom was a school teacher. It was the first time a non-trained astronaut had been invited on one of NASA's space missions, with the aim of re engaging the general public's interest in the Space Programm - which had waned since the *Apollo Moon Missions*. The incident captured my imagination and spawned an idea for a song - which I completed once I had settled into my new job at the resort on Rhodes island. The storyline is of an average person describing his trip to the moon at NASA's invitation. Maybe it was a type of escapism for me - to alleviate my anxiety regarding my new working adventure - or maybe I was just inspired by the size of the full moon that I witnessed, one night, while sitting on the pebbly, Lardos Beach. So big, I felt as though I could reach up and touch it!

Sitting on the Moon

I'm sitting on the moon
let me sing you a little moon tune
I feel like a lune
Sitting on the moon

I'm sitting on the moon
don't you know I got here real soon
my rocket's in tune
I'm sitting on the moon

I ain't no spaceman just a homo sapien
I'm a worker on a loom
I got invited and I was delighted
when NASA flew me to the moon

That's why I'm sitting on the moon
You know that it's lovely at noon
there's plenty of room
Sitting on the moon

I ain't no spaceman just a homo sapien
I'm a worker on a loom
I got invited and I was delighted
when NASA flew me to the moon

That's why I'm sitting on the moon
there's plenty of room
it's lovely at noon
Sitting on the moon

Sitting on the moon

At Brindisi we drove onto the ferry that took us across the Adriatic sea to Greece where we completed our journey by driving on to Athens. Kerryn and I said our goodbyes to Louise as she went off to a meeting with the manager of the Contiki hotel in Athens. Then we boarded the ferry, bound for Rhodes, from the port of Piraeus. My excitement grew as our ferry entered the ancient port of Rhodes, passing between the pillars that are said to have once supported the giant statue of Colossus - who's legs straddled the harbours' entrance. After a short time, sightseeing through the bustling, tourist packed town - it's Medieval castle and markets - we boarded a bus to Lindos, on the south eastern part of the island, where my "contact", Vayios, operated a kiosk on the beach. Upon arriving at the kiosk I was disappointed to be told that Vayios was away for a few days and that I should go to the B&B owned by his aunty - up on the hill towards the castle that overlooked Lindos Bay - where he would contact me on his return. So Kerryn and I climbed the hill towards the castle - winding our way through the skinny lanes between the glaringly white houses with their pastel coloured window shades and doors - and found the little old aunty and her B&B, and along with an Aussie couple whom we'd met on the ferry, rented two rooms.

I was relieved when Vayios finally tracked me down at his Aunties' *pension* but was disappointed to be told that his cousins' resort

Celibate Summer? Entertaining some Aussie visitors in my Hut

was not ready to open and the final stages of construction might take a few more weeks to complete. In order to ease my concern and to welcome me and my friends to his town, Vayios, then, rolled and lit up an enormous joint - of, what he boasted was,.. "the best *gear* to come out of Morocco" - for us to smoke. All I remember of the rest of that night was the cheeky smile on Vayios's face - as he left us in our "mind blown" state - and lying in bed, next to my "plutonic" friend, Keryn, listening to the Aussie couple, in the adjoining apartment, bonking their brains out! I lay there, awake all night, as horny as hell, struggling with my conscience, wanting to *make a move* on Keryn but reminding myself that she was going out with Charlie, my ski instructor friend back in Hopfgarten. My celibate resolve was certainly tested on that long sleepless night - especially with all the moaning and groaning coming from the other side of the wall! I felt like giving myself a swift uppercut, months later, when Kerryn confided to me how surprised, and slightly offended, she was that I didn't proposition her, that night - particularly as her affair with Charlie was, all but, over at that time!

That night of *missed opportunity* seemed to set a precedent for *any* amorous activities during that hot summer in the Greek Islands, and although being surrounded by bikini clad, oiled up, suntanned women of all nationalities, I, completely, bombed out in the bedroom! Maybe it's because I spent most of my time, clad, in tiny red, (*budgie smuggler*) Speedos. A poor fashion choice but one made out of practicality as it was just so bloody hot! Either way, they certainly didn't enhance my chances of attracting the opposite sex. Even when an old flame, whom I'd met in Austria, came to stay with me at the resort for a few days, she was content to end our night's out with just a hug and kiss good night! What ever the reason, my summer in Greece, that year, was a lonely, loveless one. There was an ancient magic in the air surrounding the island of Rhodes, but despite being the realm of the Greek Gods of love - Aphrodite and Eros - in my case, it unfortunately had no influence on *my* sex life!

Celibate Summer

*Terrible, it's been unbearable
I'm like an animal locked up in a cage
dreadful, I've got a head full
I feel a big pull, pulling me back to you*

*Celibate summer said ooh what a bummer it's been
celibate summer so dial me the number for sin*

*Outrageous, I hope it's not contagious
I've been through stages but not as long as this
disgusting, my balls are busting
I'm only lusting, your body is my wish*

*Celibate summer said ooh what a bummer it's been
celibate summer so dial me the number for sin*

*Set me loose take the juice
come on and cool my heat
come on and do it I wanna chew it
I wanna bang 'till my heart wont beat*

*Please, please don't tease
I'll go down on my knees
to go down where you need
Unbelievable, it's inconceivable, my heart is bleedable
but still you let it bleed*

*Celibate summer said ooh what a bummer it's been
celibate summer so dial me the number for sin*

If I'd known how loveless that summer was going to be, I'd probably have not waited the three weeks it took, before the resort – where I was to perform - would be ready to accommodate me and the tourists. I spent two weeks holidaying in Lindos with Keryn and other Aussies - who had also worked in Hopfgarten and followed us down to the Mediterranean - before moving in with Vayios and his girlfriend, Vera, at his home in the small village of Lardos. *That week* was *also* torturous for me, as - after sharing a joint of the *lethal Moroccan weed*, with Vayios and Vera, in the cool of each evening on the front porch - I would have to listen to *them* making loud passionate love on the other side of my bedroom wall while I tried to go to sleep!

Eventually, his promise of employment came good as Vayios took me to the partially completed resort at Lardos Beach and introduced me to his cousin, Vassilli - who eagerly offered me six gigs per week and accommodation at his exciting new business venture and pride and joy, called, *"Camping Lardos"*. Situated at the bottom, south eastern, end of the island - about an hours drive from the capital of Rhodes - this, somewhat, isolated couple of acres, was Vassilli's dream… *"to be the next great camping experience in Greece"*. It featured a large swimming pool, restaurant and taverna with alfresco dining - on an elevated terrace that overlooked the resort and down to the coastline. It offered a range of accommodation - from tent camping sites to modest, self contained bungalows - most of which, at this stage, hadn't been completed. I came to learn that *"Partially Completed"* was a common occurrence in Greece. Even Vayios's house had rusting steel Reo rods protruding from the flat concrete roof - in anticipation of building an extra floor on top. A sight, not uncommon, throughout much of Greece! It fell inline with some Greek phrases that I became very familiar with, such as… *"siga siga"* and *"entaxy"*, which translated to… *"slowly, slowly"* and *"OK"* - Being the Aussie equivalent of.. *"she'll be right mate"* and *"all in good time"*. I called it.. *"Greek Time"*. One of the *few* buildings that *had* been completed in the resort was a bamboo hut that stood, one and a half meters above the ground, on stilts, and had a view across the marshland to the beach and Lardos Bay. It was one of many planned to be dispersed throughout the resort, but they were to come, "in *Time*"..in…*"Greek Time!"*. That hut was my accommodation for the summer…From a broom closet in London, to a cellar in an eight hundred year old Austrian Inn to a Polynesian fale in the Mediterranean – the variety of my abodes was fascinating! It was so unique but simple, and it was my refuge in that remote and mostly uneventful location. I used the woven bamboo walls of the hut to store the US dollars that Vassilli paid my wages in each week. I slid them between the layers of thatching, and, with cassette sales and tips, I had well over $7000US lining those walls by the end of the season. I have a photo of that hut with me in my skimpy Speedos, proudly standing on it's steps, surrounded by a group of bikini clad Aussie girls who had come down from Austria to stay with me for a few days. It completely sums up the irony of that frustrating summer, depicting me as some sort of playboy, when I actually felt like a tortured monk undergoing "mortification of the flesh" as punishment for my lustful behavior in the past. Even the male staff members of the resort looked on with envy, jibing me with the taunt of "Kamaki", the Greek term for "Lover-boy" which, although I took as a compliment, only served to heighten my frustration. Still, it was better than the alternative of being called a "Malaka" or "wanker" which would've been closer to the truth! I truly was that *kid in the lolly shop,* who wasn't allowed to taste the goods! Never the less, as *one* of my senses was denied, *other* senses, for my surrounds, were heightened, and, as if to calm myself down, I expressed my appreciation for my new environment - in *this* song;

Living in a Hut

Green, green leaves
swaying in a tropical breeze
dance for my eyes
looking down on a sleepy blue sea
relaxing me

Blue, blue sky
"slowly" as the moment goes by
play with my soul
and the worries of the world will fly
Bye, bye, goodbye

Life is so good
living in a hut

It's like I'm dreaming
I'm always dreaming
the way I'm feeling
Life is so good
living in a hut

Sweet, sweet night
I've never seen the moon look so right
shine with the stars
bathe my hut in a magical light
Bamboo delight
it's a bamboo delight

Life is so good
living in a hut

Living in a hut

Turning up the Heat

That European summer in 1986 was the hottest I'd ever experienced! Even the five minute walk down to the beach was like walking through a furnace. The pebbles on the beach were like hot coals, making it necessary to wear my leather sandals right to the water's edge before hobbling in to cool off. My attire for performing at night on the terrace was, usually, shorts, singlet top and sandals. At lunchtime, by the pool, when *day bus tours* would drop in for a swim and meal, I usually sang in my Speedos, stopping to dive into the pool every half hour to wash off the sweat!

Engaging with the audience was a lot harder here for me than it had been at Helmut's Pub. The majority of the holiday makers were German or Greek who spoke little or no English, so I, mainly, just sang to them - omitting my *trade mark* "banter" between songs. As always, music was the common denominator in communication and my repertoire of hits by Bob Dyan, Cat Stevens, The Beatles, Neil Young, The Eagles etc, etc, did all the talking for me and kept my audience on side. While I had their attention I'd slip in one of my own songs and promptly hold up my cassette album, indicating it was for sale. If not for the musical value, many of the tourists simply bought my album as a memento of their pleasant holiday in the Greek Islands and their encounter with the diminutive, scantily clad, Aussie entertainer who sang for them.

As the long hot days rolled on into weeks I gradually became restless about being stuck in this quiet little resort - where I was merely a human juke box, churning out songs to a docile audience but not really engaging and having fun with them. I also became bored with the same, pebbly, beach that had no waves on which to body surf and the bland surrounds of bare, stoney, hills dotted with dried out scrubby bushes or ancient,gnarled olive trees. I wanted out. I felt trapped. Enslaved. It was ironic that, at this restless time, I happened to be reading a novel called "Mandingo" - about the American slave trade - and although *my* situation could never be compared to the horrors those African slaves endured, I did manage to mention a few of my woes in lyrics - that the book inspired me to write.

Slave Trade

My Muma sold me to a man
my brother chained to my hand
the other died along the way

I never had a father
I never took a lover
whenever I could I'd hang my head and cry

I couldn't run, couldn't hide, I was never free
In the field with the sun beatin' down on me
workin' for the master in a world of slavery

Brought up in the slave trade
brought up in the slave trade

They stripped me they had me shown
they whipped me whipped me to the bone
they ripped my heart out and sold it to the devil

My muma sold me to a man
my brother chained to my hand
the other died along the way

Brought up in the slave trade
brought up in the slave trade

Captain Costa (white shirt) watching over me and local guitarist (white pants) entertaining Pommie tourists aboard the S.S.Bruna

When I told Vassilli of my desire to leave, his reaction stunned me. He took it as an insult and his pure Greek passionate emotions spilled out as anger and resentment - that he viciously spat at me in a convoluted mixture of Greek and English insults and threats. The first threat of.. "You fuck me and I'll fuck you! ".. was worrying enough, but the second one, of.. "I have a cousin who works in customs at the airport who'll confiscate all those American dollars you plan to smuggle out of my country in your suitcase!".. really made me reconsider my resignation. I found out later that his bark was probably worse than his bite, when the kitchen staff told me he was in tears, later that night, telling them how much he needed me - to remain for the rest of the summer as a unique feature of his beloved resort. The following day, in a much calmer state, he had breakfast with me and renegotiated the terms of my employment - as a peace offering and incentive to get me to see out the rest of the season with him. The terms he offered were very enticing and included a pay rise plus three free meals a day and unlimited use of the resort's mini moke - to tour the island in my free time. He had also arranged for me to play, occasionally, at another Hotel, owned by his cousin, near Rhodes town - which included accommodation, meals and a higher pay rate. Finally, the clincher of the negotiations, was a two day gig, each week, on a charter boat, owned by another cousin, that operated out of the port

of Rhodes. The charter boat gig also provided me with my own cabin aboard, while docked at the marina overnight. I happily accepted his generous offer which gave me the freedom to see much more of the island, exploring the ancient ruins of amphitheaters and castles and meeting more people. Hooning around the island, one day, in my mini moke, wearing nothing but my speedos, sunglasses and viser - feeling like some sort of celebrity parading the Cote d'azur in an Aston Martin - I was promptly brought back to realty as I almost lost control of the vehicle on a gravel road that led down to an isolated beach on the western side of the island. Shaken 'n' Stirred, I took solace in knowing that I now shared something in common with one of my idols, Robert Plant [Led Zeppelin], who was also involved in a car crash, albeit a much more serious one, on this island, eleven years earlier.

The Hotel gig - at a beach resort on the northern part of the island - turned out to be just an upmarket version of the Camping Lardos gig and the tourists, there, were a bit stuffy and even harder to get to know. To sour the deal further, my accommodation turned out to be a dark old storage room with no windows, in the middle of the five story building, with only air vents for fresh air - which served as entry points for the army of cockroaches that would run across my face while I tried to sleep! I only stayed there once! Renegotiating to add that night away from Lardos Beach to the Charter boat gig. That gave me three days and nights playing and staying on the boat. *That gig* became the highlight of my stay on the island of Rhodes.

Early each Monday morning I'd leave Lardos camping ground with my guitar and suitcase, packed with a few clothes, drum machine, leads and cassette tapes to sell, and

Returning to the port of Rhodes

hitchhike, or catch the bus, to Rhodes. I usually arrived just in time to board the charter boat before it departed the port, full of tourists, on a day cruise along the north eastern coast of the island. My stage on the boat was the raised bow section of the converted fishing trawler, where I'd stand - in my Speedos - legs spread wide to brace and balance myself against the wind and oncoming swell. Like a modern day parody of a Pausarius conducting the oarsmen on an ancient Roman battleship, I'd ride the bow, playing my guitar and singing into the microphone that were both plugged into the boat's rudimentary public address system which was powered by the vessels generator. Subsequently, the volume of my performance often fluctuated depending on the revs of the engine or the pounding of the wind and waves at my back. On many occasions, when returning to port in blustery conditions, my guitar and I would be showered by the salty sea spray as the bow plowed through the oncoming swell. I figured the effect of the sun and sea spray on my early '70's Gibson Hummingbird acoustic guitar must have aged it by fifty years or more, therefor adding to it's warm tone. The effect of performing out in these challenging conditions was much less warming for me - but totally exhilarating! My audience on these cruises were often young, pale skinned, Pommies who would've been more at home in a disco in Corfu or Ibiza. They were more intent on getting pissed and suntanned than singing along with any of my "easy listening" repertoire, so, once again, engaging with my audience wasn't a priority on these trips. I used this gig more as an outlet for me to just enjoy being on the water, taking advantage of the water skiing and windsurfing activities when the boat moored in a secluded cove for a BBQ lunch of grilled lamb and Greek salad at a wharf. The favorite time for me, working on the "SS Bruna", was when, after reversing the boat into it's berth back at the main promenade of the port, I and the crew would lounge in the cockpit, sipping on Scotch or beer and Ouzo - telling stories while watching the endless passing parade of locals and tourists as the sun set and the nightlife of Rhodes came alive. By far, the best story teller, in this scurvy crew of drunken sailors, was the captain of the boat, Costa. Captain Costa - the thickset, weather beaten, suntanned hulk with legs like posts from years of standing at the helm in mountainous seas - was an ex merchant seaman who had, as he told me, "sailed ships all over the world, on every sea and ocean, into nearly every port of every country" and, as well as being, "an international man, a twenty first century man and a big Kamaki " was a lot of fun to have a drink with. The time my zany friend, Marie, from Bachus Marsh in Victoria who was living in London, came to visit me and stay on the boat, was unforgettable. She, like Costa, was loud and larger than life, both figuratively and literally!, and the two of them hit it off like a house on fire. The parties on the Bruna, those nights, as Marie and Costa competed for centre

stage, were epic, and often became the focus of attention on the busy Marina. Despite all the fun and frivolity, there was a serious side to Costa. He was a skilled sailor and captain, so when he roared an order at the crew, it was for a good reason, and that order was meant to be obeyed! I would often be woken in my cabin - extremely hungover - by the sound of his voice, bellowing over the boat's PA system, ordering me to wake up and come on deck to sing. That was because I'd slept-in, and the boat was already full of passengers and steaming out of the harbour!

The Captain's Mad

The Captain's mad and I'm so sad
he said to me "I ain't gonna stand for none of this treachery
I think we've got a mutiny
I'm gonna stand my ground before we set to sea"

The captain's mad, now that's too bad
He's a good man
but he changes tune when you don't do a job like he knows you can
He's got to use a firm hand
He's the law at sea and more when he's on land

When I lost ya I met a Greek called Costa
An international man-no problem
If you find me I'll be a big kamaki
An international man of the twenty first century

The captain's mad, stark raving mad!
the ship's on course
but the next porto'çall is the scene of a crews' remorse
the captain is a powerful force
the captain's mad and I'm so glad that I'm not the cause

The captain's mad, the captain's mad
The captain's mad, the captain's mad

My time on Rhodes, although not as socially exciting as my experiences in the Austrian Alps, was, however, rewarding for me. The ancient mystery that permeated the air there stirred the artistic potential inside of me and inspired a different style of songwriting that evolved in the years to follow. I could see why famous artists such as Leonard Cohen, Robert Plant [Led Zeplin] and David Gilmore [Pink Floyd], to name a few, chose to spend so much time in the Greek islands. I was told that Gilmore actually owned a property right near Camping Lardos but, unfortunately, I never investigated that claim to confirm it. One visiting musician I *did* see and get to perform with was my old mate, Weza, who came over from London to check out my gig. The couple of shows we did together during the last week of my time at the camping resort were the most enjoyable of my whole tenure - except on my last night, when he and the staff threw me in the pool, and I completed my set, shivering, in wet dripping clothes. *That*, was the *only* time, throughout the whole Mediterranean Summer, I actually felt cold!

I happily saw out the remaining month of that summer sharing my musical services between the camping ground and the charter boat, before I flew out of Rhodes airport back to Athens. With my stash of American dollars, rolled up into bundles inside my socks and undies in my suitcase, I nervously passed through customs at Athens airport to board a Lufthansa flight to Vienna. Security was tight in Athens, as a number of terrorist related hijackings and bombings had recently occurred, so my heart missed a beat when I was asked to open my suitcase. For an instant I wondered if Vassilli *had* actually carried out his threat to inform the authorities of my international money laundering activity but it was merely the fact that my drum machine had caught the guards attention on the xray machine. I was eventually allowed through after explaining my status as a traveling musician. My only other concern was that my baggage might get lost in transit and I would loose all my income from that grueling summer. I breathed a sigh of relief as the plane rose from the tarmac, and, banking to adjust it's course for Austria, it gave me a spectacular view of Athens' sprawling metropolis with the ancient Parthenon atop the Acropolis rising from it's clutter.

Thankful for the Greek island experience, I was glad to be heading home.

TONY JOHNS — THE BOY'S BACK

SIDE A:
THE WAY I LIVE (JOHNS) — NAME GAME (JOHNS) — BREAKFAST WITH THE BITCH (JOHNS) — MR BOJANGLES (WALKER) — YOU ONLY WANT ME FOR MY BODY (JOHNS) — STUBBO'S BAR (JOHNS)

SIDE B:
DOCK OF THE BAY (REDDING/CROPPER) — CELIBATE SUMMER (JOHNS) — MARIJUANA COOKIES (JOHNS) — CLIQUE (JOHNS) — APRIL (JOHNS) — SITTING ON THE MOON (JOHNS) — THE HUT (JOHNS)

PRODUCED & ENGINEER AT STUDIO 21, NEWCASTLE, AUSTRALIA BY C. TEGG & T. JOHNS
COPYRIGHT © 1986 FUNKY GIBBON PRODUCTIONS

Sept'-Dec' 1986 Darby St. Newcastle

The Boy's Back [Again!]

Having flown out of Greece back to Austria, I spent a pleasant week hiking, bike riding, playing tennis and generally relaxing with Helmut and Anne and other Aussies who had worked in Hopfgarten for the summer, before flying back to Australia. The alpine Summer climate was much milder than in Greece and it was wonderful to experience the lush greenery of the Tyrolean hills - as compared to their total, snow covered, white-out in winter. Before leaving for home I renegotiated with Helmut to return in four months time for the next winter season. While preparing to catch my flight out of Munich Airport I withdrew all of my winter wages from my savings account at the local bank and rolled them up, with my American dollars from Rhodes, into my socks and undies and buried them in the middle of my suitcase. I was hoping to cash in on a favourable exchange rate back in Australia when I deposited them into my Commonwealth Bank account at The Junction branch in Newcastle. I was unsure of the limits of foreign currencies that could be brought back into Australia at that time so I decided to run the gauntlet, and smuggle the almost ten thousand dollars of cash back into the country, rather then risk loosing some of it in penalties or tax. It was another nervous walk through customs for me at Sydney airport, but, looking like just another suntanned Aussie tourist returning from his European holiday, I strolled through, unquestioned. Letting out a massive sigh of relief, I firmly grabbed my suitcase and guitar at the luggage carousel and made a hasty exit!

This brief, four month, visit home was a carbon copy of my return home twelve months earlier, catching up with friends and keeping my foot in the door at all the local venues where I performed, as well as recording another cassette album to take back to Austria as merchandise. This cassette featured the artwork from the poster that Rock City Promotions had printed for me on my return to Newcastle the previous year, but this time, "The Boy's back", would refer to my return to *Hopfgarten,* for the third time, later that year.

As with my previous cassette album, I utilised my free studio time at Studio 21 and paid Col Tegg, for his time, to help me produce and engineer the project. I also enlisted the services of local musicians such as Greg Bryce, from DV8, and Denis Butler, from Atlantis, for lead guitar solos, as well as Dean Tolhurst on keyboards. I performed the rest of the backing on acoustic and electric guitars and harmonica as well as programming the drums and bass on my Yamaha RX7 drum machine which I affectionately referred to as Rex. Rex had become an integral part of my live performance banter - who even received heckles and complimentary drinks from the audience on occasions!

Most of the songs on the cassette had been written by me during the previous twelve months while living in Austria and Greece - except for Marijuana Cookies, which had become a standard in my repertoire for the last five years. The other two songs, Mr Bojangles and Dock of the Bay were popular covers in my set list and I released the later on a single while I was home. The airplay and publicity *it* received kept my name fresh on the local music scene - even though I'd been absent for much of the previous two years. Releasing *that* single was a clever ploy by Peter Anderson and the team at Rock City as it was becoming harder for them to keep my profile high, with *me,* being overseas most of the time. Pete explained all this to me over lunch, a few days before I was due to fly out of the country. He asked me to consider settling down for a while, next time I was home, to record and promote a proper, vinyl album, so as to really have a go at taking my singing/song-writing career to the next level. I reluctantly agreed to his suggestion, for, as much as I loved playing in Helmut's Pub, I knew it wouldn't advance my career, and the chance to make a professionally recorded album was what appealed to me the most.

Darby's Pies

My transient lifestyle was making it harder to find somewhere to call home. On *this* return visit, after staying a few nights at my parents house in East Maitland - where I'd left my car and P.A equipment - I found myself sleeping on a mattress on the floor in the spare room of a friend's house in Stewart Avenue, Newcastle. A week later I accepted an offer to rent a furnished room at a house in Darby street - that had a notorious reputation among members of the Cook's Hill Surf Life Saving Club. My old shit stirring mate, Baza - the one who gave me the nickname of "*The Funky Gibon*" - currently lived there, along with a legend of the surf club and Vietnam veteran who we simply called Jack. *This* was "*Animal House*" all over again, and if not for the fact that I would only be living there for a short while I might not have moved in. Nothing was sacred. Jack and Baz where the high priests of pranks who revelled in toying with my, somewhat *OCD*, habits of keeping my room tidy, making my bed and allocating various articles of my clothing to separate draws. This meant I would often come home to find my room had been ransacked, the bed short-sheeted or stripped and my socks and undies relocated to other parts of the house. It was harmless fun that infuriated me, but not so bad that a few beers on the front verandah with the boys - watching the passing parade of beach babes walking to and from Bar Beach - couldn't calm me down.

Although Hunter street was made famous by Bob Hudson's hilarious "Newcastle Song" in the 70's, I believe Greg Bryce, from the band DV8, described the true heart and soul of Newcastle when he wrote about Darby street in his song called "Darby street Blues". The street, renowned for it's restaurants, cafes and the Delany Hotel, provided the boys and me, residing at 36 Darby Street, with unlimited choices when it came to feeding time. As diverse as our options were, concerning fine dining, it was ironic that most of our food budget usually ended up in the till of the tiny shop directly across the road from our dwelling. Darby's Pie Bar. Darby's meat pies had, and still have, the reputation for being the best in the land but I have serious doubts about *that* being a good reason for us to have purchased breakfast, lunch and diner *there* on way too many occasions!

Life wasn't *all* "meat pies and tomato sauce" at the Darby Street Hilton. Baza, being a keen fisherman, ensured our diet was supplemented with a healthy dose of prawns, oysters and fish - that we'd eagerly cook on the BBQ when he'd triumphantly return with his catch. My favourite angling outing with Baz was when we drove his runabout up the Myall River from Tea Gardens to Tamboy, where his friend, Mark, had a hut on the river from which he operated a licensed prawn shot. Mark was a professional fisherman who was authorised to run a net across the river to catch prawns. It was a long night of laughs and lager when we set up camp at his hut, hauling the net in to shore every few hours to sort through the tangled mess of weed, prawns, fish and eels, all the while being wary of the spiked Bull Routs. The boys delighted in warning me that they would have to cut *it* out of my hand if I mistakenly grabbed one! The highlight of that long sleepless night was being able to help myself to those delicious Myall River Prawns - as they cooked, beside the sorting table, in a forty four gallon drum positioned over the camp fire. Sitting under the stars that night in the absolute serenity of the Myall Lakes National park - listening to the camp fire crackling as it cooked our catch while the river slowly gurgled past and the cicadas buzzed in the paperbarks surrounding us - is a priceless memory of those most carefree of my youthful days.

"*Carefree*" also summed up my attitude to romance at that "*nomadic*" time of my life. There's is no doubt that my occupation certainly made it easier for me to meet women but my constant migration between towns and countries wasn't conducive to long term affairs. That's why I was always surprised when one romantic interest that I'd been involved with, during that time of constant travels, was always available and willing to reconnect with me each time I came back home. I don't think *Julie* was saving herself for me, she wasn't that naïve, instead, like me, I think she was just letting our affair run it's natural course in between my overseas jaunts. Still, I couldn't help feeling a tinge of guilt each time we got reacquainted, knowing I'd fly out of the country within months. In fact, that sense of guilt also transferred to my relationship with my friends and family - as I dropped in and out of *their* lives. I justified this part-time existence by convincing myself that *this* was my *journey*, my *career*, and I had no expectations of, or demands on, anyone who was part of that journey. It was who I was.. and the way I lived.

The Way I Live

Say goodbye my friend
I don't have a home
only you again
is all I need to hold

I watch the seasons change
they tell me when to go
sometimes it feels so strange
I wish that you could know

It's the way I live
I don't take
so don't make me give
it's the way I live

Where will I be next year
I'll write and let you know
Wether far or near
it's just another show

It's the way I live
I don't take
so don't make me give
it's the way I live

I'm not asking you to wait for me
all I want in life is to be free

It's the way I live
I don't take
so don't make me give
it's the way I live

Say goodbye my friend

January-April 1987
Hopfgarten

Winter Season #3 in Hopfgarten

My flight from Sydney to Munich airport in mid December of 1986 was my fifth international flight in two years and the third to be paid for by Helmut, who was, once again, there to pick me up and take me back to his pub in Hopfgarten. As we did eleven months earlier, we stopped at the cassette manufacturing company in Munich to give them my latest master tape and order two hundred copies - that I would return to pick up in a weeks' time. On that return visit I was accompanied by George, the manager of the Offenlach disco - situated across the street from Helmuts Pub - who had kindly offered to drive me there as Helmut had other business on that day. Thankfully, George and I had no dramas at the border, *this time*, when returning with my concealed imported product. I wasn't too concerned at *this* border crossing as the box of cassettes just looked like blanks because I'd taken the precaution of printing the labels back home in Newcastle, at *Instant Print*, and brought them over in my suitcase. When we got back to Hopfgarten I assembled the cassettes - with their labels and covers - in my room at the pub. It was a tedious task but helped me avoid paying customs duties and earned me an extra $4000 that season – by selling *all* the cassettes. In return for his friendly gesture, George simply asked me to mention his disco during my performances each night at Helmut's. I had many nightcaps at Disco Auffenlach that season - few of which I had to pay for!

My accommodation, *that season,* was in, the notorious, "Stubbo's Bar" - the converted attic in the ceiling space of the pub building which faced directly across the street to the belfry of the Catholic church. As if to mock me - for writing "*The Bellringer*" song - the clanging of those church bells was even more pronounced and seemingly persistent from my new abode, causing me to rise from what little sleep I could get, much earlier in the mornings than I would have preferred. The only advantage being that I spent much more time on the ski slopes than in my room. A particularly pleasant memory I have of looking out my window at *that* bell tower was on Christmas eve, around midnight, when, instead of seeing those massive cast iron domes swinging from side to side - emitting their deafening thunder - I saw, through the lightly falling snow flakes, three brass trumpets poking out of the belfry window like clandestine barrels of snipers rifles, quietly playing "*Silent Night*". It was the most surreal and magical Christmas image I have ever witnessed - and made me feel so glad and privileged to be back in this Tirolean Winter fantasy.

The *fantasy* continued as I skied each day and performed each night to enthusiastic audiences who sang along to the covers in my repertoire and warmly applauded my originals. Their appreciation also extended to buying my new cassette album and shouting me an endless supply of drinks. It wasn't uncommon for my mixing desk to be buried under a legion of beer, bourbon and schnapps glasses - standing like toxic sentries, guarding my settings and awaiting the command to inebriate me. They were very efficient troupes! - and I was a very obliging *P.O.W.* who rarely repelled an alcoholic attack! It wasn't until the next morning, as those church bells rang out their unique style of reveille, that the extent of my injuries, from the previous nights' *battle of booze,* became apparent. Splitting headaches and nausea were a regular feature of my mornings - until I staggered up the road, to the cafe near the ski lift station, for a strong coffee - before gingerly hitting the slopes.

It was on one of *those,* grossly hungover, mornings that I began to piece together this ditty - about a poor Aussie wretch who couldn't come to terms with his own, self inflicted, misfortunes.

The Ballad of Wallaby Ted

I feel like Wallaby Ted's brother, I feel like his brother, Roo
I'm stuffed I'm buggered I'm nackered I'm mothered
worn out, washed up, I'm through
I feel like I've been through the ringer
like I've been hit by a truck
I feel like Wallaby Ted's brother
I feel like I couldn't give a ffff

Feel like Wallaby Ted's brother, feel like his brother Roo
got the shits, in the pits, got the jack, had a stack
I feel like I couldn't give a poo
I think my days are numbered
I think my time has come
I feel like I've been on a binge for a week
on a gallon of Bundaberg Rum

I'm Wallaby Ted's brother
Roo was his name they said
I'm Wallaby Ted's brother
so I guess that makes me
Roo Ted

I feel like Wallaby Ted's brother, I feel like his brother Roo
hung up, strung out, dead broke, "who's shout!"
got bugger-all to do
Now you might think I'm a winger
but I've got good cause to scoff
çause I feel like Wallaby Ted's brother
I'm totally pissed off

I'm Wallaby Ted's brother
Roo was his name they said
I'm Wallaby Ted's brother
so I guess that makes me
Roo Ted

And so, that's how I felt, most mornings, for the next three months - until the warm spring air began to melt the snow and the tourists trickled away like the run-off from the slushy ski runs. That's when the sing-alongs and the Schnapps, the yodelling and the Yaegermisters, the schussing and snow ploughing and the skolling and prosting, finally stopped - as the season drew to a close, and it was time for me to return home.

It was with a heavy heart that I packed my bags, this time, because I'd reluctantly decided to follow Pete's [my manager back home] advice and settle down to have a serious go at establishing myself in the music business - with a properly recorded album of my new songs. This meant no more popping in and out of the country every few months, but, instead, focussing my time and finances on a long term goal to cement my career as a singer/songwriter. I was twenty eight years old now, and, realistically, knew my chances of making the *Big Time* were very slim - but I also knew it had to be *now or never* to give it a go. After all, I knew my body [especially my liver!] couldn't handle the hammering I gave it every winter season in Austria! I was given a sobering reminder of my precarious existence the day I slipped, while skiing over a large area of ice that had formed on a ski run, and landed heavily on the base of my spine. As Helmut carried me to the local doctor for an injection to ease the paralysing pain, I saw by the look of dismay on his face that, not only had I jeopardised his investment in me, but, I'd risked loosing my most valuable asset... my health and well being. It made me realise that I needed to curtail some of my riskier behaviour if I wanted to enjoy longevity in the career that was giving me so much satisfaction.

Narrowly surviving my third European junket I sadly said my goodbyes to all the wonderfully warm friends I'd made in Hopfgarten. I used the local dialect term of "Servus", for goodbye, rather than "Auf Wiedersehen", which translates to "until we meet again", because I wasn't sure if that would ever happen. In fact, I wasn't sure of many things concerning my future, and, although I was willing to give anything a try, I was beginning to succumb to niggling thoughts of doubt.

What I'm Gonna Do Tomorrow

I hate being told what I'm doing wrong
don't you try and tell me how to sing my own damn song
stand there and complain and stomp the floor
but before my time is up you're gonna hear it more and more

I wake up every day and draw the blind
to let the sunlight in chasin' those shadows from my mind
I wonder and I hope this is the one
the future in my dreams may have just begun

But I guess it's just the same for you
fillin' your days with thoughts of somethin' new
look all around, beg, steal or borrow
but you aint never seen nothin' like what I'm gonna do tomorrow

What's to do today? Work to be done
nothin' I can't do later time to have myself some fun
but the more I put it off the more I find
that the time I had for fun has somehow slipped behind

But I guess it's just the same for you
fillin'your days with thoughts of somethin' new
look all around, beg, steal or borrow
but you aint never seen nothin' like what I'm gonna do tomorrow

Why is everybody singing those sad songs about yesterday
paintin' a picture grey and full of sorrow
don't you think it's time we took a look at life 'round the other way
çause you aint never seen nothin' like what I'm gonna do tomorrow

I hate bein' told when I'm gonna fall
I hate bein' told just about anything at all
I wake up every day and close the blind
to sleep a little longer, dreamin' the future in my mind

May 1987-Dec'1989
Newcastle/Sydney Merry-Go-Round

Kitchener Parade. The Hill. Newcastle

Upon arriving back in Newcastle my first attempt to establish a more sedentary existence was to move into a one bedroom apartment in Kitchener parade near the NBN television studios. Considering that this was to be my first real serious crack at breaking into the Australian music scene, the coincidence that my new street address was the same as the town near Cessnock - where I began my musical journey in a high school rock band - was notable. The apartment, being unfurnished, aided my *settling down* plans as I began to acquire items of furniture, including some heirlooms from my grandmothers estate that my uncle John generously transported from Maitland in his work truck. If I'd foreseen how many times I would need to transport *that furniture* between my numerous addresses - in the subsequent months and years - I might have more wisely chosen a fully furnished abode!

Having been overseas for most of the previous three years, I had an unnerving sense of feeling like a stranger back home, so I was delighted when I found UJ Neil was living in the flat right next door to mine. Neil and I first met several years earlier in the Paterson Tavern where I was playing one night and he was out drinking with fellow students from the Tocal Agricultural College. After deciding that the farming life wasn't his forte he chose a similar path to mine as a solo entertainer - confiding in me, years later, that I was his role model. We remained friends and often discussed the challenges of our anomalous careers over a few beers while fishing in the Hunter river or in Shoal bay at Port Stephens sharing a bottle of Green Ginger Wine. His notorious residency at the Grand Hotel superseded my halcyon years at the Cricketers Arms. His band, The Funbusters, with Phil Screen, Dave Carter and Mick Stove - that unmercifully and hilariously mocked every aspect of music and entertainment - tested the capacity of the Cambridge hotel in a residency that would last more than ten years and go down as legendary in local music folk lore. Neil also had an interest in a small recording studio situated on the top floor of an old bank building in high street, Maitland, with his mate "Hilly". "Hilly",[Andrew Hill], was also a muso from Maitland who played in a local band called Attic Fanatics. On one occasion he accompanied me and UJ on a fishing trip to Shoal Bay, sharing in the lethal Green Ginger wine! It was a night that all of us would recall with laughter for many years to come. Hilly recently paid homage to that outing, and his departed friend, when he brewed his own special port/wine concoction - bottling it and printing labels naming it "Lovely Boy" - in memory of one of Neil's signature salutations. The day I dropped into their studio to record one of my songs still brings tears of laughter to my eyes. I recall trying to sing my

heartbreaking lyrics, of yet *another lost love,* watching Neil in the control room, in his usual madcap persona, pull grotesque faces of feigned grief, until we both broke down in convulsive hysterical laughter. The atmospheric feel of the tune was reminiscent of the Roberta Flack hit called "The First Time Ever I Saw Your Face" but it was *his* face that had me doubled over with belly aches of laughter, turning the session into a fruitless, fun filled, fiasco! The laughter we shared that day is one of my finest memories of my mate, Neil - the atypical comedic genius, masking a gentle, troubled soul.

This is the song that made us laugh so much that day, and, which he ensured, I could never seriously sing again without chuckling ;

It's Gone

As I sit by my window
I cry and know
it's gone

As you lie in your bed at night
turn in your sleep and wake in fright
and know
it's gone

As I sit by my window
you cry into your pillow
and we know
we know
we know

It's gone

{ Dedicated to the memory of Neil Unicomb aka UJ Neil 1964-2013 }

It was a heartbreaking honour to be asked by Neil's wife, Rachel, to perform the eulogy at his funeral in 2013- undoubtedly my toughest gig - recalling this and many other anecdotes of our brief time united by our common appreciation of music and entertainment.

***

To have moved home and serendipitously landed right next door to my old mate and comrade seemed like a sign of good things to come but my hopes were dashed when he and his girlfriend, Amanda, informed me they had just bought a house in the industrial harbour-side suburb of Carrington and would be moving out soon. I sensed that, the some what possessive, Amanda, was glad to be removing Neil from the possible temptations that my proximity may have offered him. Her concerns were justified after my first night of residency - preceded by a night of reacquainting myself with the wildlife at Newcastles' nightclubs - when she found, not one, but two pairs of high heels sitting on the step at my front door the next morning. I was content to let her think of me as some sort of globe trotting playboy - as she dragged Neil away from trying to peek through my screen door to asses my catch while giving me a congratulatory wink - but the truth of my nocturnal adventure was much more mundane. I had offered an old friend and her companion somewhere to stay overnight instead of them driving back to Maitland. Admittedly, there was *some* amorous activity but only with my friend. The three of us sharing the only piece of furniture that I had managed to move into the unit - being the double mattress - did, however, add some spice to the occasion!

I must add that Neil certainly didn't need *my* encouragement to get up to his own mischief. I was made well aware of *this* in our time performing together, in subsequent years, with Phil Screen and Mark Tinson as the Tex Pistols. *That band* was almost a *country/rockabilly* spin off of the Funbusters but with cowboy hats and accents and a bit more musical integrity - having Tinno as M.D. and songwriter. Performing alongside these stalwarts of the music industry was like reaching a summit in my musical *ascent* - which I'll talk more of later. It was the *after gig* activities with Screeny and UJ that symbolised more of a moral *descent* that tested my integrity the most! It opened my eyes to that bubbling cauldron of debauchery that churns the myth of *Rock'n'roll* - and I was easily lured into it's bubbling froth. It made me understand Amanda's mistrusting and suspicious nature and had me pondering aspects of loyalty and fidelity in my own life.

The song I wrote around these thoughts had an appropriately levered heavy rock edge that was inspired, subliminally, by the Billy Squier hit of 1981 called The Stroke. Just as much as the *heavy rock* style didn't really fit in my *Easy Listening* repertoire, neither did the aspects of infidelity sit well in my conscience and personal life.

Don't You Trust Me

I've got a problem with my woman
that lady loves me so fine
but like my shadow she's always around
you know it's cruel to be so kind
I can't breath, I can't sneeze without her knowing
she's got to know my every move
but I'm a man who needs some freedom
I wish she'd tell me what she's tryin' to prove

It makes me wonder when I see her acting like a spy
babe are you my lover
or just some kind of private eye

Don't you trust me?
Don't you trust me?

You look so good when you're out on the town
but baby you don't look so good when you follow me around
now how can I say this to you?
I know that you'll think I don't care
but baby when I sing it's my living
and when I go to work I don't need my lover there

Don't lock me in çause honey I'm lookin' for another way out
you've got me cornered
and I need to know what it's about

Don't you trust me?
Don't you trust me?

Ain't got no problem with my woman
çause we sat down and talked it through
now she understands I need my freedom
and honey that's why I'm free tonight
to be here with you

If she finds out about the two of us we're dead
that's why I ask her every night before we go to bed

Don't you trust me?
Don't you trust me?

Trust issues in their relationship a few years later had Neil often trying to patch things up with Amanda who had moved to Queensland. This meant he wouldn't turn up for our Tex Pistol's gigs so we recruited Brien Mcvernon to stand in for him. The running joke in the band at that time was when Brien would ask over the microphone "where's lil'ol' UJ tonight?" and we would all reply in unison to the tune of the Marty Robbins' classic, North To Alaska,…"he's gone…North…to Amanda!".

The direction of *my* personal life, in Kitchener Parade, took a more Southerly course as I struggled to re-establish my social connections. A lot of my friends were settling down with partners, so my nights out on the town, just like my career, became more of a *solo* experience. Often ending in lonely, stumbling, walks home from night clubs at three am, wondering where the good times had gone and where my life was heading. This resulted in me spending more of my nights *off* at home. Contemplating my life over a beer or bourbon and rolling myself a small joint. A vice I'd previously reserved for more social occasions with friends. Watching the sun set behind Mount Sugarloaf, casting a rusty glow over the city and suburbs that sprawled out below me, as I vegetated on my lounge.

Mount Sugarloaf was the iconic geographical landmark of the region. Every TV aerial, on every rooftop, pointed towards *It* - because of the two huge transmitter towers located on it's summit. It was a symbol of home to me. I saw it from the back verandah of my family home in East Maitland as I was growing up and it was the first thing my eyes were drawn to when driving back from gigs outside the Hunter Valley. It was *Our Mountain,* and, even though it was a mere foothill compared to the ones I'd become familiar with in Austria, it had monolithical status in my memories. I clearly remember, as a six year old, waking up at my grandmothers' house in Greta, to see a light dusting of snow on the ground and hearing the radio announcer exclaim that Mount Sugarloaf was covered in snow!

It was an expansive view - through the large window of my lounge-room - that entertained me, in my blissful state, until the room darkened and the city lights began to switch on, snapping me out of my melancholy trance. Those contemplative, glowing, sunset-scaped evenings were special moments at my new address but eventually, only served to heighten my growing sense of loneliness.

Somewhere

*Somewhere in the world, someone
is somewhere all alone like me
somewhere in the world someday
together we will be*

*Someone in my life is missing
someone I don't even know
and that day when I find my someone
only time will show*

*You're somewhere in the world
I'm somewhere out there too
somewhere, somehow, some day
I'll be with you*

*We shouldn't be alone so long
it's such a sad waste of time
we shouldn't be alone at all
but we're both so hard to find*

*Somewhere in the world, someone
is somewhere all alone and blue
somewhere, somehow, some day
I'll be with you*

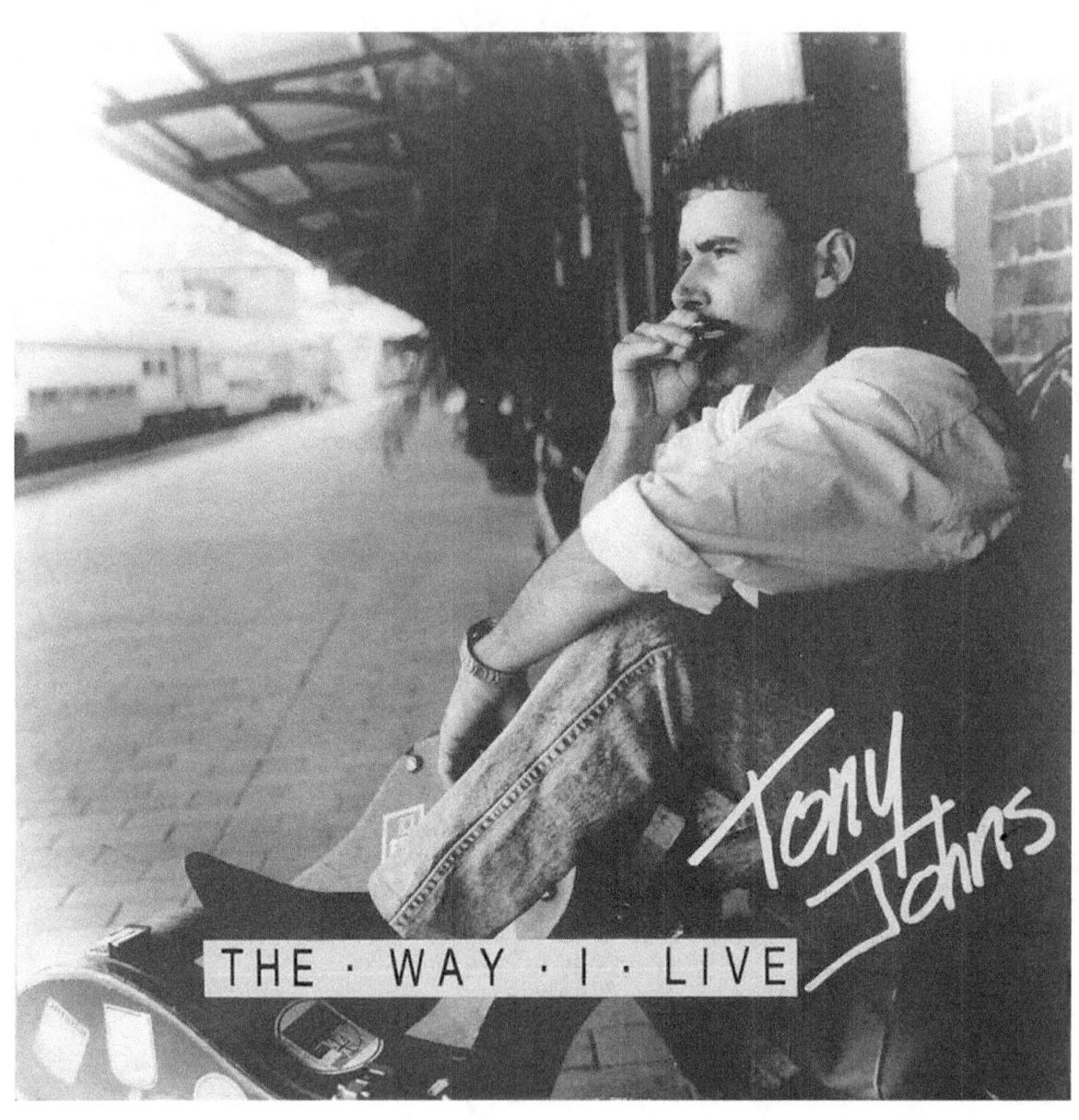

The Way I live [Album]

The couple that moved in to the apartment next door to me - when Neil and Amanda moved out - were from my hometown of Maitland, and, although I didn't know them well, they would sometimes share those *sunset watching sessions* with me. As well as some of their *pot* stash! We shared a lot of laughs on those irregular smoko sessions and as much as I dearly appreciated their companionship, I had an uneasy sense of how unproductive and unhealthy this pastime was for me. My salvation came in, what are now, two outmoded forms of entertainment media; The *first;* was a video cassette of a movie about the life of Gandhi, starring Ben Kingsley. After watching the movie, late one night, from the lounge I'd been glued to since sunset that afternoon - and realising how fruitless my own existence currently was - I promptly got up and flushed my remaining half bag of weed down the toilet. *That* gesture didn't totally end my use of illicit substances but it did break the regularity of it. A quote of Gandhi's, at the end of that movie, particularly caught my attention and I wrote it down with the intention of composing a song around it;...

> "…...In the end they always fall
> when I despair
> I remember that all through history
> the way of truth and love has always won
> there have been tyrants and murderers
> and, for a time, they can seem invincible. But,
> in the end……they always fall.
> Think of it – Always
> They always fall."
> [Mahatma Gandhi]

I never did write that song, and I was no tyrant or murderer either, but I did feel I had been neglecting aspects of Truth and Love in my life and sensed my impending Fall. That Fall eventually came, ten years later. Ironically occurring, at a morally productive time in my life, when I had addressed most of my issues and shortcomings and settled down to raise a family. It seems the Karma Bus has no particular timetable, but it will, eventually, get around to picking you up!

The other item that helped lift me from my slump at that time was a vinyl LP record. With the guidance of a young man from South Africa called Kevin Shirley, I had begun to record ten of my original songs at studio 21. My manager at Rock City Promotions, Peter Anderson, had recently recruited Kevin [or the Cave Man as he referred to himself] to engineer and produce a few recording projects for some of his acts. One of which was the popular local Scar/Reggae band, Vegemite Reggae and their new album.

Unlike my previous, low budget, cassette albums - hastily thrown together to sell as merchandise at my European gigs - this project was much more meticulously planned and budgeted for. It also consumed most of my spare time - and cash - for the remaining months of 1987 and into 1988.

Apart from a few ballads, most of the songs we chose for the album had a bluesy feel - highlighting the influence that bands such as *Little Feat* had had on my song writing. This favoured Kevin's musical preference and allowed him to recruit the members of, Sydney based, blues band, "Chasin' the Train" - whom he'd previously worked with - to provide backing. Although I financed the sessions, it was a great privilege and wonderful experience for me to watch Ian Lees [bass] and Mark Meyer [drums] lay down the rhythmic foundations while Kirk Lorange provided his *magic* on slide, electric and acoustic guitars. The musical fraternity associated with Rock City Promotions, at that time, ensured I had a diverse choice of other fine musicians to contribute to the album, including; Vegemite Reggie's Tony Heaney [Keyboards], Kim Pink [Sax/Clarinet],and Jason Nelson and

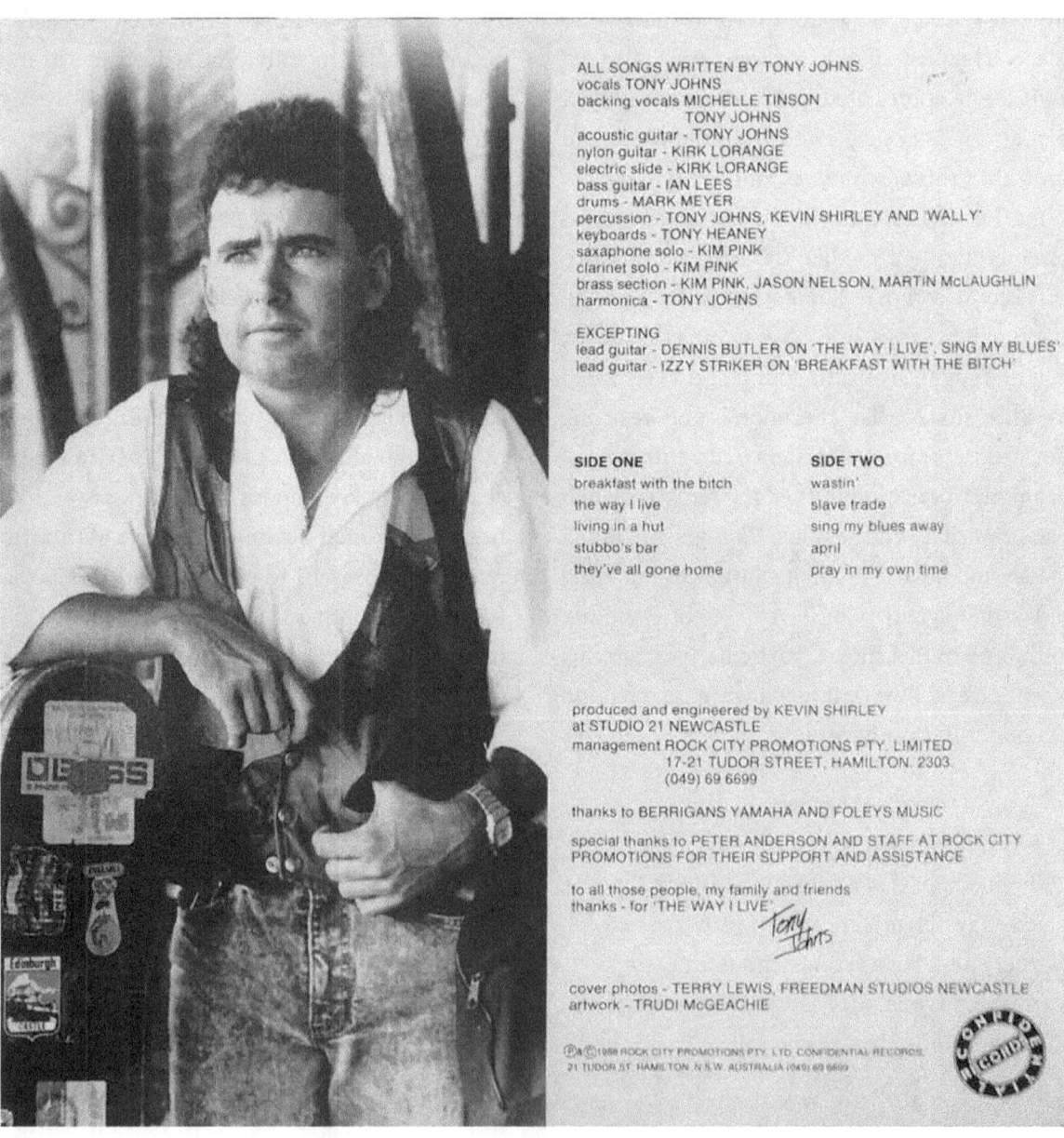

ALL SONGS WRITTEN BY TONY JOHNS.
vocals TONY JOHNS
backing vocals MICHELLE TINSON
　　　　　　　　TONY JOHNS
acoustic guitar - TONY JOHNS
nylon guitar - KIRK LORANGE
electric slide - KIRK LORANGE
bass guitar - IAN LEES
drums - MARK MEYER
percussion - TONY JOHNS, KEVIN SHIRLEY AND 'WALLY'
keyboards - TONY HEANEY
saxaphone solo - KIM PINK
clarinet solo - KIM PINK
brass section - KIM PINK, JASON NELSON, MARTIN McLAUGHLIN
harmonica - TONY JOHNS

EXCEPTING
lead guitar - DENNIS BUTLER ON 'THE WAY I LIVE', SING MY BLUES'
lead guitar - IZZY STRIKER ON 'BREAKFAST WITH THE BITCH'

SIDE ONE
breakfast with the bitch
the way I live
living in a hut
stubbo's bar
they've all gone home

SIDE TWO
wastin'
slave trade
sing my blues away
april
pray in my own time

produced and engineered by KEVIN SHIRLEY
at STUDIO 21 NEWCASTLE
management ROCK CITY PROMOTIONS PTY. LIMITED
　　　17-21 TUDOR STREET, HAMILTON. 2303.
　　　(049) 69 6699

thanks to BERRIGANS YAMAHA AND FOLEYS MUSIC

special thanks to PETER ANDERSON AND STAFF AT ROCK CITY PROMOTIONS FOR THEIR SUPPORT AND ASSISTANCE

to all those people, my family and friends
thanks - for 'THE WAY I LIVE'.

cover photos - TERRY LEWIS, FREEDMAN STUDIOS NEWCASTLE
artwork - TRUDI McGEACHIE

Ⓟ & © 1988 ROCK CITY PROMOTIONS PTY. LTD. CONFIDENTIAL RECORDS.
21 TUDOR ST. HAMILTON. N.S.W. AUSTRALIA (049) 69 6699

Local singer's album hits the spot

TONY Johns' debut effort *The Way I Live* is a complex, ever-changing album that features spirited playing and heart-felt lyrics.

Each song is a different entity — each has its own character and feel and that makes for interesting listening.

But with all this moving and changing between tracks there is an underlying current of beauty and thoughtfulness.

The album's best song is *They've All Gone Home*, a wistful track about loneliness dominated by Tony's sweet voice and some beautiful acoustic guitar.

The same pensive mood is picked up again in *April* where the vocals float into a watery harmonica. This sad, poignant song is about a love that can never be.

And the mesmerising sway of the percussion on *Living In A Hut* reflects the dreamy, relaxing lyrics:

"Green green leaves, swaying in a tropical breeze,

dance for my eyes looking down on a sleepy sea.

Relaxing me."

Stubbo's Bar also has a very strong atmosphere. With its bluegrass harmonica and piano, it sounds like an old drinking song.

Percussion is used to great effect on much of the album's material.

The thrusting, knife-edge drums on *Wastin'* drive home the realisation that "I've been wastin' my life away", while the writhing percussion on *Slave Trade* reflects the anger of a degraded and miserable life in chains.

But just when things are getting a bit too down, along comes *Sing My Blues Away*, a classic, uplifting blues number with a screaming chorus.

The Way I Live is mostly mellow, a bit funky in places and overall very soothing to the ear.

A lot of work has obviously been put into production because the sound is crisp, lively and squeaky clean.

The album will be launched at a special celebration at Fanny's this Saturday night. If you're busy that night you can always catch Tony at the Hotel Delany on Thursday evenings.

— Michael Parris

INXS kick back to Australia

Martin Mclaughlin [Brass], Dennis Butler [ex Atlantis] and Issy Osmanovic [Screaming Jets] were also recruited to add their unique styles of guitar to two of the tracks, and Michelle Tinson [Mark's wife at that time] sang backing vocals. The whole project was masterfully coordinated and conducted by Kevin with an immense passion and humour that was infectious and that drew the finest and most creative performances from each musician. Kevin and I shared a common sense of humour and a taste for bourbon - often celebrating a successful day of recording with a shot or two of Jack Daniels, in the control room at night, while remixing tracks. It was on one of those late sessions that we decided to include "Wally" [the stage name I'd given my RX7-Yamaha drum machine] on the list of credits on the back cover of the album. On that occasion, Kev and I took turns in tapping on the pads of the drum machine to add exotic percussion sounds to a couple of the tracks. ["*Living in a Hut*" and "*Slave Trade*"].

I chose the *number one platform* of Newcastle railway station as the backdrop for the album's cover - to symbolise the beginning and end of my life's journey up to this point in time. Choosing *this* iconic landmark turned out to be a timely decision, now that the rail line has been removed and the station has been preserved as a heritage site used for public markets and entertainment.

Working with Kevin on *that* album was a wonderful experience. He taught me invaluable lessons in recording studio techniques and disciplines and produced a *marketable* hard copy of my musical abilities at that time - for which I'll remain forever thankful. His burgeoning talent and enthusiasm eventually lead him to America where he has worked with the likes of Joe Bonamassa, Iron Maiden and Led Zeppelin. He subsequently returned to Australia, working with Silver Chair and, more recently, with Jimmy Barnes at his studio in Manly.

My album was favourably received by my audiences and sold well - mainly due to a marketing campaign orchestrated by Peter Anderson in which he called in a few favours from his business associates at the NBN3 television station. This resulted in commercials for the album being run each night, for weeks, after it's launch - often during prime time, when the six o'clock news was on, and during highlights of the Seoul Olympics. One of the news presenters, John Church, also featured the album on his late night current affairs programme. He even organised video clips of me singing some of the tracks - in the NBN studios - which he used to close his show each night. With all *that* television exposure - and some airplay on local radio stations which saw it make the number 10 position on local charts - my songs, and my name, became re affirmed in the local entertainment scene – So vital, after my long absence abroad.

Despite the album's success in reigniting my career, I always considered it a reflection of the artist I dreamed of being, rather than who I really was. Among all the incredibly talented musicians who played on the record, I saw myself as the weakest link. That's because I was trying to be the musician I imagined, and not the one that was really inside of me. It would be another *six years* before that part of me finally emerged - on an album that I recorded in Mark Tinson's studio in Cook's Hill, Newcastle. It took me *those* years to realise that writing songs that were fundamentally just rehashes of old blues tunes wasn't going to make me stand out, and that I needed to stick with the style of songs that showed the real me. I'm sure it's not the first time an artist has tried to pinpoint and market his uniqueness - and not just copy something that's already been done.

```
PRINTER'S COPY         Friday, 01 Jul, 1988    28 JUL 1988
THE SINGLES

   TW   LW  Record                                    Artist Cat-No.
    1   ---- GOT TO BE CERTAIN ********    KYLIE MINOGUE FES K 571
    2    1  I WANT YOU BACK                   BANANARAMA CBS LS 2007
    3    3  COULD'VE BEEN                       TIFFANY WEA 7-53231
    4    2  THE FLAME                        CHEAP TRICK CBS 651466
    5    4  WHAT A WONDERFUL WORLD         LOUIS ARMSTRONG FES K-514
    6    5  PINK CADILLAC                    NATALIE COLE EMI MH 2072
    7   10  THE WAY I LIVE                     TONY JOHNS IND CR 709
    8   12  BLUE MONDAY                        NEW ORDER CBS FAC73-7
    9   29  HOLD ON TO LOVE ****             JON ANDERSON CBS 651514 7
   10    8  (SITTIN' ON)THE DOCK OF THE BAY  MICHAEL BOLTON CBS 651387 7
   11    7  I SAW HIM STANDING THERE            TIFFANY WEA 7-53285
   12    9  WHEN WILL I BE FAMOUS?                 BROS CBS 651270 7
   13   --- BETTER BE HOME SOON *****       CROWDED HOUSE EMI CP 2100
   14   19  FAST CAR *                      TRACY CHAPMAN WEA 7-69412
   15   11  LOVE IS A BRIDGE             LITTLE RIVER BAND WEA 7.53291
   16   28  THE VALLEY ROAD **              BRUCE HORNSBY BMG 104865
   17   13  NEW SENSATION                           INXS WEA 7258016
   18   16  IT MUST BE LOVE                   EUROGLIDERS CBS 651557 7
   19   15  TELL IT TO MY HEART              TAYLOR DAYNE BMG 104796
   20    6  GET OUTTA MY DREAMS               BILLY OCEAN CBS LS 1999
   21   30  ROOTY TOOT TOOT *        JOHN COUGAR MELLENCAMP POL 870 327-7
   22   31  MOTORS TOO FAST *                  JAMES REYNE EMI CP-2093
   23   33  TOGETHER FOREVER **                RICK ASTLEY BMG 104862
   24   20  ENDLESS SUMMER NIGHTS            RICHARD MARX EMI MH.2066
   25   18  RISE TO THE OCCASION            CLIMIE FISHER EMI EMI 2087
   26   17  NOTHING TOO SERIOUS                  ICEHOUSE FES K-535
   27   --- ALWAYS GOT THE BLUES **      CEBERANO/MATTHEWS FES K453
   28   24  SIGN YOUR NAME              TERENCE TRENT D'ARBY CBS 651315 7
   29   14  ONE MORE TRY                    GEORGE MICHAEL CBS 651532 7
   30   --- TOMORROW PEOPLE **   ZIGGY MARLEY & THE MELODY MAKERS EMI VS 1049
   31   26  YOU'RE NOT ALONE           AUSTRALIAN OLYMPIANS CBS 651556 7
   32   21  FOR YOU                            JOHN DENVER BMG 104841
   33   39  LOYAL *                            DAVE DOBBYN CBS 651558 7
   34   25  LOST IN YOU                       ROD STEWART WEA 7-27927
   35   37  LOVE TAKES CARE/BE WITH YOU       THE ANGELS FES K-543
```

Already Been Done

I wanna be the first, I don't wanna stand in line
I want everybody to know the whole idea was mine
I wanna do somethin' that no one's ever done
I wanna be some one and not just a bum

Right back through my life always feelin' small
lookin' for a trick or two to make me stand out tall
I wanna say somethin' that no one's ever said
I wanna be remembered when I'm long gone dead

But it's
already, it's already, it's already been done
It's already, it's already, it's already been done

I've been beaten to the punch çause there's nothin' left to do'
everything I try is old, gotta get somethin' new
I wanna make somethin' that no one's ever made
I wanna be wealthy, I'm sick of bein' underpaid

But it's
already, it's already, it's already been done
It's already, it's already, it's already been done

I wanna be the first I don't wanna stand in line
I want everybody to know the whole idea was mine
I wanna sell somethin' and see my money spent
I wanna live in a mansion, I don't wanna pay rent

But it's
already, it's already, it's already been done
It's already, it's already, it's already been done

Although my tongue was firmly in my cheek when I wrote that jazzy little number, there *was* a hint of desperation in the lyrics. I was twenty nine and owned little more than my car, PA equipment, guitar and a bit of furniture, and was probably wondering if the ten thousand dollars I had just spent on my album had been a wise investment. My concerns were addressed in a meeting - arranged by my brother-in-law at that time, Mark, who was a fervent supporter of my music - with the manager of *Crowded House*, Brent Murphy. Brent had hired Mark to oversee plumbing and renovation projects at his home in Rose Bay, Sydney, and they had become good mates - so, on Mark's request, I was invited over for a chat and a bit of advice regarding my career. Brent complimented me on the effort I'd put into making my record but gently pulled my head out of the clouds by informing me that the chances of making a fortune out of chart success were akin to winning the lottery. He did, however, praise me on my work ethic and how booked up I was with live performing - noting that what I was currently earning was much more than some of the high profile touring acts were pocketing. He encouraged me to keep on writing songs but to take pride in knowing that simply by being gainfully employed, [full time], in the music business, was a major achievement in itself. As I left his house with my feet firmly back on the ground I realised that the journey I had embarked on, almost ten years earlier, *was* going pretty much to plan; I was making a good living from doing what I loved - so I resolved to stay on track and see what lay ahead. To paraphrase Oscar Wilde....I was content to stay in the gutter but continued to look at the stars. {At the time of releasing my Album, Compact Discs were just beginning to replace Vinyl records and cassettes. Unfortunately, having exhausted my finances, I could only afford to manufacture vinyl LP's and cassettes. The consensus among most musicians at that time was that people preferred vinyl to CD's. That theory was disproved by the end of that year[1988] when CD sales outstripped vinyl. Despite this, my record sold well and I easily recovered all the costs involved in producing it. In recent years, vinyl records have enjoyed a resurgence in popularity. After storing *mine* in boxes under the house for thirty years, sometimes using them as place mats and drink coasters, it's surprising to be selling them once again!}

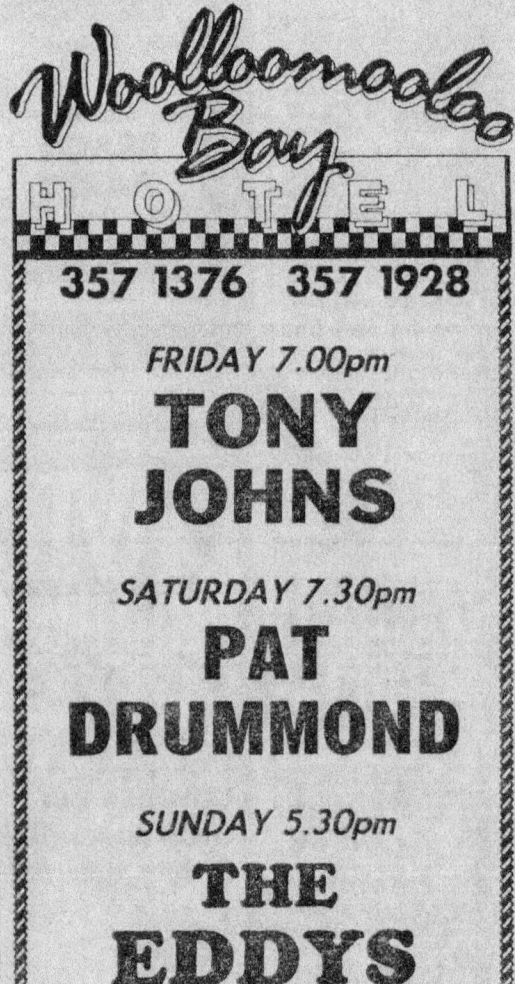

Wentworth Avenue. Hillsdale. Sydney.

With my confidence bolstered by the release of my new album I bravely - and naively - set out to conquer Sydney. Rock City Promotions had booked gigs for me in The Rocks, Woolloomooloo Bay, Palm Beach, Rockdale, Epping, Randwick, Coogee Bay, North Sydney, Middle Harbour, Parramatta, Cabramatta and even as far out as Windsor. With all the recent time spent in the recording studio and the long hours I was spending in the car - commuting between Newcastle and Sydney - my social life really began to suffer. That's why I decided to move to Sydney to live with some of my old travelling companions from my time in Europe.

I hired a small Pantec truck to relocate my newly acquired furniture, and my old mate Brownie and his wife, Lee, came along for the ride and to help with the lifting. Brownie was a talented photographer who, in years to come, shot many promotional photos for myself and the Tex Pistols, as well as the cover for my next album [*The Valley*]. He was a mischievous character who loved to see me *loose the plot* when he got me stoned on his wicked supply of weed. Unfortunately for me, he succeeded in doing it again when he lit up a joint and passed it around - as we were half way to Sydney on the Motorway. He and Lee howled with laughter as I screamed in paranoid terror, weaving the ungainly truck through the congested traffic along the narrow lanes of the Pacific Highway from Hornsby, through Pymble, down to Chatswood and eventually across the harbour bridge and onto the Eastern Suburbs. That journey was harrowing enough, but even more memorable was the *next time* I hired a flatbed truck - with Brownie as my sidekick – a few years later, driving to Sydney to pick-up an above ground swimming pool for my new home in Belmont. On that occasion we ended up covered from head to toe in mud as we dismantled the partially drained pool, often sinking knee deep in sludge as we struggled to retrieve the buried steel support struts. Driving home with our rusty, mud coated load, exhausted and hungry from our eight hours of *toiling in the trenches,* we stopped at the McDonalds' restaurant in Pennant Hills. Still stoned from the celebratory joint that Brownie suggested at the completion of the pool extraction - blissfully unaware that we resembled crazed warriors of some ancient tribe of mud-men from the mountain forests of Papua New Guinea - we walked up to the counter to order our food. It wasn't until we got back in the truck, with our burgers, that we both broke into hysterics, realising the chaos we had just caused, as mothers frantically gathered their children away from us and the staff stared in disbelieve at the two filthy vagrants ordering enough food to feed a bus-load of tramps.

My new address was a three bedroom house on, the busy, Wentworth Avenue in Pagewood - that I shared with a friend I'd made whilst living in London, Darlene, and her best mate Kathy. It was, conveniently, just around the corner from my old Hopfgarten ski buddies, Stubbo and TB. They had lived in the Maroubra area all their lives and together with their large circle of friends, who often came to my gigs, my social calender was rarely vacant! The parties that TB and his housemates, Marto and Blinky, held in their bachelor pad - affectionately known as "The Mansion" - on Bunnerong Road, were legendary, and that was where Stubbo and I spent most of our weekends. I was such a *regular* visitor that I earned the title of "Half Tone" - being half the size of TB [a former front row footballer with the Eastern Suburb's Roosters] who's name was also Tony. He and Stubbo were like my *city brothers,* and the great times I had with them, that year, were some of the best in my Bachelorhood. Darlene and Kathy were like my *city sisters* and together with my actual sister, Lyn, living close by in Rockdale, I finally felt the comfort,warmth, and empathy of friends and family, that had been absent from my life since returning from my travels abroad. I began to feel grounded.

    I had no doubt that I'd moved to the *big smoke* when I woke on my first morning at the new address to find we needed milk for breakfast. Walking outside, I tried to cross the six lanes of peak hour traffic, to buy a cartoon of milk from the, massive, East Gardens Shopping complex across the road. As I dodged the chaotic traffic in bare feet, boxer shorts and singlet, I noticed the 747's taking off and landing just down the road at Kingsford Smith Airport. As my eyes and ears processed this maelstrom, my nose detected the unusual combined scent of roasting tobacco and cornflakes, wafting through the air, from the nearby WD&HO Wills and Kellogs factories. Sydney - with all it's noise, odours and traffic jams - was now my home.

    I had *many* weird and wonderful experiences in that year of being a city dweller; My resident Sunday afternoon gig at the Stardust Hotel, in Cabramatta, ranks high on *that* list. I recall how one of the local drug dealers - a short, stocky, South American guy who reminded me of Al Pacino in Scarface - use to conduct his business in front of me on the stage. While I performed, he stood with his back to the audience, laying out his chattel of weed, coke, speed and pills, on the floor at my feet near my guitar effect pedals. As I looked down at his illicit market stall, neatly arranged on either side of the base of my microphone stand - my eyes wide and bulging from their sockets - he would quietly, but firmly, instruct me to "Keep playing!, Don't stop!, Just keep singing!". So, while I dished out the tunes, he dished out the goods - to a steady flow of customers wandering up to him, selecting their preferred poison and slipping twenty, fifty or hundred dollar bank notes into his hand, then nonchalantly strolling back to their stool at the bar. Fortunately, his business operation had a positive flow-on effect for me, as many of his customers would look up and notice my *Album* being displayed for sale and purchase *it* as well. It was like their *one-stop-shop* for drugs and music! Occasionally the *stage front trading operations* would be interrupted by the local constabulary - wandering through the bar with a sniffer dog - but *Scarface* always seemed to know when those raids were about to happen and would close up shop early and disappear out the side door and away through the back car-park. That same car-park had a notorious reputation for car thefts, so I always parked my new Mitsubishi L300 Van in the lane beside the pub - where I could see it from the stage through the large glass windows! Despite the seediness and dark criminal undercurrents that pervaded the venue, I made some good friends and loyal fans at that gig which became one of my favourites. Some of those locals even travelled up to Newcastle, the following year, to help me celebrate my thirtieth birthday. They were good, hard working, salt of the earth characters who reminded me of the friends I'd grown up with in East Maitland. Enlightening me to some of the less successful aspects of multiculturalism in Australia, they bemoaned the gradual demise of their suburb, claiming the influx of *so many* mixed nationalities, religions and cultures, placed critical pressure on even the most tolerant of long term residents.

A couple of my other gigs had a much more health related aspect. The first, being when I played in a very upmarket fitness gym in Bondi. I'm sure it was much more entertaining for me, as voyeur, than the sweaty, scantily leotard-clad, socialites all busting their guts to keep up appearances. Serenading the exhausted temptresses, I gallantly resisted the urge to sing *"Show Us Ya Mota"*! The second gig, was a cafe overlooking a squash court on the first floor of an office complex right in the heart of Sydney's CBD. Only a glass wall separated me and the cafe' patrons from the barrage of squash balls being relentlessly splatt against it. The *constant pounding* often providing a rhythm pattern for me to play along with. The challenge and stress of finding a car park at peak hour on a Friday afternoon and trying to avoid a ticket from a parking officer while carrying my equipment up stairs to the venue was barely worth my performance fee!

I really started to feel like a part of the vibrant Eastern Suburb's scene when I scored residencies at The Duke of Gloucester in Randwick on Fridays and the Clovelly Hotel every Saturday. The "D.O.G.", as the locals referred to it, reminded me of my old Friday night residency at the Cricketers Arms in Newcastle a few years earlier and was also my brother-in-law, Mark's *"local watering hole"*. As always, he flew my banner for me and sang my praises to the publican and the regular patrons, many of whom were his mates. As a result, I was warmly received and often doubled my night's wages in album sales.

The Coogee Bay pub, on the other hand, was a completely different experience for me that took quite a bit of adapting to - before I felt comfortable. The management of *this* venue operated it more like a nightclub by having a resident DJ who played upbeat dance music in my breaks. It was a strange juxtaposition of musical genres. Going from my folkie, accoustic, sing-a-long style straight into loud, thumping, dance oriented, rock and techno, every forty five minutes when I took my breaks. It was even harder to re connect with the audience after they'd been stirred up on the dance floor. Now, more intent on refilling their drinks at the bar and chatting up the person they'd been dancing with, rather than listen to my "easy listening" tunes. In desperation, I tried to match the driving beat style of music that the DJ was pumping out but my acoustic guitar was no match for his highly produced vinyl LP's spinning on his turntables and shaking the foundations through his massive sub woofer speakers. Just as I was about to concede - and cancel that gig - a new, resident DJ was hired, who, luckily for me, played a style of music that complimented my repertoire rather than competing with it. In between my sets he played more of a country rock style of music that enhanced what I was doing. It was only at the end of my performance that he would put on the *dance music* to really rev up the crowd that I'd been limbering up for him. His name was Scott - and over the few months that we both resided at *that* venue we became good mates. He totally understood my performance regime and worked with me to help me fully connect with my audience. Only turning the venue into a dance club at the end of my show. I'd often stay on to watch him weave his musical magic at his desk, after which we'd head out to parties or other late night venues with his wife and friends. I became absolutely besotted with one of those friends, a gorgeous, long legged, five feet ten brunette with the most apt name of Cherry. Cherry was the first girl to make me aware of the term…"Punching above your weight". She was an absolute stunner with a figure that turned heads whenever she sauntered into a room - and I was a long way down the line of guys vying for her affections. My short stature also meant that I was a long way down from her line of sight, which wasn't all bad because it meant my vision was in line with her perky breasts! The issue of *height* seemed inconsequential when I was out with Scott and his entourage. That was because Scott was a Dwarf! He even made *me* feel tall when I walked beside him! His charming and attractive wife, although not a dwarf, was short but still taller than him - and *that fact* seemed to give me hope in my pursuit of the tall, tasty Cherry. I thought my luck had turned - the night she agreed to my offer of coming home with me - after a particularly late night, partying at a house full of Kiwi expat's in Randwick. She was having trouble getting a taxi, so I said I'd drive her home to Bondi in the morning. We were both fuelled up on pot and speed and I figured I had a better chance of finding *my* house than *hers*. As we climbed into bed and she modestly removed her dress - revealing a sexy, hot pink, laced Teddy negligee - I truly thought my wishes had been granted. That wasn't to be, as she insisted we keep to our own sides of the bed and that I keep my promise of driving her home at daybreak. It was clear I wasn't getting a bite of this cherry! I was devastated, shunned and dejected, and lay on my back - jaws clenched in my *amphetamine induced* condition - staring at the ceiling. The only thing to distract me from my thoughts of disappointment and sexual frustration for the next four hours - knowing I was only inches away from my wildest fantasy - was the sound of the old man next door, pottering in his back shed. It was something he did regularly and usually late at night. Mumbling to himself as he rummaged through whatever he had in there, often hammering and sawing to fuel my insomnia. I had never spoken to him and only occasionally caught a glimpse of him, collecting his mail, which added to his mystique. His nocturnal nuances puzzled me and teased my imagination, and, since Neil Diamond had already composed a song about my alluring but aloof bedmate [*Cherry Cherry*], I began formulating lyrics about my, equally intriguing, neighbour.

The Man Next Door

Midnight and lonely, alone in bed
wide awake with the noise coming from the garden shed
in my neighbour's yard, so close I fear
for my sanity and life from what I hear

Full moon and thunder, I'm a child afraid
of the monster beneath my bed my mind has made
But this is real, just outside my room
The monster who waited so long is coming for me soon
so very soon

Do you know what it's like to be afraid?
I don't think I can take much more
something so bizarre is going on
each time I hear the man next door

Sound's like he's digging. Did he kill his wife?
Sounds like wrapping up the pieces and cleaning the knife
He talks to himself, I'm sure he's mad
The voice of a lonely old man is frightening and sad
Frightening and sad

Do you know what it's like to be afraid?
I don't think I can take much more
something so bizarre is going on
each time I hear the man next door

In an age where murder breeds
a thrusting knife will sow the seeds
A twisted mind will break the law
I wish I knew the man next door

Midnight and lonely, a days old age
Reading between the lines on an empty page
from the book of life, when life is gone
So hard to live in a world where you don't belong
Where you don't belong

Do you know what it's like to be afraid?
I don't think I can take much more
something so bizarre is going on
each time I hear the man next door

Sure, those lyrics may have been a bit melodramatic but local media reports, at that time - about corpses being found in houses in the suburbs, and nearby residents having no idea that their neighbours had died or been murdered - really spooked me. Maybe I was watching too many horror movies - a favourite late night past-time of mine. After all, my mother chose my name while reading a magazine article about actor/singer, Anthony Perkins, who was best known for his role as the schizophrenic, [*Norman Bates*], in the classic Alfred Hitchcock thriller called Psycho! Although I was christened Anthony, I was always called Tony, and it was a badge of honour to know I'd been named after a Hollywood star - except I sometimes wished I'd been named after someone with less dubious notoriety, like, let's say... *Tony Curtis*. My chance to act out a role in a *real life melodrama* presented itself to me while living in Sydney - but didn't win me any acclaim. In fact, it was a performance that almost cost my life! It really did show me that *this city* was full of strange and sinister people who I was far better off *not* knowing! I'm referring to one Saturday night when I met a charming and attractive young lady at a wine bar on Canterbury Road - where I was singing - who invited me back to her apartment. I'd had little luck in the way of romance since moving to the Harbour City so I was an easy target for *this* classy enchantress, who, after the obligatory nightcap, soon had me naked and rolling around under the doona in her four poster bed. It was shaping up to be a long, lusty night, when, suddenly, there was loud, frantic, knocking on her apartment door. From that instant, everything seemed to speed up, as if the *fast forward button* had been pressed. As the knocking on the door increased in intensity and a male voice on the other side began to call out her name, my seductress sat bolt upright and frantically whispered "That's my boyfriend!, he's a cop!,he should still be on duty!, he's got a bad temper!, he'll have his gun!, you've gotta go!, quickly!, grab your clothes and go out over the balcony!" As shocked as I was, I couldn't help thinking that she'd rehearsed those lines and this wasn't the first time she used them. Never the less, fearing for my life, I promptly obeyed her commands. Snatching my clothes - strewn along the floor between the bedroom and living room - I managed to slip on my underpants in a mad, hopping, scurrying scramble that ended on the balcony. Luckily, for me, the unit was on the first floor of the four story complex so I flung the rest of my apparel over the railing then pursued them by climbing over. I then lowered myself down, letting go and praying that the concrete driveway wasn't too far below my short, dangling limbs! As I felt the cement make contact with the soles of my feet I attempted a *commando style role* - to break my fall - which resulted in losing skin off my bare back and elbows but I was thankful not to hear any bones breaking. As I fumbled around in the shadowy driveway, collecting my boots, socks, shirt and jeans, I glanced upwards to see my *"Juliet"* retreating from her balcony through the glass sliding door. Silently biding her "adieu", I hastily retreated to the safety of my van parked down the street. The drive back home, that night, was a long one - as I didn't even know what suburb I had been in -

so I simply headed east, using glimpses of the city skyline to get my bearings. Finally calming down from my ordeal and finding major roads to get me back to familiar territory, I had plenty of time to contemplate the next phase of my life. That's when I decided it was time to move back to the safety of my old stomping grounds - Newcastle.

I'll never know if I'd been the unwitting participant of some weird, kinky role play between two bored lovers or simply a victim of an unfaithful girlfriend, but that late, one-night stand, soapbox drama, was the *beginning of the end* of my lecherous and sometimes treacherous, bachelorhood behaviour. My lusty, late night, post gig rendezvous' became less frequent and much less dramatic, until, within six months of moving back to Newcastle, I finally decided to take the plunge and settle down.

Sydney

Sydney, it's a great place to visit it picks me up when I'm blue
Sydney, it's a great place to visit there's always something to do
Well now if you're bored, things are too slow
Come down to Sydney it'll get you on the go
Sydney, it's a great place to visit but I wouldn't wanna live there too

Sydney, I drove into the city in the traffic at the end of a queue
Sydney, I got lost comin' home and that was in a taxi too !
Well you can drive around for hours on end
not know where you're goin' or knowin' where you've been
Sydney, it's a great place to visit but I wouldn't wanna live there too

Sydney, I went to Centre Point Tower, took an elevator right to the top
Sydney, they said I'd get a great view but I couldn't see a thing for the smog !
Well I wouldn't care if I didn't live there
Just let me live where I can breath the air
Sydney, it's a great place to visit but I wouldn't wanna live there too

Well every traffic light that you come to is red
Everyone you meet wouldn't care if you were dead
Every single day all I want to say is give me the country instead

Sydney, and into Kings Cross for a midnight fling
Sydney, or to the Opera House but opera really ain't my thing
Well I know all the night spots there's none I ain't been
Some'll cost you the world and that's just to get in !
Sydney, it's a great place to visit but I wouldn't wanna live there too

Well I've been to Bondi, Toronga Park Zoo, screamed in Luna Park, what more can I do ?
I'm your typical tourist with my Kodak too but I think I'll leave Sydney for you
I Think I'll leave Sydney for you
I Think I'll leave Sydney for you

Dangar Street, Wickham. Newcastle.

My relocation back to Newcastle was a gradual process, transporting a few of my possessions, in my van, along with my PA equipment, whenever I had gigs up there. En route to my gig, I would drop off my things at a house in Dangar street, Wickham, that I was to rent with my old *Belair-motorcycle-stunt -mate*, Ringa. The rustic, Federation Style, dwelling had been purchased by our mutual friend and my European Contiki Tour companion, Gluey, as an investment property. We were his first choice as tenants. A decision I'm sure he came to regret as tales of our flamboyant nocturnal activities filtered back to him through our circle of friends. His chief informers would certainly have been our neighbours, Mungo and his partner Di. I would often see them, bleary eyed and exhausted, leaving for work in the mornings, casting accusatory glances at me and Ringa, as we merrily farewelled our party guests from regular, all-night swarays - involving loud music, alcohol and elicit substances that ensured we wouldn't nod off and miss any of the festivities!

My time for *settling down* may have been just around the corner but living in this house ensured I would exit the *single life* in a *blaze of glory*!...An "*inglorious blaze*" might be a more apt description!

The location of our Dangar street den was ideal for me and Ringa as it was within walking distance of our favourite nightclubs. At worst, a very short taxi ride, if the bourbons and Drambuie's rendered us incapable of efficiently putting one foot in front of the other! It was just behind Wickham railway station in a grimy, dockside precinct comprised of weather-beaten cottages and light industrial warehouses. It was also within view of the Floating Dock "Muloobinba", where my father worked shifts as a painter and docker. As he toiled to restore the rusted, stinking hulls of those massive ships, I shamelessly partied on, just a few hundred metres from him, in our dilapidated cesspool. Considering all the mayhem and mischief we got up to in that abode, the term... "Being on the wrong side of the tracks" was most apt. As well as extending invitations to the bands, DJ's, bar staff and females we'd meet on our nocturnal bar and dance floor reconnaissance missions, it wasn't uncommon for taxi loads of our mates to pull up at the front gate, knowing they still had a chance of *some action* at our place after 3AM. The looks of jealous bewilderment from the store-men and truck drivers, working in the warehouse across the street, fuelled my amusement as the wobbly parade of giggling, mini skirted girls, carrying their high heels, followed closely by long haired, lecherous Casanova misfits, stumbled onto our front verandah. Night after night, after night.

I managed to sleep off *my* hangovers, but it amazed me how Ringa dutifully went off to work on the week days, with, sometimes, barely an hours sleep! In order to maintain some semblance of health, to offset our punishing lifestyle, we often rode our bikes along wharf road up to Nobby's and Newcastle Beach as well as played squash in local competitions. My *last* game of squash was particularly memorable as I succumbed to a bout of diarrhoea in the middle of a game. Shitting your pants in front of an audience is something you don't easily forget!

The Tex Pistols [Ye-ha!]

Mark Tinson[guitar], Me[overalls], Phil Screen[drums] & UJ Neil[bass guitar]

Despite all the late nightclubbing and Dangar street debauches, I still managed to maintain a solidly booked roster of solo and band gigs around the Hunter Valley and Sydney. My career and social life merged, most nights, into a blurred fantasy of songs and seduction. It wasn't uncommon for me to finish my resident Friday night gig at the Woolloomooloo Bay hotel in Sydney at 11.30pm then drive back to Newcastle to meet up with Ringa and his party recruits at Fanny's Nightclub. This would be just before closing time, after-which we would head back to our house to *party-on* 'till dawn.

Throughout this chaotic period, I was invited back to do some guest spots with The Colours band who had recruited the services of my friend and mentor, Mark Tinson. He knew I'd been burning the candle at both ends and surprised me, the day he dropped me off at my Dangar street house - after a sound check for our gig that night at Fanny's - by suggesting I don't get stoned *before* the gig!

The success of the Colours gigs led to a brief reformation of the *Tony Johns Band* to promote my new album [*The Way I Live*]. *That campaign* ended disastrously at the Newcastle Workers Club one Saturday night in 1988. The venue was a popular haunt for mature age punters - many of whom were divorcees looking for a new partner or a fling - who just wanted to hear songs they knew while they danced and romanced. It was affectionately known as the Parachute Club or Jump Club, and local *cover* bands such as Baron and Nodes Levity were firmly entrenched there and footed the bill perfectly. That's why - when *we* walked on stage and started playing all of my *original, bluesy, laid back sludge* - the packed auditorium emptied itself of patrons within ten

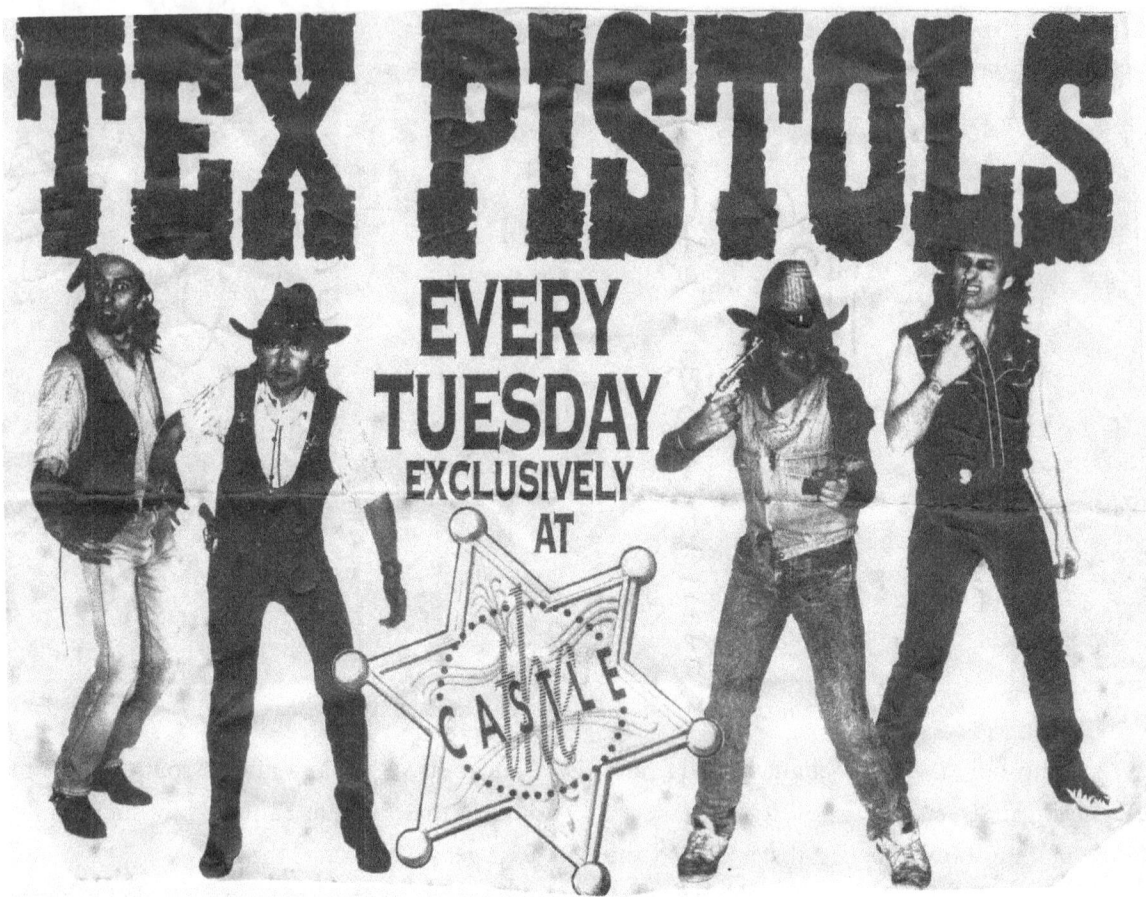

minutes. It was *so* bad that we cut our performance short and barely salvaged the night - by ditching *my* last four songs for some *standard* rock'n'roll numbers to try and keep the remaining fifteen people on the dance floor. It was my *worst* moment on stage! Much too similar to my last, *stinking,* game of squash!

The following year an earthquake reduced *that* club to rubble, sadly taking the lives of nine people. A disaster, that for years after, I would associate with my dismal performance that night.

Later that year - as if to rescue me from the ruins of my humiliation - Tinno asked me to be a part of his new concept, comedy cowboy, rockabilly band. Along with UJ Neil and Phil Screen I became one of *The Tex Pistols*.

The Tex Pistols was the perfect tonic to perk me back up. It put the *fun* back into music for me. We dressed up in cowboy hats and boots and talked like the rootin' tootin' gunsligers that we'd seen in all those John Wayne movies when we were kids. Laughing 'till we cried, we took the piss out of every cliché' associated with that genre. Our repertoire was a killer, crowd pleasing mixture, of classic country and western and rockabilly hits. It was also complimented by some *tongue in cheek* originals - penned by Tinno - to exploit our *concept* into a viable marketing product.

Our *first* merchandising exploit was a cassette album of covers, called "*Never Mind the Bullocks*" in honour of our namesakes, *The Sex Pistols*. It featured a, 2/4 time signature, version of *their* hit, [Pretty Vacant] and a similar conversion of the Rose Tattoo classic, [RocknRoll Outlaw]. Two of the more quirkier songs on the album, that I had the pleasure of singing, were [Chew Tobacco Rag] - written in 1951 - and [The Man Who Comes Around] - written in 1937. *Those songs* were a delight to perform and I revelled in adopting a *deadpan* stage persona while singing them. They also fitted perfectly into my *solo* repertoire, alongside my own novelty originals, which lead to *me* including *them* on *my* next cassette album called "*Tony Johns in Helmut's Pub*". I also took the liberty to *rustle* a few more songs from *that Tex Pistol* album, including; "*Chicken Train*" by the Ozark Mountain Daredevils, "*40 Below*" by Canadian band, Gary Lee and The Showdown, and our kick-arse version of "*Ghost Riders in the Sky*" by Stan Jones and his Death Valley Rangers. Screeny had a subtle dig at me for *re-marketing[stealing]* that Pistols product, and, admitting my guilt, I playfully justified my deed as being "*common among outlaws*"!

Is that a gun in their pockets?

FOUR Newcastle musos who say they're all cowboys at heart, have formed a new band, The Tex Pistols, to play at the Castle on Monday nights.

All seasoned musicians, the Tex Pistols are UJ Neill, Phil Screen, Mark Tinson and Tony Johns.

Yes you've seen them all before, by themselves and in other bands, and they are going to keep that up.

'Forming the Tex Pistols is just so we can act like cowboys,' Phil Screen told *T.E.*

'We're all old Coalfields boys and we've wanted to do something like this for a while.'

UJ and Phil play in the Funbusters and Mark Tinson is in the Colours, while Tony Johns mostly plays solo.

And the result is a kind of fusion of all their interests.

'What we'll play won't be really mainstream stuff,' Screen said.

'Some of our stuff is 50 years old, like real Roy Rogers songs, and the Sons of the Pioneers.

'There'll be a few 2/4 pieces, the odd ballad, maybe even a waltz, but certainly some up-tempo stuff as well.'

Well they've got me intrigued. See the Tex Pistols at the Castles on Monday nights from this week.

Chew Tobacco Rag [Billy Briggs][1951]

Well I like to smoke my old corn pipe
but I've chewed tobacco nearly all my life
ah Pwtt ting, pwtt tung, pwtt, ting p'ting
chew tobacca chew tobacca chew tobacca rag

I even like to smoke cigarettes sometime
but when it comes to dipin' I'll draw the line
ah Pwtt ting, pwtt tung, pwtt, ting p'ting
chew tobacca chew tobacca chew tobacca rag

If ya chew tabacca don't spit on the floor
expectorate in the cuspador
ah Pwtt ting, pwtt tung, pwtt, ting p'ting
chew tobacca chew tobacca chew tobacca rag

If ya never had a chew in ya life before
why don't ya try it you'll sure want more
ah Pwtt ting, pwtt tung, pwtt, ting p'ting
chew tobacca chew tobacca chew tobacca rag

Just take a big plug and bite of the end
let it run down and off your chin
ah Pwtt ting, pwtt tung, pwtt, ting p'ting
chew tobacca chew tobacca chew tobacca rag

If ya chew tabacca don't spit on the floor
expectorate in the cuspador
ah Pwtt ting, pwtt tung, pwtt, ting p'ting
chew tobacca chew tobacca chew tobacca rag

Well you can smoke cigarettes while the sun goes 'round
while I chew tobacca and spit on the ground
ah Pwtt ting, pwtt tung, pwtt, ting p'ting
chew tobacca chew tobacca chew tobacca rag

Well all day long you can smoke your pipe
while I chew tobacca and spit all night
ah Pwtt ting, pwtt tung, pwtt, ting p'ting
chew tobacca chew tobacca chew tobacca rag

*If ya chew tabacca don't spit on the floor
expectorate in the cuspador
If ya chew tabacca don't spit on the floor
expectorate in the cuspador
ah Pwtt ting, pwtt tung, pwtt, ting p'ting
chew tobacca chew tobacca chew tobacca rag*

Singing that song - with all of it's sound effects - was like performing oral gymnastics! I always had to give my microphone a good wipe down with my handkerchief after spitting out those lyrics!

The Man Who Comes Around [Bud Green & Tommy Tucker][1937]

There's a man comes to our house every single day
papa comes home and the man goes away
oh papa does the work and moma gets the pay
and the man comes around when papa goes away

Now the man that comes to our house he's a very nice
he comes in the summer time and brings moma ice
just a little teeny weeny bit that soon melts away
he has to come back again later in the day

There's a man comes to our house every single day
papa comes home and the man goes away
oh papa does the work and moma gets the pay
and the man comes around when papa goes away

Now the man that comes to our house comes to sell a brush
he comes in a hurry and he leaves in a rush
and every time he goes away moma's in a fit
if she didn't get everything she thought she ought git

There's a man comes to our house every single day
papa comes home and the man goes away
oh papa does the work and moma gets the pay
and the man comes around when papa goes away

Now the man that comes to our house drives a cadillac
he runs around the corner and he parks it out the back
moma comes to the door he's always sure to greet her with
open up honey bunch and let me check your meter

There's a man comes to our house every single day
papa comes home and the man goes away
oh papa does the work and moma gets the pay
and the man comes around when papa goes away

now when I grow to be a man I'm not gonna be
a plumber or a janitor no sir-ee
I won't be a doctor with an office down town
no I'd rather be just the man that comes around

There's a man comes to our house every single day
papa comes home and the man goes away
oh papa does the work and moma gets the pay
and the man comes around when papa goes away

I wonder if my grandfather, Perce, ever heard that song? I could imagine him singing it as he rode his push-bike – from Greta to Hawks Nest!- to go fishing, in order to feed his family, during the depression years.

All the songs in our show may have had a country theme but our live performances had a kick-ass, rock'n'roll edge, reminiscent of Tinno and Screenies former band, The Heroes.

As we refined our act, at resident gigs at The Cambridge Hotel and The Castle Nightclub, eventually wowing audiences at the Tamworth Country Music festivals, I revelled in sharing the stage with some of the finest musicians and sharpest wits in the business. Mark Tinson, Phil Screen, UJ Neil [RIP] and, later on, Brien McVernon became my rock'n'roll family. It was a welcomed relief - discarding my "Solo" obligations - to do some hootin'and holerin' with lil' ol' MJ[Tinno], lil' ol' UPJ[Screeny], lil' ol' UJ and lil' ol' cousin Whan [Brien] - *They* were our *stage names*, that, to this very day, we still use to greet each other!

Although I may have been in a *Country/Cowboy band* I felt I was living the *Rock'n'Roll dream*. I was *still* enjoying my solo gigs, singing my original songs and promoting my record. I was still enjoying the night life at the clubs and back at the parties in Dangar street and recuperating during the days by sunbaking up at Nobby's beach. The biggest thrill, however, was performing with the Pistols, both on and off stage. Screeny and UJ were seasoned party animals and although Tinno distanced himself from their post-gig antics, *I* was an all too easy and willing participant. This song - that Tinno wrote for me to sing on our "Squel.Like.A.Pig" album - poked fun at our randy, rootin' tootin', cowboy-rockstar aspirations.....

Stereo Blonds [Mark Tinson]

I want stereo blonds in the back of my Cadillac
with the top pulled back so every one can see
one to the left of me
one to the right of me
real high fidelity
I want stereo blonds in the back of my Cadillac

I've been watchin' those long haired boys on the TV screen
They've been playin' their guitars and singing
not a whole lot better than me
I wouldn't cross the street to see them play
but when it's party time they really got it made
They've got stereo blondes in the back of their Cadillac

I want stereo blonds in the back of my Cadillac
with the top pulled back so every one can see
one to the left of me
one to the right of me
real high fidelity
I want stereo blonds in the back of my Cadillac

I've been listen'n to those preachers on the radio
they could save my soul if I help out a little with their cash flow
now I don't know if I believe what they say
but brother Jimmy, well he sure knows the way
He's got stereo blondes in the back of his Cadillac

I want stereo blonds in the back of my Cadillac
with the top pulled back so every one can see
A woman to the left of me
a woman to the right of me
real high fidelity
I want stereo blonds in the back of my Cadillac
I want stereo blonds in the back of my Cadillac
I want stereo blonds in my Cadillac
yeah, come over here baby
and you too honey!

We never quite made it to the level of owning Cadillacs - but a motel room with a spa bath and a few, naked, groupies wasn't a bad consolation prize!

There was no question about the success of The Tex Pistols, especially when we took the show to Tamworth for the country music festival. Still, even the best acts can crash if booked to play for the wrong audience. I'm referring to our one and only disastrous gig when we were booked to play at the Imperial Hotel in Tamworth at a time of the year when the country music festival *wasn't on*. On this occasion we learnt that when the festival is over, the pubs and punters in Tamworth revert to favouring good old hard rock and roll bands. Even our good friend, Mike Vee - who was the booking agent for the pub - knew this, but omitted to inform *us*. He even disguised our act by advertising us as a hard core punk/scar band from Melbourne, but also omitted to inform us of this. I'm sure his intentions were honourable. Fulfilling his role as agent by providing us with work and supplying entertainment to the venue. Not realising he was effectively sending us [*The Lambs*] to *The Slaughter!* Needless to say, when we graced the stage in our cowboy hats and boots, babbling on about *attractive sheep* and broken down *John Deere* tractors, in our mock yankee accents, the hostile audience of long haired, nose pierced, tattooed thugs all but nearly lynched us! Of all the occasions to require the *Blues Brothers Chicken Coup Wire* in front of the stage...this was it! My last moment on stage was graced with a half full can of beer narrowly missing my ear as it whizzed past. Retreating to the managers office, we sat stunned as he pleaded with us to..."Loose the hats and accents and go back on and just play some rock and roll music!" The same manager who only a few months earlier, after our show during the festival, had been buying us rounds of drinks and pleading with us to come back and play in his pub as soon as possible!.. We reluctantly appeased him by returning to the stage - playing some *Stones* and the *obligatory* Lynard Skynard's "*Sweet Home Alabama*" - which managed to placate the, somewhat, diminished crowd. It was like reliving my dismal gig at the Newcastle Workers Club but I was consoled to know it could happen to even the best - such as The Pistols. We cancelled the following night's show and drove back to Newcastle with our tails between our legs.

Accused of being "*Too Country*"! - we rode out of the *Country Music Capital* before *Sunset* the following day. A three hour drive I enjoyed with Screeny as we laughed about the ill fated booking and how I'd given up a solo gig - worth four times the money! - to come to Tamworth for a *good ól' arse wooping*!..

The End of an Era-Painting the Town Yellow

As I neared the end of my *"Twenties"* I sensed a change in my lifestyle approaching.

For the previous ten years I'd lived the most wonderful, care-free, existence. Intuitively steering my musical career whilst recklessly sowing the seeds of my bachelorhood. I wasn't particularly proud of some of the mischief I'd gotten up to - but vainly tried to justify it as a means of relieving the pressures of self employment. Apart from the *physical* hammering that my body had endured, the *moral* part of my psyche was telling me to slow down and start taking life a little more seriously.

Conscience

Hey you! Who, me? Yeah you!
Don't you think I know what you're trying to do
You told me I'd be fine
wasn't that your favourite line?

Looking for a life of your own
you're looking everywhere but it's right at home
stop asking everybody else 'cause they're talking nonsense
just ask your conscience

Having the time of your life
no kids, no home, no wife
don't you think it's time you settled down?
put both feet back firmly on the ground?

No guilt when you make mistakes
when you do, well they're the breaks
stop blaming everybody else when you're tired of all the nonsense
just ask your conscience

How long will you live this way?
Can you afford the price you'll pay?
An old fool living in the past
blaming time - that went too fast

Blame a dream that never came true
don't blame me it was up to you
you always said you had no time for a conference
with your conscience

The timing for this change of direction also seemed perfect as I'd just settled into a relationship with, my soon to be wife, Jacqui - with whom I'd just begun to look for a house to buy.

Coincidently, at this time, I was just about to turn thirty, and the party I held to celebrate this milestone symbolically also farewelled my careless, carefree, bachelor odyssey.

The party for this momentous occasion was held in the backyard of our Dangar street residence in Wickham. A modest patch of ground, roughly 12 metres square, that was bordered by the brick walls of neighbouring warehouses on two sides - enclosing it into a type of amphitheatre. The theme of the party revolved around the colour yellow - being a bright, happy colour - to symbolise that I was *mellowing yellowly* [*as Donovan had sung*]. I even advertised the event on leaflets that I'd printed and distributed at my gigs. Subsequently, scores of people - from every stage of my life - turned up, decorated with yellow hair and clothes and costumes including; Frangipani flowers, yellow pages phone books and bottles of Galiano. Old friends - from my childhood, through to current mates and musical collaborators - made the night one of my best, making me appreciate every one of the thirty years I'd been alive! The crowning glory of the celebration was the band called *Men Without Shame* - that I'd hired to perform on a makeshift stage along the back fence. My muso mates, Mick Punch, Matty Munroe, Ed Peters and Ross Peters, were the perfect catalyst for the best party I'd ever attended. Everyone danced and sang so enthusiastically that by the nights' end, the small backyard became a dust-bowl. Every blade of grass in that yard was pulverised by the stomping feet of the enormous crowd packed in there.

The huge number of people that attended my 30th bash had the effect of making our location more conspicuous. For months afterwards, we had total strangers knocking on our door, at all hours of the night, asking..."*was there a party happening and could they score some good drugs?*". My decision to move out to my own house was validated the morning I walked out the front door and looked down the street to see a dozen cops, with sniffer dogs, knocking down the door of the house on the corner with sledge hammers. If a raid, such as that, had ever been carried out at *our* address I would've been writing a *lot more* songs about "*Doin'Time*"!

And so, just like when Ringa and I headed off in different directions,eight years earlier – that Saturday afternoon when he took me on a crazy motorbike ride through the Bel-Air hotel - we amicably parted ways again. We were leaving behind a haze of wild memories within the walls of that decadent dwelling in Dangar street, Wickham.

With the celebration of my first thirty years completed - and figuring I'd be around for another thirty - I withdrew all the funds from my life insurance policy to use as deposit on a house in Hamilton - into which I moved with my fiancee. Once again, an uncanny coincidence being, that the street, this house was in, had the same name as my *musical* grandfather - Percy!

And so began the new phase of my life and career. A change for the better. Something worth holding onto...

Hold on to You

My heart is beating again
I've found a true friend
at a time in my life when timing is everything
you found the time
I found the place
warm in the smile that shines on your face

My soul is washed in your love
so clean and shinning
shinning like a new star burning forever more
never to fear darkness again
those days are gone now I hold your hand

I'll hold on to you in my arms this way
I'll hold on to you
every new day

My mind is free to decide
it's clear and made up
you're the one I've needed - the one I've been waiting for
you are my love
you are my friend
sharing my life from now 'till the end

I'll hold on to you
in my arms this way
I'll hold on to you
for together we both know the way

Within a year, Helen Grogan and Jus Gordon performed *that song* at my wedding. An event that Jacqui and I celebrated with close friends and family while cruising around Lake Macquarie on a floating restaurant. It was a symbolic occasion - as we sailed away on a journey that offered smooth seas and fine weather. That was until an *emotional storm* caused us to founder on rocks, ten years later.

Chapter 4
1990's

Adopting to Adapt

Purchasing our house and *moving in together* had an instant settling effect on me and Jacqui. The old, federation style, two bedroom cottage in Percy street, Hamilton, was solid, but in need of a face lift, so most of our spare time and cash was spent on restoration and renovation projects. Suddenly, our priorities shifted from nightclubs and parties to paint charts and picket fences. It was a productive lifestyle change, and just as Newcastle was entering a new phase in the entertainment industry - with the construction of the Entertainment Centre at Broadmeadow - I felt my life taking a more responsible course towards growth and maturity. As I scraped and plastered and painted the *interior* walls of our new dwelling, the *exterior* steel walls of the Entertainment Centre rose into the sky in view of our front verandah - across the railway tracks near Broadmeadow station.

My parents, relieved to see me opting for a more conservative lifestyle, took a keen interest in my new relationship and real estate purchase, visiting often to contribute furnishings and manual labour to some of the renovation jobs. I particularly enjoyed reconnecting with my father when he assisted me in painting the corrugated iron roof, just as I had done with him, as a teenager, at our family home. His unique concept of a *safety harness* was a long, thick rope - that he'd acquired from a ship while working at the dock yards - which was tied around my waist as I stood on the steep pitched roof. It would then run over the gable and down to the back yard where he'd wrap it around *his* waist to act as an anchor. It allowed me to move freely across the corrugated iron without slipping on the wet paint and falling off.

Dad's acquisition of that ship's rope was just one of many items he procured in his tenure at the Dockyards. In fact he was regarded by his co-workers as "the man to see" if you required any *foreign orders* or items, hence his nickname – *Smoothy*. His association with the *Wharfies* and the Painters and Dockers union had endeared him with a sense of entitlement and an ethic of..."what's on the ships and wharfs is ours" and, consequently, my garage is still cluttered with enough rope, wire, paint brushes and paint to open a small chandlery store! My passion for yachting began back then and Dad was an invaluable assistant when the time came to service my vessels on various slipways around Lake Macquarie. One of the most expensive items required when maintaining a yacht is the anti-foul paint needed to stop marine growth from fouling the hull. I only recently discovered just how expensive that paint was, as my father had supplied me with enough of *it* to last the past thirty years and the five different boats I had owned! Scraping the barnacles and preparing my yachts' hull for anti fouling is a stinking chore that, oddly enough, evokes the sweetest memories of my generous, contemplative father and his strong, calloused hands.

Just as I was re-establishing *my* family ties, Jacqui was also searching to mend a maternal bond that was severed in her infancy. Although raised in Belmont, NSW, by her loving *adoptive* parents, Dave and Marie, she now felt the need to find out more about her birth mother and father. Her quest was achieved after being registered with an agency that assisted in reconnecting adoptees with their biological parents. Over the next few years, as we nurtured *our* three children, she became initiated with *another* family - that included her *natural* mother, father and five younger sisters who were born after she was adopted out. Colleen, Jacqui's birth mother, became pregnant with her in the early nineteen sixties at a time when *pregnancy out of wedlock* was a socially taboo subject.

Her boyfriend and their parents convinced, and somewhat coerced, her to leave Brisbane and spend the the remains of her term in Sydney at a facility for unmarried mothers. There, she gave birth and relinquished the child for adoption. The practise was common at the time and left deep emotional scars for many of those women, particularly Colleen, who complied with the process with much reluctance and regret. She eventually married her boyfriend and bore five more children to him, leaving her with a lifetime of wondering whatever became of their first offspring.

The song I wrote about Colleen's story was an attempt to describe emotions from someone else's perspective and my heart literally ached whenever I sang it. Particularly the night my 25 year old daughter, Sophie, sang it with me at Lizottes Theatre restaurant in 2017 to launch my last album. The song's performance evoked many emotions from the audience that night – one person in particular - Colleen!

Dad helping me out with boat maintenance

Natural

If I had held you in my arms
I might have never let you go
If I had listened to my heart
and not the voices saying no
If I knew without you
the pain would break my heart
I would have stayed, I would have prayed
that we would never be apart

And now as winter fires burn low
the embers glowing in the dark
'though it was many years ago
a longing yearns within my heart
to hold you, to tell you
why I let you go
It was so wrong to break that bond
that's why I've got to let you know

It's only natural to cry
only human asking why
It's just as natural as can be
Natural
You should be with me

If I knew without you
the pain would break my heart
I would have stayed
I would have prayed
that we would never be apart

It's only natural to cry
only human asking why?
It's just as natural as can be
Natural
You should be with me

I eventually got to know and become friends with Colleen and the rest of Jacqui's biological family. I was also well accepted by Dave and Marie and her adopted brother, Steve. A few years later, after settling into married life, I would boast cheekily that I had the unusual and unfortunate predicament of having, not one, but, two *mother in laws*!

Austria Calling

Of *all* the enquiries I ever received to book me for a gig, *this one* takes the cake!

It was winter, 1989, and as well as feeling the chill in the air, a shiver was running up the spine of my musical career as I sensed an ominous change approaching. I was performing in the front bar of the Bel-Air Hotel at Kotara to a small, uninterested crowd one Thursday night. It was a regular, alternating, Thursday gig that I'd secured through an agent. It was generally uninspiring and uneventful, but consistent, and vital in paying my new-found home loan. As I played to the transient audience - mostly late night shoppers from the Kotara Fair shopping complex across the street - I reminisced about the full house I used to play to, out back in the lounge area every Saturday, eight years earlier. I occasionally threw one of my original songs into the set list just to see if I'd get a reaction, but, apart from my old "*Hungry Creek*" mate, *Captain* - heckling from the bar - it went unnoticed. Suddenly, my day dream was interrupted by the barman calling out to me - holding up the telephone connected to the wall behind the counter by a long curly black chord - saying... "it's for you!" The distressed voice at the other end of the line was that of an elderly woman. She excitedly proceeded to explain to me how an Austrian man had been calling her every night *that* week, asking for "Toorny Joohns, the singer", and how he needed me to come back to his pub in Austria to perform. Having no luck in explaining to him that I didn't live with her and that she didn't even know me, she undertook the task of finding me, through the local *Gig Guide*. Relieved to have finally tracked me down, she then stipulated that I contact the Austrian gentleman to stop him from calling her at all ours of the night!

Of course it was *Helmut* trying to contact me and I have no doubt he was probably half pissed when he made those calls, making the communication process even more arduous for that lovely old woman! It was very flattering to know Helmut was so keen to have me back in his pub, especially when so many of my Newcastle gigs seemed to be heading the way of *that* Bel-Air Thursday night. I had begun to doubt my ability to entertain a crowd - as I had in the past - but reassured myself that returning to Helmut's Pub, for a season, would bolster my confidence. I wondered if the *local scene* was changing or if it was *me*. That question was answered a few years later when the Bel-Air Hotel was demolished to make way for a MacDonald's fast food restaurant. It was a sad indictment on the Newcastle music scene and the iconic venue that had hosted so many of Australia's greatest bands, touring in the 70's and '80's, such as INXS, Australian Crawl and Midnight Oil.

Having just taken out a mortgage on our new residence in Hamilton, my return to Austria was a bit more risky, so to ensure the bank loan repayments would be met we acquired tenants to occupy the house in our absence. Capitalising on Helmut's enthusiasm to re-hire me, I upped the stakes on my employment conditions to include return air-fares, employment for Jacqui [in the bar or kitchen], an apartment for us and season

Tony Johns IN HELMUT'S PUB

SIDE ONE
1. SHOW US YA MOTA
2. THE MAN THAT COMES AROUND
3. WALLABY TED'S BROTHER
4. MARIJUANA COOKIES
5. CHICKEN TRAIN
6. THE BELL RINGER OF HOPFGARTEN

© 1989 All Rights reserved. Funky Gibbon Prod.'s.

SIDE TWO
1. CHEW TOBACCO RAG
2. HUNGRY CREEK
3. THE 8 DAYS OF SKI LESSONS
4. 40 BELOW
5. P.C.A. THE EASY WAY
6. GHOSTRIDERS IN THE SKY.

ski passes. Ironically, as we departed to spend the winter in Europe, our Tenants were a couple just arriving from France to experience a Summer in Australia! Unfortunately for them they were also about to experience an earthquake - the first to cause major damage and loss of life in Newcastle's history! On that fateful Thursday morning in December 1989 our French guests felt the house shake and move on its concrete piers, causing the brick chimney to crack and fall to the ground. They moved out shortly after to venture to other, safer, parts of Australia and to allow my parents to arrange repairs with the insurance company. Seeing the headlines of the event in Austrian Newspapers, I initially passed it off as, probably, a coal mine collapse or explosion but was mortified as the true cause became clear.

The shocking news put a damper on our trip as we both felt we should've been there when it occurred. Especially as some of the worst damage occurred in our new home suburb of Hamilton.

The devastating incident back home seemed to set a forlorn precedent for the rest of our time in Hopfgarten. It was one of the worst ski seasons in years, being too warm for any decent amount of snow to fall. By February in 1990 we were going for bike rides and hikes up the mountain instead of shushing down the slopes on skis. Tourist numbers were drastically down and my performances in the bar had as much atmosphere as elevator music. It was difficult to be motivated, watching the few punters that remained, drowning their sorrows and becoming as messy as the muddy pistes on Mount Hohe Salve!

One peculiar and flattering highlight of that season was when the two owners of a nightclub in Florence, Italy, made a special visit to Helmut's Pub. They'd come to offer me the job of resident entertainer, for the upcoming summer, at their venue called The Red Garter. They were known as The Two Francos and had heard about me through Contiki drivers and reps who regularly took tours to The Garter, for a night out, while staying at the Contiki Villa in Florence. It was a nice boost - for my faltering ego - to be wined and dined by those, very determined and persistent, Italian gentlemen. After serious consideration, I eventually declined their lucrative job offer, explaining to them that I just wanted to go home and re-establish my life and career in Australia. I'd visited the Red Garter several years earlier, as a tourist - when on my epic Contiki tour - and even got up and sang a song with the resident performer. Having seen the style of entertainment required there, I knew it didn't really suit my performing format. The last thing I wanted, after the dismal season I was currently experiencing in Austria, was to go to Italy for the summer and fail there as well! Despite their persistent pleas and increased monetary incentives I stood my ground and managed to halt their badgering by suggesting they employ my good mate, Jus Gordon. They reluctantly agreed to my suggestion only after I promised to bring him to Florence to let them hear him perform. So after contacting Gordon, who was currently in London, I arranged for him to spend a weekend in Florence - when he was due to visit Hopfgarten later in the season. The rest is history - as the two Francos absolutely fell in love with Gordon's entertainment style and continued to employ him for five more years! His tenure at the Red Garter paved the way for other

Newcastle Musician's to perform there, including Jim Overend, Michael Mills and Daniel Arvidson - forging some wonderful, lifelong, international connections and friendships!

That weekend, when Gordon drove me and Jacqui to Florence for his audition, was probably the most enjoyable few days of that disappointing winter - Getting lost on the Italian motorways and Venetian canals, flooding the bathroom of our poorly plumbed hotel room and even loosing Gordon's car in the multi-story parking station near Florence! The hangover I left Florence with - after a night of celebrating Gordon's new gig, drinking Zombies and Black Russians at the Garter - was the worst I'd ever experienced!

Helmut's investment in me that season became a huge deficit as he paid me to play to a handful of people in his bar - while paying high rent on the brand new apartment he'd provided for me and Jacqui. Jacqui became despondent as she spent more time in that apartment because Helmut had no work for her. That, in turn, placed a strain on our relationship. As a consequence, I would go straight back to the apartment after gigs, to keep her company, rather than frequenting the disco's across from the pub. As a result of this, I lost touch with a lot of the locals I had befriended in past seasons. Most hurtful, was being chastised by my old friend, George, the manager of Offenlauch Disco - who had driven me to Munich to smuggle my cassettes over the border. He accused me of "ignoring him, after all he had done for me in the past!". The final humiliation was when I found Helmut commiserating his failed venture while on a bender at The Silver Bullet Bar. As I told him of my decision to return home early I was met with cold indifference as his forlorn gaze never left the beer glass that he was clenching in both hands.

I must've played over ten thousand songs, in my gruelling schedule, throughout the four winters seasons I spent in Hopfgarten. Ninety percent of my heart and soul went into each of those performances. The other ten percent being the alcohol content! The sad truth is knowing I left a big part of myself - in that quaint mountain village - that will live there forever. Leaving a silent void within me that no song can fill.

Just as George Harrison had sung, "All Things Must Pass", my golden times in Hopfgarten were over. It was the saddest way for some of the best times in my life and musical career to end. Hopfgarten - the charming little village nestled in the, fairytale like, Tyrolean Alps - symbolised the freedom of my youth. It was there I was truly free. Living a bohemian lifestyle, free to make music, free to make friends, free to make love, free to make mischief in the snow and free to make a mess of myself on a daily bases for months on end. Although I've smiled many times recalling those magical seasons, the thought of ever returning has filled me with trepidation - unsure of whether I could bare the flood of bitter, sweet memories!

Returning to our repaired but slightly crooked home, and assuming that if our relationship could survive that dismal season abroad it could survive anything, Jacqui and I prepared for married life. We sold the Percy street house, increasing our mortgage for a house in Belmont - that overlooked Belmont Bay, Lake Macquarie.

It was a time of contentment!

Belmont Bay

Green waves, white sales, easterly breeze
ripples the water, shuffles the trees
dangling my toes from the edge of the pier
drifting away
On Belmont Bay

Blue skies, grey clouds, sunshine between
shadows and sloops sailing by on a lean
view from the ridge, ocean blue lake and sky
day after day
on Belmont Bay

Sometimes I feel like a stranger
Sometimes I feel like I've always been here

Salt air, gum trees, blue mountain haze
Green point at sunset on still summer days
bush tracks that lead to the shores of the lake
keep it this way
on Belmont Bay
day after day
on Belmont Bay
drifting away
on Belmont Bay

Domestic Bliss

It was now 1991. We were married and expecting our first child. Suddenly the weight of responsibility dawned on me. It was a comfortable weight and one I felt I was finally prepared to carry. Just as Jacqui was feeling the kicks of our daughter within her womb, I was feeling a new sense of morality kicking into my lifestyle. I slowly began to pull back on social sessions with my friends, particularly if it involved consumption of alcohol and drugs. Not that I was making judgement on my friends but I just wanted to clean my act up in preparation for the arrival of my children. The past ten years of my life had been pretty seedy at times and I just wanted to give my kids the purist possible atmosphere for them to be raised in. This was a very foreign concept for me to implement, and, as my will was very undisciplined, I chose to distance myself from my *partying* friends to avoid the temptation of regressing. These friends were good, well intentioned, people with productive careers who, socially, enjoyed the occasional herbal cigarette or line of nose candy. I was fine with that, having partied often with them over the years. Understandably, some of them took offence to my perceived snub, but I saw it as more of a remedy to a weakness in *my* personalty rather than a flaw in *theirs*.

Making the effort to try and eliminate the toxins we'd been ingesting prior to the term of Jacqui's pregnancy also made me aware of the number of pregnant women I noticed who still smoked cigarettes and drank alcohol. Prompted to take a moral high ground stance, I penned this passive protest song;

Give Me a Chance

*I live inside you curled up and warm
your womb my world until I'm born
You are my keeper, my only friend
just to survive in here on you I depend*

But you're too selfish to change your ways

*'cause from the day I was conceived
I've had to live the life you lead
and cigarettes don't help me breath
and the wine won't help me grow
and though the drugs may ease your mind
they don't make me feel so fine
and if I'm born before my time
I won't be surprised
please open up your eyes
look in the mirror take a second glance
and give me a chance*

*You are my keeper, my only friend
just to survive in here on you I depend*

But you're too selfish to change your ways

*'cause from the day I was conceived
I've had to live the life you lead
and cigarettes don't help me breath
and the wine won't help me grow
and though the drugs may ease your mind
they don't make me feel so fine
and if I'm born deformed or blind
will you handle it
as a mother you're not fit
look in the mirror take a second glance
and give me a chance*

Give me a chance

Sophie and the Seven Dwarfs

The arrival of my first child, Sophie, was an almost surreal experience that transported me into a child's fantasy world while simultaneously terrifying me with the enormous pressure of responsibility that parenthood brings.

The importance of maintaining a regular income from my music was now paramount in order to provide for my family. Every gig had to be a success to ensure being rebooked and I began to book myself months in advance for security and peace of mind. For the first time - since leaving my *stable* office job at the Newcastle Steel works over ten years ago - I sensed the riskiness of my occupation. Although it bolstered my resolve to succeed in the entertainment business it also left an uneasy tingling sensation in the pit of my stomach. The same feeling I imagine a tight rope walker might feel when he performs without a safety net.

I'd always appreciated my career but it's longevity was a much more serious matter now. All this added pressure made me a much more serious person - and the most effective and enjoyable way to relieve that pressure was playing games with my child. The story books, the dress-ups, the make-believing, the tickles and laughter, made me forget the pressure - and took me back to my own idyllic childhood where I had been so content and happy. The wild, irresponsible, days of my bachelorhood certainly took a back-seat now, as, for the first time, I began to feel like a mature adult. That is why it was so significant the day I took Sophie to the Belmont 16foot Sailing Club to see a live performance of Snow White and the Seven Dwarfs. One of those dwarfs, acting in the show, was my old DJ mate from the crazy times when I lived and performed in Sydney. The look of utter surprise and excitement on Sophie's face was priceless as I took her backstage to meet *Scott* and the rest of the cast. Sophie was extremely devoted to childhood fantasy fairytale stories - as her bulging closet of costumes attested to - so meeting those characters, in real life, was almost unbearably fantastic. She literally quivered with delight as the dwarfs cheerily greeted her,

some of whom were barely taller than her! Most surprising, was when Scott suggested I apply for the role of Prince Charming, as *that* cast member was leaving for other work. He assured me I'd be a shoe-in for the part - knowing my singing ability, and - as they where midway through their Australian Tour and had no other options. I declined the offer - having solid bookings of my own for months ahead - and still wonder what direction my career may have taken had I accepted.

It reminded me of when I knocked back my manager's suggestion to take on the role as *Big Dog*, a character in the children's programme "*Romper Room*" at the NBN television studios. I'm sure *that* costume would've been too big for my diminutive stature! Sophie appeared on the show with other infants and I smile now considering that I could've been right there beside her, stumbling around in that big, brown, woolly costume!

It was an absolutely wonderful experience to guide my daughter through her childhood years. Years that, when I recall them, evoke as much sorrow as they do joy. *Joy* for the privilege and fun it was to be there with her and *sorrow* that they are gone, forever. My initiation into fatherhood left me with more questions than answers and more doubts than confidence but I vainly hope that Sophie considered me to be her *fatherly* Prince Charming and Hero. Literally taking on that *actual role* in the Snow *White Pantomime*, however, may have been taking *that* concept just a little too far!

Up until then, my life had been a dress rehearsal. Sophie's birth raised the curtain on the *real* show.

Sophie

Third of December, Nineteen ninety one
made me a father and my wife a mum
She made her debut on this stage of life
I wiped the tears away and hugged my wife

I cut the chord and blessed that day
clear in my mind just like yesterday
She came on stage into this show of mine
Her name in lights just like her eyes that shine

Sophie, beautiful Sophie
We made you
made me so happy

Her opening number was a baby's cry
so sweet the melody it captivated me
showed me how good life could be
just bouncing on my knee

Sophie, beautiful Sophie
We made you
made me so happy

Third of December that each new year will bring
I'll light a candle, just for her I'll sing

Sophie, beautiful Sophie
We made you
made me so happy

One Day Away

So there it was. The seemingly impossible had occurred. I had started my own family.

What surprised me *most* was how comfortable it made me feel. My family and home became my comfort zone and the most valued possession of my life.

We were lucky that my performance income was enough to allow Jacqui to give up her job and become a *full-time mum* and I was privileged to be like a *stay-at-home dad,* only leaving the house to go off to my gigs, usually after our baby was in bed for the night. I had an abundance of solo work in local venues as well as weekly gigs with the Tex Pistols and was in the process of recording my next album. Life was good.

Everything was rosy. In fact, the only aspect of my life that did cause me some discomfort was when I had to leave my cosy home to perform out of town for a few days. I had established a regular schedule of gigs further afield of Newcastle, which included the upper Hunter and New England districts as well as further Northwest out as far as Cobar. These gigs were useful as promotional tours allowing me to trial the new songs going on my album as well as sell my previous recordings. These mini tours were also extremely profitable, sometimes earning me as much as $500 per night with meals and accommodation included. The average solo performers fee, at that time, was somewhere between $150 and $200 so it was well worth my while to hit the road.

In order to keep the family together while I traversed the countryside, I bought a small, pop-top, caravan, allowing me to take my wife and child with me. The caravan gave those work trips more of a holiday feel but it wasn't without it's share of dramas. Like the night we almost froze in it, camping on the outskirts of Armidale in June. The morning after performing at the Wicklow Hotel, shivering our way through a bitterly cold night, we woke to find one of Sophie's fury toys was stuck to the wall with ice that completely lined the vans interior. Subsequently, I didn't always take the family away with me and that's how this song came to be written - while driving the straight, flat, roads near Werris Creek, flanked by endless golden acres of sunflowers.

One Day Away

*One day away from my love
is one day too long from my love
One cold night in a lonely hotel room
one thought to hold while I dream
just to know I'll be home soon*

*One day away from my home
is the longest day I have known
Mile after mile of these New England farms
one day away when I'll be lying in your arms*

*One day away from my love
I'm just one day away from my love
one country mile is like a million more to me
one country smile of goodbye
oh how I miss my family
one day away*

Scottish Superstition

As a young man, my father's father left the town of Dunfermline, Scotland, to come out to Australia in 1912. Twenty three years after settling down in the small mining town of Greta, NSW, where he married and reared seven children, he died in a tragic and mysterious drowning accident. My own father, being an infant at the time, had little chance of getting to know him. Discovering this sad part of my family's history helped me to appreciate the struggles my dad must have faced as a boy, that moulded him into the stoic man he became. It possibly also explained the loving but awkward relationship that existed between us.

As the birth of my second child approached I vowed to myself that if it was a boy, I would strive to make *this father-son relationship* a closer one than in the preceding two generations. I clearly remember the disappointment I felt as a child, the day my father was about to take me fishing in the river at Morpeth on his friend's boat but I fell ill. He sat by my bedside for the rest of the day promising to take me fishing another time, but that opportunity never arose. That's why I had a standard reply to enquiries as to the sex of the – soon to be born - baby..."well if it's a boy, I'll have someone to go fishing with!".

Having written a song to celebrate the birth of my *first* child, I had set a precedent that would be unfair to my *second* child if he wasn't dedicated a song as well. Up until the day of his birth, I had no idea what theme that song would have. That was until the midwife assisting in the delivery handed me my son,

cocooned in a blanket, and spoke to me in a broad Scottish accent. She explained to me that while she was cleaning the baby, after the birth, she had to remove a thin membrane - residue from the birthing sack - from his face and head. This membrane or caul, as she called it, was considered by Scottish fishermen to be a sign of good luck. Most surprising was that she asked me if I wanted to keep *it* as a good luck charm - which was also a common practise back in her homeland. I thanked her, but declined the offer, content in knowing I finally had the theme for my *son's song*;

Fishin' With Jack

How much better does it get?
You say I ain't seen nothin' yet
I've seen enough to be content
and thank my lucky stars for what they have sent

I've travelled far and I've survived
and now I feel like I've arrived
there's only one place left I know
where every son and father one day should go

I'm goin' fishin', fishin' with Jack
I'm gonna wear my lucky fishin' hat
Jack's goin' fishin' with me
we'll drop a line where the fish are gonna be

Out in our boat we'll cast away
Off Fishing Point or Wangi Bay
or Swansea channel on a drift
when I get down one thought will give me a lift

I'm goin' fishin', fishin' with Jack
I'm gonna wear my lucky fishin' hat
Jack's goin' fishin' with me
we'll drop a line where the fish are gonna be

How much better could it be
a rockin' boat, the salt and sea
Jack's a lucky fisherman I'm told
But I'm gonna have to wait and see
He's only two days old

I'm goin' fishin', fishin' with Jack
I'm gonna wear my lucky fishin' hat
Jack's goin' fishin' with me
we'll drop a line where the fish are gonna be

Meg & me at Poley's property at Barrington near Gloucester

Man's Best Friend

Keeping in line with the fishing theme, a vivid memory springs to mind of a sunny day out, on our recently acquired, twenty seven foot, steel motor/sail yacht, fishing near Pulba Island in Lake Macquarie. It was before our children were born, so it was just me and Jacqui and her large, ungainly, black Labrador retriever who answered to the impressive title of *"Benson"*.

Benson was part of the package when I moved in with Jacqui, and instantly became my permanent shadow. He was the first pet dog I'd owned since loosing *Zeus*, my bitsa poodle, back in high school days. Weighing well over thirty kilograms, he was an awkward passenger, especially when it came to transferring him from the tender to the yacht. A back breaking exercise, as I wrapped my arms around his four legs and lifted him from the dinghy onto the transom at the stern of the yacht. This risky manoeuvre was attempted several times, embarking and disembarking for the voyage, as well as when he needed to go ashore during overnight stays, to do his business. To his credit, he only once defecated on the deck of the boat, and that was because I refused his constant barking pleas to take him ashore because I was in bed, trying to sleep.

On *this* particular outing, after having no luck with the fishing and opting to weigh anchor to head for home, Benson decided to help himself to the piece of squid that I'd left dangling on the hook from my fishing line. The shock and horror I felt as I turned to see him chomping on his tasty treat was only matched by the look of distress in his eyes as the large hook embedded itself somewhere at the back of his throat. My mind raced and my heart ached as he writhed and gagged - trying to cough out the sharp piece of steel - knowing we were hours away from the nearest veterinary clinic. In those seconds of seeing him in so much discomfort, I loudly berated myself for leaving the bait on the hook where he could get to it, and knew that it was up to me to help the poor suffering creature. That's when I pried his jaws open, and, following the fishing line with my fingers, manoeuvred my hand to the very back of his tongue where I felt the hook firmly dug in to the flesh. My immediate instinct was to pull the hook toward me, but the blood chilling groan from Benson, as the barb dug in further, stopped me. That, and the searing pain I felt on my wrist as his jaws and teeth clamped down in reflex, made me reverse my action and push the hook further down his throat. It was a sickening moment as he gagged and convulsed with half my arm lodged in his mouth but it worked and the hook mercifully dislodged.

That traumatic incident was a strong bonding moment between me and Benson. As he gently licked the slime and saliva from my hand, as if to show his gratitude, I had no idea what an integral part of my life and family he would become in the following years. Apart from being a companion and playmate for me and my kids, he became their guardian when I was away on tours.

Benson lived a long and comfortable life

Sea dogs - Me & Benson on Lake Macquarie

with us and passed away, peacefully, in the care of my father-in-law, while we were away on holidays. A sad event for which I'm grateful that I and my family were spared the grief of being present. Dave, who was elderly and quite frail, had the unenviable task of digging the large hole in our backyard and burying Benson. We planted a tree in that spot to honour him.

Years later, when *that* tree was quite large and my kids were young adults, I found myself digging another hole under it. This time it was to bury the dog we had rescued from the pound, as a puppy, to replace Benson. We named her Meg. She was a Border Collie, and, true to her breed, she used to round-up the kids in the back yard when they were toddlers, like a sheep dog would do with her flock. Meg was, absolutely, *one of the family* and literally helped me raise my kids - especially through the dark years when my marriage disintegrated. Little wonder that I, unashamedly, bawled my eyes out as Sophie helped me lay Meg in that hole - sobbing as I shovelled the soil and vowing that; "she would be the last pet dog I would ever own".

Although I wrote this song, in mind, for Benson, my heart will always dedicate it to Meg.

One of the Family

Let me tell you 'bout a friend of mine
a better friend I'll never know
He's been with me for a long long time
and we've got a long time to go

'cause he's one of the family
more than a friend to me
yes he's one of the family
he's part of the family tree

I trust him with my wife and children
and he protects them when I'm gone
and late at night when I return to them
he's there to welcome me home

'cause he's one of the family
more than a friend to me
yes he's one of the family
he's part of the family tree

I almost forgot to mention
he's one of a kind our Benson
and I am a firm believer
that man's best friend
is a Labrador Retriever

'cause he's one of the family
more than a friend to me
yes he's one of the family
he's part of the family tree

The Valley album

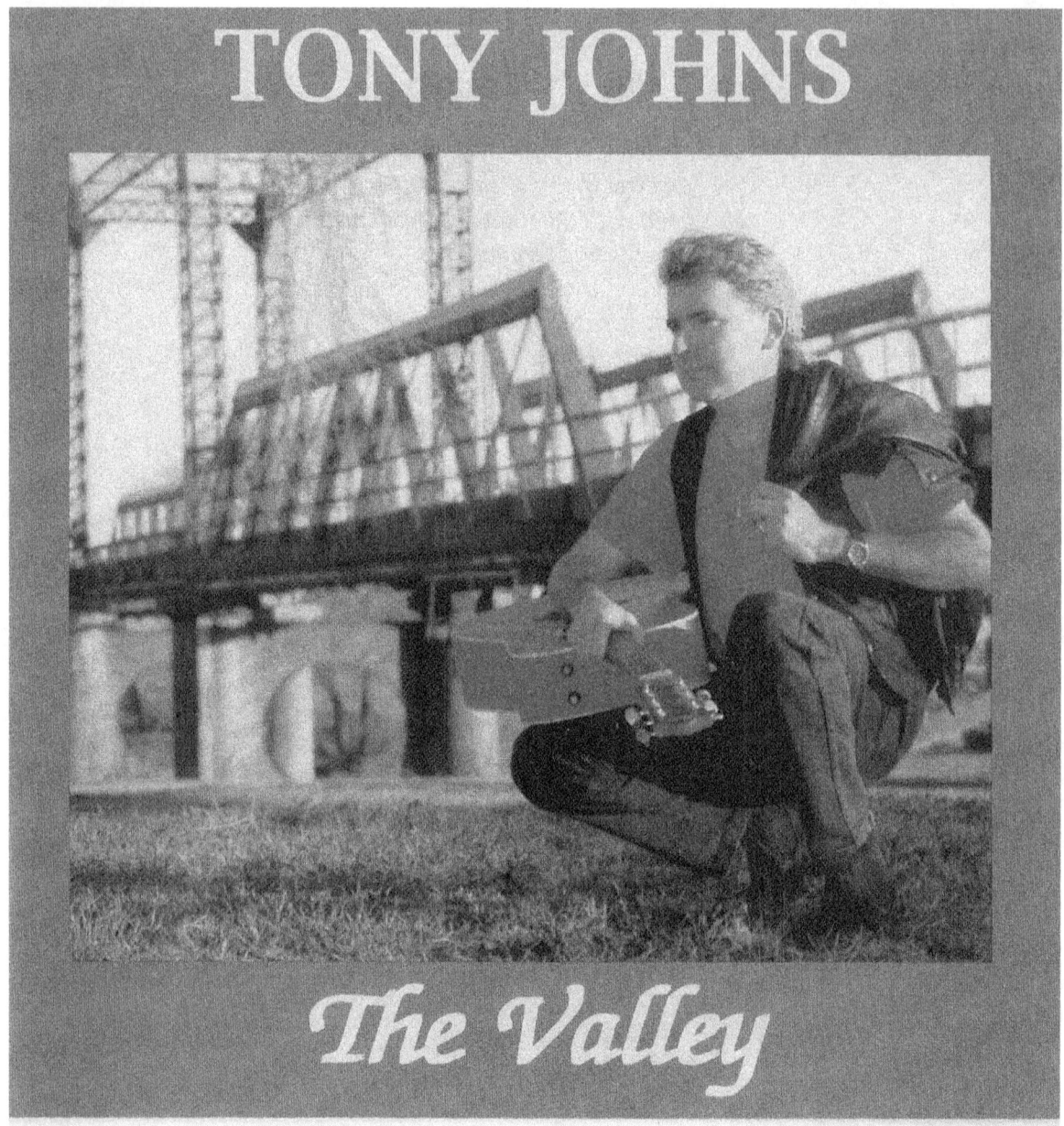

One of the most pivotal and significant years in my life was 1994.

As my thirty sixth birthday approached I had the firm impression that all aspects of my life were finally in order. I felt it was *my time*, as if the planets had all aligned for me. My personal life was wholesome and productive, happily married with two beautiful children and making plans for a third. Financially, I was earning a good, steady, income, so much so that I was well ahead in my home loan repayments and had even taken out a second mortgage on an investment property. A remarkable achievement, having recently endured *the,* Paul Keating's, "Recession we had to have" and home loan interest rates of 17%! Professionally, I was still firmly entrenched in the local music scene, performing up to five nights a week in and around Newcastle as well as regularly touring throughout country regions in NSW.

One resident gig in Newcastle, at a venue called The Crazy Cow, was paying me $300 per night, which was twice the average fee paid to soloists at that time. It was a restaurant/bar annexed to the Sydney Junction Hotel, in Hamilton, that had a casual, *Tex/Mex,* western style theme. It was furnished with solid, rough sawn bench design tables and chairs that I often walked on while performing. As I sang and played guitar, I carefully stepped between the diners meals and drinks, crushing the peanut shells, under my boots, that the customers were encouraged to discard on the tables and floor. *That gig* was one of my favourites, as the management appreciated my inclusive style of entertainment - wandering through the room and adjoining beer garden, equipped with my wireless microphone and guitar - actively engaging with the patrons and enticing them to become part of my performance. It was reminiscent of the antics I got up to when I performed in Austria at Helmut's Pub and my intention was to make it part of my act in all the venues that I played back at home.

That plan completely backfired on me the

All songs written by Tony Johns

TONY JOHNS:	*Lead vocals*
RITA SCOTT:	*Backing vocals*
TONY JOHNS:	*Acoustic guitar*
IAN LEES:	*Bass guitar*
MICHEL ROSE:	*Pedal steel & Dobro*
WAYNE GOODWIN:	*Fiddle & Mandolin*
MARK TINSON:	*Mandolin*
GARY WILSON:	*Drums*
TONY AZZAPARDI:	*Percussion*
TONY JOHNS:	*Harmonica*
WAYNE GOODWIN:	*String arrangements (on "Somewhere")*

Produced and recorded by MARK TINSON at OVERHEAD STUDIOS, NEWCASTLE
Mastered by DON BARTLEY at STUDIO 301

"The Valley was inspired by my wife and children and the beautiful life we have in the Hunter Valley."

Special thanks to MARK TINSON, without whose help these songs would be nothing but notes in my scrapbook!

Tony Johns Aug. '94

Cover photos - MICHAEL BROWN

day I was booked for a lunchtime show at The Buttai Barn, another rustic venue located on a property near Kurri Kurri that had more of a traditional Australian Outback theme. On *that* occasion my audience was a bus-load of senior citizen women, some quite frail, who almost had heart failure when I jumped up on their dining table to serenade them. Unbeknown to me, the tables, disguised by large white paper clothes, were merely planks resting on folding trestles, so as I stepped onto one end, the other end rose up like a see-saw, hurling plates and food and drinks into the air and showering down on the unsuspecting sea of blue rinse hairdo's below me. Needless to say, it was my *last* solo performance at Buttai Barn. I returned many years later to perform in my *duo* at a wedding and was re-acquainted with the manager/owner who promptly advised me to refrain from walking on the tables!

My regular stream of solo work and weekly gigs with the Tex Pistols enabled me to finance my *next* album. A collection of original songs that I'd been working on with Mark Tinson for the last few years and was finally ready to release. Tinno and I had carefully chosen the songs for the album to fit in with the theme of *my life and family - living in the Hunter Valley*. I called the album "The Valley" which featured songs from my past, such as; *Back in the Hunter Valley* and *The way I live*, right up to my latest works, such as; *Fishin' With Jack* and *Belmont Bay*. The album effectively encapsulated my life and career over the previous fifteen years and was, by far, my best work to date.

The quality of the album was undoubtedly due to Tinno's engineering and production skills - at his home studio in Cook's Hill - as well as his recruiting and conducting prowess in mustering the team of gifted session musicians who provided the magical backing music.

The studio musicians - that any artist would give there right arm to perform with - included;

Ian Lees on bass guitar[*Moving Pictures*], Gary Wilson on drums[*Lonnie Donegan band*], Wayne Goodwin(RIP) on fiddle, mandolin & strings[*Emmylou Harris band*], Michel Rose on pedal steel & dobro[*The Catholics*], Tony Azzapardi on percussion[*Doug Parkinson band*], Rita Scott on backing vocals[*JAB*] and Mark Tinson on mandolin[*Heroes*].

The final touch on the album was provided by my good mate, Michael Brown, who took the beautiful photos of the historic bridges at Hinton and Morpeth - not far from where I grew up - to grace the cover.

I released the album in August 1994 on CD and cassette and it was well received by the country music community, especially after radio presenter, Nick Erby, played it on his syndicated country music programme, allowing it to be heard right throughout Australia on dozens of community based radio stations. Some of the songs on the album won song writing awards in regional contests around Australia and New Zealand and also earned me a finalist place in the TIARA Awards in Tamworth that year.

The Valley album truly represented my singing/song-writing career up to that point and is still one of my proudest achievements. Most rewarding is, even after 26 years, when I hear that one of my songs from *that* album is *still* receiving airplay. A recent phone call from a presenter on a Brisbane community radio station, requesting to buy my album, is testament to this.

My home in Crown street, Belmont - situated on a high ridge that ran west and down to Green Point - had a magnificent view looking south over lake Macquarie all the way down to Gwandalan and south-est toward Swansea Channel and out to the Pacific Ocean. At night, lying in bed, I could look out the large bedroom window at the stars and moon, just like I had done, as a child, at my grandmother's house. I suppose it was my way of praying and giving thanks for the wonderful life I had - as I lay there gazing at the night sky until I fell asleep. Time could have frozen at that point - and I would've been content.

Things couldn't get any better.

I'm Satisfied

I look up to Heaven and the soft starlight
'till sleep comes drifting
and I dream all night
morning greets me with a sky of blue
I watch another sunrise
and see my dreams come true

I'm content here where I stand
I've made my peace with who I am
I could have more if I tried
but there's no need
çause I'm satisfied

I spent my life searching for a pot of gold
but the colours of the rainbow
were washed out and old
funny how I found it in that clear blue morn'
it had always been there
since the day I was born

I'm content here where I stand
I've made my peace with who I am
I could have more if I tried
but there's no need
çause I'm satisfied

If I could climb a mountain
if I could reach the top
It doesn't mean I'd be any closer to God

I'm content here where I stand
I've made my peace with who I am
I could have more if I tried
but there's no need
çause I'm satisfied

Circle of Life

As my life and career steadily and happily ploughed through 1995 the *euphoria* I experienced at the birth of my third child, [Brady], in October, was matched only by the *anxiety* I felt for the recent diagnosis of Mesothelioma in my father.

The ironies and contradictions in life were never made more obvious to me than the day I watched my ailing father cradle my one day old son in his thinning arms, knowing that, once again in my family, this child would never get to know his grandfather.

Despite his failing health, my father's stoic and nonchalant demeanour ensured that the celebration of Brady's arrival into the world was a joyous one. A beautiful baby, in perfect health, with two inquisitive and loving siblings as well as doting parents and grandparents, Brady had it all!

The only thing he didn't have at this point was a song from me. Having written songs to celebrate the births of his sister and brother I now felt myself under pressure to come up with a tune to honour this new family member. The stark contrast of seeing Brady surrounded by so much love and affection in his first hours of the wonderful life that lay ahead of him, in the arms of my father who was preparing to loose everything, painfully provided the song's theme to me.

I'm sure I'm not the first son to say that his father was the hardest person to buy gifts for. Dad seemed to have all he wanted in life; his car, a few tools in the shed to tinker with, a bet on a Saturday morning at the TAB and a few beers at the Windsor Castle Hotel, and he was happy. That made Christmas shopping an impossible task as I struggled to pick him a gift that he could use. I still have a fishing rod and toolbox in my garage that I bought for him and he never used! He was the epitome of the cliché..."what do you buy for someone who has everything?" It was that phrase that came to mind as I gazed into my new son's blue eyes, the same striking blue as my father's - and Brady's song proceeded to write itself.

Someone Who's Got It All

Blue eyes from his father
his mother's pride and joy
an angel wrapped in linen
balloons saying "it's a boy!"

Birthday cards and flowers
on the bassinet and pram
blue bear from his sister
little brother holds his hand

What do you give to someone
who's got everything he'll ever need?
to take what the world has to offer
and go wherever life may lead
What do you give to someone
who leaves you feeling ten feet tall?
Love is all you can give
to someone who's got it all
Love is all you can give
to someone who's got it all

Photographs and heirlooms
Heaven blessed by Aunty Fran
the sweetest new born babe
and he's Nana's little man

And Brady is maybe the luckiest one
Surrounded by so much affection love and fun
and his life has just begun!

What do you give to someone
who's got everything he'll ever need?
to take what the world has to offer
and go wherever life may lead
What do you give to someone
who leaves you feeling ten feet tall?
Love is all you can give
to someone who's got it all
Love is all you can give
to someone who's got it all

Tree Change?

So there we were. The five of us and our dog. In the house overlooking the lake, with the pool and cubbyhouse in the backyard. *His* and *Her* cars in the driveway, parked next to the wheely bins. The yacht moored near the Sixteen Foot Sailing club just down the road. The investment property, slowly gaining value, a few blocks away in central Belmont near the Coles supermarket where we did our weekly shopping. *That* was our domesticated life. Our contented and happy existence - living in the '*burbs* -... Or was it?

Not that we weren't grateful for our wonderful lifestyle. After all, how could it get any better? It was our kids future that had us concerned. The increasing urban population, sadly, saw the parcel of bushland at the end of our street being bulldozed for a new housing estate which became the theme of my next song, called, "*Walkin' Track*". *That*, and the increasing crime statistics, began to make us question the quality of life our children would have growing up here. So, we started considering a move to the country.

I suppose being an idealist isn't all that bad, but I suspect my vision of country life was more influenced by TV shows such as "Green Acres" than from any practical knowledge of farm management. Still, the thought of giving our children an upbringing in clean, fresh air, surrounded by farm animals and wide open spaces, was an admirable objective. Which is why we began searching for *our* country Shangri-La.

We knew the sale of our house and investment property would see us in the market for a small acreage, house and barn, somewhere in the hinterland of the Newcastle region. Location that would have little effect on the mileage I was already clocking up travelling to my gigs. I figured that my musical income would still support us even if I couldn't manage to derive an income from my property, so out we went to look.

We spent days, sometimes weeks, travelling around and camping in the countryside, to properties in Mulbring and Stroud, and as far away as Dubbo. Although we never committed to the move, they were, at the least, wonderful family outings.

The whole idea and experience was great fodder for a song that I was writing to add to the collection for my *next* album. An album I was aiming at the Australian country music market even though I didn't consider myself to be a country singer. I referred to my style of songwriting as "suburban country", and this song was my way of saying...."you don't have to be a cowboy to sing country songs". Tinno and I were close to completing *this album* in his studio at that time. A wonderful time, that, had I known was soon to come to an end, I may have spent more time in the studio and less in the country-side!

Tradin' Places

I never rode a horse, I never milked a cow
I couldn't shear a sheep and I wouldn't work a plough
but I'm movin' out of town çause I need a little space
and I wanna raise my kids far from this rat race

So I'm...tradin' places with the land
leavin' suburbia when I can
tradin' my back yard for those wide open spaces
movin' out and I'm tradin' places

But I've got to mow the lawn and weed beside the fence
suburban rituals that just don't make much sense
like takin' out the garbage and bringin' it back in
man I tell ya where I'm goin', aint no question..."where's ya bin?"

So I'm...tradin' places with the land
leavin' suburbia when I can
tradin' my back yard for those wide open spaces
movin' out and I'm tradin' places

There'll be a dam to replace the swimmin' pool
muddy eels and yabbies in the creek
there'll be a river on the south boundary
so I can still go fishin' once a week

Well I know it won't be easy, I've got my work cut out
everything to learn 'bout nothin' I know much about
but I read the magazines "First Farmer" right through
and they tell me how they did it
Lord and tell me I should do it too!

So I'm...tradin' places with the land
leavin' suburbia when I can
tradin' my back yard for a paddock full of spaces
movin' out and I'm tradin' places

Movin' out and I'm tradin' places

Hard [studio] Time

[Top left] Dad at Greta

I was surprised by my reaction the day my father died.

As I, my mother and sisters, sat at my fathers bedside in our family home, assisted by a registered nurse, we said our goodbyes and watched him breath his last breath. It was at that moment the sadness and grief, that had been churning inside me since hearing of my father's fatal diagnosis, was replaced by a strangely beautiful and calming feeling of peace. It was as if I was experiencing the release of the pain he had endured over the previous months and I was glad he was finally free of all his worldly suffering. It was an almost euphoric sensation - that confused me to the point of guilt - which I eventually passed off as my minds way of dealing with the loss of my father. A father who I never really knew all that well and who, now, I never would.

Visiting my father in the weeks leading up to *that* day, I struggled to connect with him in intimate conversation. Both of us had always been awkward in *that* way. The bond and love had always been there, just not in a verbal format. It was usually expressed in a practical way, like when we worked together on servicing my first car or renovating my first home, or repairing and painting my yacht. *They* were thoughtful occasions of few words but full of love - in actions. My last recollection of one such action is of helping him change a washer on a leaking tap in his bathroom. It broke my heart to see this, once so strong and powerful, man barely able to turn the wrench to loosen the nut on the tap - so I completed the job for him. Every washer I've changed since that day reminds me of our

Dad at the Newcastle Floating Dock

delicate filial relationship.

In the weeks leading up to his death in February, 1996, I resolved to honour him with a song that I planned to sing at his funeral. I wrote the song on my yacht. The same yacht, that only months earlier, he had helped me paint at the Green point slipways in Belmont. I treasure the photo I have of him standing on scaffolding with a paint brush, gingerly reaching up to paint the gunnel's - the weight loss, from his illness, unmistakeable.

I completed the song just days before he passed and my plan of singing it for him at his bedside was abandoned, particularly as I couldn't even rehearse *it* without breaking down in tears. *That* made the idea of performing the song at his funeral even more unlikely, as I knew I'd be too overwhelmed with emotion to sing. My only alternative was to record the song and play the CD at the church service.

Once again, my mentor and friend, Mark Tinson, came to my rescue in this urgent matter. Being an old family friend, it was particularly relevant to have his involvement. The very next

Mum & Dad

The whole family at Pam's wedding

day, after I had *said* goodbye to my father, I was in Tinno's studio *singing* my goodbye. *Singing*, might not be the apt word to describe my performance in the studio that day. I tended to blubber and choke up through each line, trying to suppress my raw emotions. It was difficult for me and undoubtedly an uncomfortable experience for Mark. Avoiding contact with my tear filled eyes, he quietly sat slumped over the controls, elbows on the desk, with his forehead cradled in the palms of his hands. I was sorry to put him through such a grinding and deeply personal task but he graciously endured the session. He even composed and played some mandolin to give the song a decorative and sensitive touch of class.

I completely broke down when the song was played over the PA at the funeral service - justifying my decision not to perform it live. Afterwards, at the wake, many of dad's friends and co-workers from the dockyards complimented me on the song and asked where they could purchase a copy of it. Although flattering, it felt extremely inappropriate to be discussing marketing at such an occasion. It would be another twenty years before I would release it for sale. Over that time, many of those fellow workers also contracted and died of *Mesothelioma* - due to coming into contact with asbestos while working at the dockyards. Compensation was available for sufferers of this insidious disease, and, as sick as my father was in the last few months of his life, he diligently attended legal proceedings to expedite *financial support* for my mother after his death. In years to come, when I fell on hard times, my mother passed on *that* support to *me*, making me feel as though my father never really left me. Always there by my side, looking out for me.

Tribute

Just an ordinary man
a worker all his life
provider for his children
life partner for his wife
I took so much for granted about this hard but loving man
and never knew that one day
I'd be as grateful as I am

And this is my tribute
it was easier this way
to open up my heart to him before he goes away
'cause there's no one else quite like him
in all the world there's only one
he is my father, I am his son

Such a thoughtful easy man
it comes as no surprise
It's like looking in a mirror when I look into his eyes
There are mysteries about him
things I'll never know
but all men have their secrets
to take with them when they go

And this is my tribute
it was easier this way
to open up my heart to him before he goes away
'cause there's no one else quite like him
in all the world there's only one
he is my father, I am his son

The scars will fade like the time we had
but there's time to say...
I love you Dad

Just an ordinary man
a worker all his days
He's done his best
he's earned his rest, respect and praise

And this is my tribute
it was easier this way
to open up my heart to him before he goes away
'cause there's no one else quite like him
in all the world there's only one
he is my father, I am his son

He is my father and I'm proud to be his son

"The human voice is the organ of the soul."
(Henry Wadsworth Longfellow)

Chapter 5
1998-2018

From Dream to Nightmare

Spasmodic Dysphonia

The loss of my father served to strengthen my resolve to live up to the role of patriarch in my family and I continued to plough into my work. I had a solid schedule of gigs booked up to twelve months in advance and was nearing the completion of my next album. By 1997 all that was needed to complete the album was to record my lead vocals. That never happened!

During the latter half of that year I began to notice small breaks in my voice while I was performing. The unusual aspect of these "breaks" was that they occurred, predominantly, in songs that I'd always found easy to sing. Songs that only required the use of the mid range of my vocal scale, the range that my talking voice would use.

The audio effect of these "breaks" was similar to my microphone cutting out for a second, then cutting back in. The best, visual, way of describing it, is to imagine the words I was singing as bold print but some letters were missing. The letters missing [or cutting out] were usually the vowels in a word but as 1998 approached, whole words began to drop out. My voice simply locked up and wouldn't allow them to come out of my throat. The whole phenomenon was painless but it did feel like invisible hands inside my throat were choking the flow of my speech. Eventually I did begin to experience discomfort as I attempted to force the words through the perceived blockage by Belting out the song - which did work but which was extremely physically tiring and often ruined the song's delivery. My constant use of *that* technique eventually caused a cyst to form on one of my vocal chords which did require surgery to be removed. Still, the underlying cause remained.

I was forced to abandon my solo singing career in February 1998. That's when the disorder also began to affect my talking voice, disrupting my communication with my audience, which, for me, was the most crucial feature of my act. The location of the last two venues I performed at was significant. One was just down the road from where I began my musical journey, with my friend Helen, in the Cessnock vineyards, and the other was just down the road from the BHP steelworks, where I'd left my "*Day Job*" to follow my musical dream.

That "*Dream*" began to disintegrate into a *nightmare* over the next few years. As I sort treatment for this strange affliction some of the best E.N.T. specialists couldn't give me a

FEATURE
weekender.

Johns rediscovers his voice naturally

BY JOSH LEESON

LOSING his singing voice almost cost Tony Johns everything. His passion, his career and eventually his confidence.

Back in 1997 the then 40-year-old folk singer was one of the most accomplished performers on the Newcastle music scene. The Arcadia Vale resident's albums *The Way I Live* (1988) and *The Valley* (1994) had sold reasonably and his tracks *Campin in the Barringtons* and *Fishin' With Jack* received radio airplay.

Just when Johns was preparing to complete his third album *Natural*, a touching tribute to his contented family life as the father of three young children, everything suddenly turned upside down. The onset of spasmodic dysphonia, quickly ended his profitable singing career and shelved the recording plans for *Natural*.

Spasmodic dysphonia is a voice disorder where involuntary movements or spasms occur in the larynx muscles during speech.

"I just had to go out and do whatever I could, which was labouring," Johns says. "I had two mortgages at the time. I had to sell one to cover the cost of the other one. I had three young kids in school. I had no skills or qualifications in anything else and the voice problem affected my confidence as well. It was like my Achilles heel.

"I thought about going to uni, but I couldn't focus on anything. I was too shot and devastated."

Johns eventually returned to music purely as a guitarist, playing in the well-known duo Empty Pockets with Emil Matla.

Along the way he valiantly tried to restore his singing voice through speech therapy, learning relaxation techniques and even receiving botox injections into his vocal chords.

"I tried that with the doctor once. You get an injection through your throat and you're awake and he says, 'Now try and sing a note so I know the needle is going through your vocal chord muscle'," Johns says. "If he misses you feel all the fluid flowing down your throat.

"I did it once and for the first three weeks I had no voice whatsoever. I was completely mute and then when it came back it worked. I sang my heart out for two weeks and did four gigs, but then it went away again."

While Johns' voice has never returned, his music refused to die. After constant encouragement from good friend and renowned Newcastle musician and producer Mark Tinson, *Natural* was finally completed and released in November.

Four of the 13 tracks used Johns' voice recorded in the 90s before he suffered spasmodic dysphonia, while Newcastle musicians Kevin Bennett, Brien McVernon, Michael Hawke, Peter DeJong, Justin Ngariki, Julie Wilson and Ty Penshorn provided vocals for the remaining songs.

Johns' 25-year-old daughter Sophie Gibbons also made her recording debut singing the title track.

"To have Sophie singing was the cream on the cake," he says. "She really changed the tone of that song with her voice and I never imagined hearing it like that, but I wouldn't want to hear it any other way now."

Johns says *Natural* was always "unfinished business" and its release has helped the healing process.

"It's such a good feeling to have the songs out there," he says. "It's not going to resurrect my career, but it's going to help those songs have a life of their own."

Tony Johns and friends will launch *Natural* at Lizotte's on February 2.

SURVIVOR: A throat disorder ended Tony Johns' singing career, but it hasn't prevented him from finally releasing his third album. Picture: Simone De Peak

---

definitive diagnosis. It would be almost ten years later, after countless treatments and procedures, both medical and psychological, before it was finally assessed as Spasmodic Dysphonia - a neurological disease that causes spasms in the vocal chords, for which there is currently no known cure!

The realisation of knowing my singing career was over had a crippling effect on me. It wasn't that I considered myself a great singer. It was more the fact that the immensely pleasurable and lucrative career that I'd established over the past twenty years was now gone. Over. In ruins! And I was lost for ideas on how to replace it and support my family. Already suffering severe anxiety and depression at my situation, the new voice that Spasmodic Dysphonia had given me was strained and shakey, which, when I spoke, only served to compound my lack of confidence.

Have you ever had those nightmares where you're in mortal danger and you open your mouth to scream for help but no sound comes out?... I was living that nightmare!

The human voice is the organ of the soul. [Henry Wadsworth Longfellow]

As a child, I had a reoccurring dream that I could fly. In those dreams I would float upwards from the backyard of my home in View street and drift across the neighbourhood, hoovering above the other houses and backyards. They were the best dreams, giving me the wonderful sensation of total freedom. Those dreams became less frequent as I grew into adulthood but I could still access that feeling of freedom - when I sang. I was a capable vocalist but I knew I wasn't particularly outstanding. The crucial aspect of singing, for me, was that it gave me wings. It allowed me to fly, to soar above the world and all it's worries. That was the magical allure and reward that singing held for me. It connected me. To God - the universe. To life. To myself. To my soul.

When Spasmodic Dysphonia took away *my* voice - leaving me with *it's* grotesque substitute - it broke all those connections. Most significantly, the one to my soul. I lost myself. My Identity. My Mojo. I lost my way. I lost my ability to fly. My wings had been cut and I fell back to earth with an impact that shattered me into a thousand pieces, like a scattered jig-saw puzzle.

I was broken and also ashamed at how completely I crumbled. It was as if my voice was my Achilles heel that the voice disorder had targeted. A seemingly minor health issue that absolutely rendered me inadequate and impotent. I constantly reminded and berated myself that, apart from a stuttery and hoarse voice, I was in perfectly good health and in the prime of my life. That I would find another direction in life and career that didn't rely on singing or the use of my voice. Those thoughts kept me *afloat* for the next twenty years - but that was all. Just treading water - never really propelling myself toward a specific destination or goal. That part of me - the source of motivation and aspiration - had died, or, at the least, had fallen into some sort of deep coma. I actually felt like I *had* died and was simply existing as some sort of ghost or zombie in my earthly body. I stopped socialising because - apart from the *physical* difficulty in talking with people - I began to feel like I was invisible. As if I was an imposter, lacking substance. A dead man walking among the living. I often wondered if I'd gone mad but reassured myself that..."mad people don't know they're mad!". It was *that* logic that kept me functioning for the next two decades. Keeping darker thoughts - such as suicide - at bay, allowing me to stumble through the fog of my life until it slowly began to lift.

The greatest tragedy of all, at this time, was the disintegration of my family. As *I* fell apart, so did my marriage. This resulted in my children becoming transient visitors, spending equal amounts of time between mine and their mother's house. It was an amicable arrangement, but a situation I never imagined for my kids - and one for which I've barely forgiven myself.

I couldn't hide my utter devastation the day I told my mother of my marriage breakup. Sobbing uncontrollably, with my head buried in her shoulder. Holding me in her arms, I could

Academic, Sophie

the bullet had mortally wounded my soul. As always, my mother was full of compassion and support. Always the perfect mix of common sense and empathy, her support through those darkest years of my life saved me from certain, absolute, ruin. I'd always been very close to my mother. I could talk to her about almost anything and what I didn't tell her, she instinctively knew anyway. To me, she'd always been the *perfect* mother and never more so than at that painful time in my life.

I take heart in knowing that those days and nights my children *stayed-over* with me, were some of the best memories I have of their childhood. Making the most of our limited time together, we played games and music and watched movies.

It was the nights they *weren't* with me, as I almost feel *her* heart breaking as she tried, in vain, to console me. To see me loose the two greatest passions in my life - my music and then my family - was just as heartbreaking for her as it was for me. I remember trying to explain to her how this calamity in my life was affecting me - how I couldn't taste the flavour in food any more, or see the beauty in nature or hear melody in music - and how her silent embrace calmed me and assured me things would eventually improve. That pathetic scene is burnt into my memory and will haunt me forever. It was the lowest point of my life. I was shattered and helpless. I was *that* little boy in the backyard, crying to my mother after the assassin had shot me in the foot with his slug gun. Only this time

Musician, Brady

Drift Car Racer, Jack

wandered through their darkened rooms, sitting on their empty beds, that tortured and haunted me most.

My kids are all adults now, each following productive paths in life. I'd been told to make the most of their childhood years because they go so fast. In my confused and anxious state, my kids went from toddlers to teenagers in the blink of an eye. Those years are such a blurred memory now, that I often question if my involvement in their lives, at that time, was of any benefit to them at all.

I'll probably never really know what effect *that* dark period in my life had on my children but I'm certainly thankful for the love we still share. This song expresses that sentiment. It was the first song I'd written in twenty years - since loosing my voice. I performed it in the Newcastle Conservatorium of Music Concert Hall in 2018, at a fund raising event for the Australian Dysphonia Network, on World Voice Day. Accompanied by my daughter, Sophie, I sang in a low, gruff, talking voice, to show the audience the effect that Spasmodic Dysphonia still had on my singing ability. It was a nerve racking experience for me - but a positive one.

The fog had finally lifted!

Always Be My Child

My first born, now 25
Has seen the world through a woman's eyes
Cradled orphans on a distant shore
From the ashes still learning more

And I'm proud of who you are
On my stage a star
Living your dreams…free and wild
But you'll always be my child

My second born, now 23
Not one for rules, not unlike me
Panels beat, pedal down, adrift
New goals achieved, more weight to lift

And I'm proud of who you are
on race track you're a star
Living your dreams, free and wild
But you'll always be my child

And the precious time I spent with them
playing games we'd sing, laugh and pretend
But just like us, games grow old and end
Is it fair?....was I really there?

My youngest boy, now 21
Party's hard, still havin' fun
Tuning craft to ride the sea
Tuning strings, not unlike me

And I'm proud of who you are
On your stage a star
Livin' your dreams free and wild
But you'll always be my child

And I'm proud of who you all are
My little ones have come so far
in time and age, …wise and trialled
Each will always be my child
yes you'll always be my child
You will always be my child

Financing the Nightmare

MT Pockets duo- Emil & me

Although my personal affairs were in taters, at the time of my vocal crisis, my financial situation was reasonably stable. A remarkable feat, considering I gave away over $12000 worth of pre booked gigs to agencies and musicians when I first lost my voice! One of my rare, wise, decisions to take out Income Protection, years earlier, ensured a reasonably adequate and steady income for the first two years of my drama. This allowed me to continue to support my family whilst seeking out medical treatment for my condition. The expenses of operations and consultations, including many trips to Sydney and even Adelaide, were all covered by my insurance. My old school mate drummer from my first rock band, Terry Lantry, was one of the agents that I passed on some of the bookings that I couldn't fulfil. Showing his concern for my tight financial situation, he offered to organise a benefit, fund raising, appeal for me and my family. I declined the offer, determined to beat this problem myself. Being *independently self employed* for the last twenty years was now an ingrained part of my personality. Nevertheless I remain forever grateful for Terry's kind offer.

To further ease the strain on the budget, we sold our family home and moved into our investment property. The financial gain of this move allowed us to purchase the property outright and even pay for extensions to

TONED UP

After **dark**
Chad Watson

BELMONT musician **Tony Johns** may have almost lost his singing voice but he has retained his sense of humour.

Johns realised his voice was failing about two years ago. A doctor discovered a cyst on his vocal cords, which was subsequently removed.

Johns has not been the same since. Now 41, he spent several months recuperating from the surgery and many more rebuilding his confidence.

'I felt crushed,' Johns explains. 'It even turned me off songwriting. My voice is a lot more stable now but it's almost like I've got RSI in my throat.

'... At least I'm still in the business.'

Having spent two decades as a lone performer — Johns was Newcastle solo artist of the year in 1982 and '85 — he has returned to the Hunter pubs and clubs circuit in a partnership.

Johns has formed a duo with singer-guitarist **Emil Matla** called M.T. Pockets, performing

M.T. Pockets

accommodate our growing family.

With no success in finding a cure for my ailment, and knowing that my insurance support was about to cease, I began to focus on finding new forms of employment - other than singing. Having operated all aspects of my own business for the previous twenty years, including bookwork, marketing and promotions, I considered my resume to be fairly impressive. Unfortunately, the recruitment officer at my first interview for an employment agency didn't share my high self evaluation. He informed me that, without formal qualifications, my skill-set meant little to the competitive employment market. His advice was to do a college or university course and come back when my resume' included some certificates. His rebuttal was cold comfort, especially coming from a fellow musician. It was particularly ironic, as he played in one of the bands that performed regularly at the Newcastle Workers Club where I had also suffered the audiences' rejection years earlier!

With my confidence shattered and my self esteem at rock bottom, I just didn't believe I could go back to the books and achieve any decent results in a course. A chance phone call from another musician - enquiring about computerised musical backing [Midi files] - steered me back toward the entertainment business as a means of employment. His name was Emil Matla, a vocalist who was relatively new to the Newcastle music scene, looking to establish himself. I'd previously met him at a few of my gigs and invited him up on stage to perform a few songs with me. It was like a strange premonition when he performed at my nephew's wedding and invited me up to play guitar for him. Telling him of my vocal problem he suggested we team up as a duo. With his voice, and my guitar, equipment and industry connections, we would both be helping each other out to find employment in the music business. Struggling to meet the financial demands of having young families, we jokingly named our duo "M.T. Pockets" and although it only earned me a fraction of my old income, it got me back on my feet and back into music! It continued to support me for the next twenty years and we still, occasionally, perform together to this day!

One particularly memorable gig of the many we did in our twenty-plus years together was at a nudist camp. On that occasion Emil decided to join in with the audience and stripped off his clothes to perform our last set of songs totally naked-leaving me as the only clothed person remaining! At that time, being in my mid fifties, it seems I'd grown more modest and less adventurous than when I was in my twenties performing at Helmut's Pub with Weza!

With all of my children now attending school, the financial commitments of school fees and uniforms began to exceed what performing in the duo was earning for me so I started looking for a day job. Initially, I started out mowing lawns and doing small handyman jobs for friends and neighbours and even at my kid's school in return for reduced school fees. I particularly enjoyed working at the school as it gave me more time with my kids in the initial stages of my marriage separation. Eventually, while doing a neighbours lawn, I was referred to their friend who operated a traffic control company and after completing a two day course, I became a Stop-Go Man.

It was a far cry from the glamour of performing on stage. I received abuse from irate motorists for interrupting their journey, and, sometimes, had empty drink cans thrown at me. On one occasion I even had to dive into a roadside ditch to avoid being run over by a flatbed truck - the driver of which had fallen asleep. A telegraph pole, a few metres away, eventually bringing his auto-cruise slumber to an abrupt, awakening, halt with a thunderous bang! Despite it's hazards and torturous, boring, blisteringly hot, long days - watching my heavy, steel capped boots melt into the bitumen - I enjoyed the work and the camaraderie of the colourful characters with whom I shared the roadside battlefield. The ten hour night shifts were my favourite. Probably because I was accustomed to night work and also because the pay rate almost matched what I used to earn as a singer. Under the cover of darkness I could also pass the long hours, listening to my concealed pocket radio with an ear piece, without being busted by the supervisor.

As unglamorous as the job was, it was a job, and being gainfully employed boosted my confidence. I got on well with the owners of the business, Greg and Kim, who had followed my musical career and sympathised with me at it's demise. They even offered to sponsor me through a course that would see me promoted to the position of supervisor, but, even then, my vocal disorder inhibited me from effectively communicating with co-workers on the noisy job sites. I regretfully declined the offer. My aim was to get back into a business of my own - as an owner/driver courier - which I succeeded in doing after a few years of twirling that red and green sign on the roadside.

So there I was, back in the real world, with a real job, after all those years of freedom in my unreal job - of music. The weekends, now, had extra special significance as I returned to the stage with the MT Pockets duo to perform George Thoroughgood's hit song…"Get a haircut and get a Real job!" Surprisingly, it wasn't as bad as I expected. A part of me even took pride in knowing I was out there, getting my hands dirty and toiling away for a quid, just like my father had done for his whole life. Another part of me saw it as life's way of having the final laugh at me for writing a song - twenty years earlier - which mocked the very same job that now filled most of the hours of my day. I re-wrote that song several times over those years, each time toning down the mocking aspect of it's lyrics. Each new version showing more respect for the person holding that stop sign. Maybe I had a premonition of what was in store for me. That I would eventually become a…Stop-Go Man!

Stop-Go Man

Some folk drive too fast some folk drive too slow
Some folk drive to get there some just drive to go
But they've all got one thing comin' one fine drivin' day
A man with a big red sign gonna step out in their way

Stop go man for the RTA
He got a plan to get in your way
He got time he's got all day
To make his stand like a stop go man

Some roads are smooth as glass some roads are full of holes
Some roads are lined with trees some are lined with telepoles
But they're all gonna need attention 'cause they're all gonna wear away
And they've all got a man with a big red sign standin' there all day

Stop go man for the RTA
He gotta plan to get in your way
He got time he's got all day
To make his stand like a stop go man

Don't slow me down get outa my way
Stop all the cars that are goin' the other way

Some cars are built for speed some cars are made for work
There's a million spinnin' wheels spinnin' round and round the earth
And the drivers of those wheels are gonna put them to the test
Until a man with the big red sign gives those wheels a rest

Stop go man for the RTA
He gotta plan to get in your way
He got time he's got all day
To make his stand like a stop go man

A Point to Prove

For the *first* twenty years as a full-time musician I dutifully paid my dues as a member of the Newcastle Musicians' Union. Over that time, I successfully negotiated my own pay rate - which was usually well above the award rate set by the Union. For *that* reason, I'd rarely called on the Union to help me out. That was until my vocal disorder demolished my career and income earning capacity. When my income protection policy expired I approached the *Union* for advice on *other* possible sources of compensation to help support me while I pursued a new career path. *Their* advice - to consult their affiliated solicitor - turned out to be timely - as it set me on a, fourteen year long, liturgical journey to prove one point; That, "Being a musician *was* a *Real* Job! "

The 1985 hit song; Money for Nothin' by Dire Straits, aptly sums up the attitude of many, regarding the legitimacy of a full time music career...."that ain't working, that's the way you do it...." and that was pretty much the attitude that my solicitor and I were up against, when we took on the insurance companies to claim for *Workers* compensation.

Having regularly performed, over many years, in venues around Newcastle, we quickly established that I *was* deemed to be an employee of those venues and *was,* therefore, entitled to Workers Compensation for my vocal disease. Proving *that* point relied heavily upon the accuracy of my employment and income records, which, due to my earlier years training as a cost clerk at the BHP steelworks, were impeccable. Unfortunately, *that* didn't expedite my claim. My case was an unusual one, which complicated the typically slow process, resulting in a decade passing before we even got *close* to coming face to face with the insurance reps to discuss a settlement. Finally - after fourteen gruelling years and almost as many boxes of photocopied files, documents and testimonials from fellow musicians - *that* settlement occurred. After deducting tax and legal fees, *my share* barely amounted to one year of lost wages! Although I had a good case to pursue the matter further in the *High Court*, I accepted it - especially buoyed by the moral victory it represented.

The settlement of *that* claim also helped give me closure to all the issues that arose from my contraction of Spasmodic Dysphonia. After sixteen long and very dark years the light was beginning to shine through and I was ready to move on. The term *"Mid Life Crisis"* very well applies to me, especially as *my* mid-life was one *enormous* crisis! - but on the other hand I also feel like I didn't have a m*id-life*. It's a very vague and confused memory to me now. I feel like I skipped *those years* and went straight from being a young man to becoming a Senior Citizen - overnight. I know I'll never get those *lost years* back but I'm intent on getting double value out of my senior *ones*!

Carol & me

Investing in the Future.

Although it was a long time in coming, the financial bonus from my compensation claim was quickly put to good use - funding projects that had sat on the back burner for many years. The first acquisition was a newer, larger, van to facilitate my courier and home handyman businesses. The second; was to fund the completion of the album of songs I had begun to record twenty years earlier - which was shelved when my voice problem put paid to my musical plans. With the remaining balance - to treat myself, as a reward, for surviving the turmoil of the previous fifteen years - I bought a sailing boat! A twenty eight foot yacht - big enough to spend days and nights out on, the beautiful, Lake Macquarie. The lake I'd lived beside for the last twenty five years. The lake I'd swum, fished and sailed in, with my kids. The lake that had inspired my music and songs - and my recovery. I could now go out and be a part of *that* lake - whenever I liked and for however long I wanted.

My partner, companion, confidant and "first mate" [where the yacht is concerned], in *all* these ventures, was Carol. Thanks to the modern phenomenon of internet dating, we became romantically involved during the early years of my crisis and have been *each others' shadow* ever since. There is no doubt her love and compassion, combined with her tireless patience, played a crucial role in bringing me back from the brink of hopelessness - and my love and devotion for her is immeasurable! She supported and advised me with all my business ventures. It was she who sort out a bigger van for my courier work when my old van was on it's last legs. Suggesting I buy a bigger model so as to be able to load it with a fork lift, rather than by hand. It was she who purchased a ride-on lawnmower for me - also to lighten my workload! At the same time, she also lined up more lawn mowing jobs, through her sisters' connections in aged care services. Finally, her support and devotion to my musical exploits was unshakeable. She accompanied me to all of my *MT Pockets duo* gigs and always invited her friends - to increase our audience and encourage the venue to re-book us. She was fond of most of my original songs and encouraged everyone and anyone to purchase my albums, often to the point of embarrassing me! She instinctively knew that I had unfinished business with regards to my songwriting and firmly encouraged me toward that goal. Meeting Carol was a pivotal moment that would eventually steer my life in a new and positive direction. Neil Sedaka said it all, when he sang... "Oh Carol"!

The next ten years, after meeting Carol, saw me develop my courier and home handyman businesses, as well as a variety of musical collaborations. Although I still suffered severe bouts of depression, I found the physicality of the delivery and lawn mowing work beneficial in redirecting my negative thoughts. The delivery work involved transporting advertising brochures from a warehouse to distribution centres throughout the Newcastle region. After a day's work of loading and unloading, up to, ten tonnes of paper, I was usually too tired to

LET LOOSE

your inner party...

TOP 40 HITS

Dear Johnsy,
Thankyou for a fantastic 5 plus years.
Trish xo

f Let Loose Duo @ letloosemusic

worry about anything more than having dinner and falling into bed! I appreciated the health and fitness benefits that the manual labour provided, especially on Friday and Saturday nights when I'd be on my feet for another four hours performing on stage with various musical line-ups. I continued to perform with Emil in MT Pockets, but, over the years, he diversified to include other musicians, forming trios and bands, such as; Dreams Trio, Sass and the Boss and the Infusion Party Band. Eventually, he fulfilled a life-long ambition by developing a Neil Diamond Tribute show that featured a six piece band, which, along with a Travelling Wilburys and Highway Men Concept Show, really tested my versatility skills on guitar and harmonica. My conversion from acoustic rhythm guitar to electric lead guitar, wasn't as successful as I would have liked but it was adequate enough to fill the roll required in all of these acts. I, optimistically, persevere with trying to master lead guitar to this day.

A rewarding consequence of working with all *those* musicians was being introduced to Trish Hart, a vibrant and sassy country rock singer, who was originally based in Tamworth. Together, we formed the *Let Loose Duo* in which we played a lively set of, covers, favourites as well as promoting our own, original, material. Trish particularly enjoyed belting out my "*Stop Go Man*" song - another of my tunes that I never imagined a female vocalist to perform! We performed together for almost five years - before she relocated to Queensland. The most memorable of our gigs was at the Seven Seas Hotel, in Carrington, where the manager, Wally - an old [Tenambit] childhood mate - organised a series of reunion nights for all my, former, Maitland friends.

Trish did most of the work on *those* nights - as *I*, mainly, reminisced with the crowd! The special significance of *that* venue was that it was my father's *favourite* watering hole when he worked at the Dockyards. Best of all was meeting some of his old workmates - who still drank there - and hearing them glowingly refer to *Him* in their anecdotes.

The "Natural" album.

Coming Back To Life

It was as if all the loose and frayed ends of my broken life were being tied back together; That's how it seemed, when Tinno [Mark Tinson] called me to suggest we pull my partially completed album off the dusty shelf and finish recording it. Unbeknown to me, somewhere between 2014 and 2015, he had been busy converting the old, analogue, 1/4" reel to reel tapes, of our sessions back in 1995, to digital format. This made it possible to resume recording the vocal tracks on his *new equipment* in the studio. All the *instrumental backing* had been completed back in the nineties and even a few of my *guide vocal tracks* were reasonably good enough to keep, but ten of the songs had to be re-sung. Seeing as I *still* wasn't able to sing without my voice going into spasms, Tinno suggested I invite colleagues from the local music scene to contribute their voices to the project. The intimately personal nature of my songs made me reluctant to invite other singers to perform my work, but, knowing it was the only way to complete the album, I agreed.

I left the coordination of *that* task completely in Mark's competent hands, as he knew the vocal capability and ranges of all the singers he intended to ask. As each vocalist turned up to sing their designated song, Mark

My musical big brother-Mark Tinson (Tinno)

guided them through the musical technicalities required, while I was on hand to advise on interpretation and lyrical punctuation. The process turned out to be an exhilarating experience for me. I welled with emotion, listening to my songs come back to life through the voices of each of these unique vocalists, some I'd only just met, others I'd known, as friends, for years in the business. Most touching of all the sessions was listening to my daughter, Sophie, nervously attempting her interpretation of the title song of the album called *"Natural"*. She'd hardly ever sung publicly, let alone in a recording studio, but, with my encouragement and Tinno's musical guidance, she delivered a performance that still melts my heart when I hear it.

Along with my daughter, the fabulous line up of singers who helped me fulfil my, 20year long, dream [my, Mr Holland's Opus as I called it!], included ; Kevin Bennett [The Flood], Julie Wilson [Andy Firth's Nova Swing], Brien McVernon [Retro Rockets], Michael Hawke [Jungle Kings and old Tenambit Tiger football teammate!], Peter DeJong [Heroes], Justin Ngariki [Rose Tattoo] and Ty Penshorn [Little Hornet]. Each singer infused the songs with their own personalities, bringing them back to life - doing the same for me and making me *so* happy they were finally able to heard again.

Complimenting the stunning array of vocalists on the album was the equally impressive line-up of musicians, once again hand picked and conducted by Tinno, including; Steve Sowerby on drums [Eurogliders], Ian Lees on bass [Moving Pictures], Rick Melick on Hammond organ and piano [John Denver/Joe Bonamassa], Bob Spencer on electric guitar [Skyhooks/Angels], Mark Tinson on electric baritone and slide guitar, mandolin and dobro [Heroes/Ted Mulry Gang], Tony Azzopardi on percussion [The Prophets/Doug Parkinson/Marcia Hines], Michel Rose on pedal steel and dobro [The Catholics/Lee Kernaghan], Mark Collins on banjo [Goldrush/Fargone Beauties], and Wayne Goodwin {deceased} on violin, fiddle, mandolin and string arrangements [Emmylou Harris/Graham Nash].

Carol put her touch on the album by taking the photos for the CD cover sleeve while strolling along Wangi's enchanting foreshore near our home, with her gorgeous, elderly, mother. Every time I pass by the unique tree that we used as the front cover photo, I'm reminded of Nancy Brown{RIP} and her zest for life and laughter.

Julie Wilson & Pam Gully either side of me

The Dream Band; (from top to bottom left to right); Pete De Jong, Dave Carter, Ty Penshorn, Jim Porteous, Michael Hawk, Robbie Long, Mark Tinson, Brien McVernon.

One Night Only!....Gratitude, Justification and Closure

My voice may have been silenced but my songs were going to have the last word!

That's how I'll always remember the night I released the "Natural" album in a live concert at Lizottes theatre restaurant in Newcastle on 2nd February 2017.

Sixteen musicians shared the stage with me that evening, filling my heart with pride as they performed my songs with passion and respect, as if it was a testimonial salute to my career. I'd never felt so privileged and proud to be a part of the musical fraternity of Newcastle!

It was difficult for me to comprehend the significance of *that* night. It virtually wrapped up my life, dedicated to song, in one concert. Propped nervously against the stool on stage, seeing the venue filled with family, friends, fellow musicians and past followers, all there as testament to my devotion and passion for music, almost overwhelmed me. On the verge of tears and total emotional breakdown, I clumsily mumbled and fumbled my way through the show, trying to give the appearance of the cocky and confident showman that I once was. Thankfully, the audience absorbed my blunders in good humour and a supportive spirit and simply enjoyed the passing parade of outstanding talent, performing my songs and refilling the void that had swallowed up my career twenty years earlier.

Infused with emotion for days and weeks after that wonderful night, I sort to disperse the aura of joy and gratitude emanating from me, by publishing an official "*Thankyou*" to all who contributed to my Album's release concert. Gushing with melodrama, *this* is how it appeared, posted on my Facebook page;

Official Thankyou to all involved in Tony Johns' Natural Album Launch at Lizottes, Newcastle on 2nd Feb 2017::

Well, I've landed safely back on Earth after being launched into orbit last thursday night at Lizottes, by the musicians and audience who participated in celebrating the official release of my new album, "Natural"! Now I have the enormous task of thanking everyone who contributed to that magical night and if I accidently omit anyone please contact me and I'll edit and republish this list! [after all, my mind is still mush from the significance of the event for me and I doubt I'll get my head straight for some time to come!]

I'm a movie buff, so I'll reference some of my favourite movies to make analogies of the effect the album launch night had on me. To begin with, the movie, Mr Holland's Opus, starring Richard Dreyfus, immediately comes to mind.... and if you didn't get emotional watching the final concert scene in that movie...then you're as dead as Patrick Swayze in the movie Ghost and, just like him, don't realise it! If that's the case, you may as well stop reading this and go find a good psychic medium!

Now, first and foremost, thanks goes to Mark Tinson, producer of the album and curator of the original 1996 recording tapes as they sat in the vault for 20 years! He conceived the album

(From top right-down); Pam Gully, Emil Matla[singing], Terry Morton[drums], Julie Wilson (singing), Sue Carson (fiddle), Justin Ngariki (singing), Sophie Gibbons (singing)

launch, nagged me for 3months to do it, recruited all the musicians [16 in all], wrote all the music scores and charts, convinced Brien Lizotte to host the show, promoted the show, conducted the band, played and sang in the band and co-compared the night [when I froze up or lost my guitar pick]. The Maestro!

Next; The Band ; Jim Porteus[the smiling bass player!], Terry Morton[drums-wrote charts and also smiled a lot!], Julie Wilson and Pamela Mary Gully[backing vocals & percussion and groovy moves!], Sue Carson [the bouncing fiddle/violin-wrote arrangements], Mick Hawke [the jigging clarinet/sax-wrote arrangements], Robbie Long [slide & electric guitars and mandolin/genius!] and guest appearance from my son, Brady Gibbons[electric gtr and nice hat!]. I can only imagine the hours these guys put in, practising at home, because we only rehearsed together for 4 hours a few days b4 the show!...except Robbie Long, who I met only hours b4 the show when he came in for the sound check!!!wow!!

Next; The Singers; Julie Wilson [also sang all backing on the album and wrote vocal charts/notes], Dave Carter[nightclubbing partner from the 1980's!], Ty Penshorn[who literally ran around the block from another gig to do his spot!], Michael Hawke [ex football partner from 1960's!], Sophie Gibbons[my daughter...in a dress!!], Peter Pete de Jong[my Heroe!], Emil Matla[my duo partner in MT Pockets for past 18years!], Brien McVernon [ex Tex Pistols partner!], and Justin Ngariki [people thought he was the security guard standing by the door at Lizottes!].

Next; The Behind the Scenes guys; Syd White [audio/video], Trevor Dare [filming video... produced video "Tribute"], Gregory James Lunn [photography and pep talk!], Steve McNulty R.I.P.—Hungry Creek Video!], and my efficient merchandise assistants Carol Lancaster [long suffering partner xox], Sophie Gibbons x, and Deb & Neil [dear friends & occasional bodyguard! lol]. Brian Lizotte and staff couldn't have been more warm and welcoming!

With my career spanning 5 decades, my last album 20 years in the making and its launch 6months in the planning, I'm in no hurry to do anything in particular except ensure my songs continue to have a life of their own and connect with people the way they have connected me to this beautiful life I've had so far!. Considering my singing career all but ended 20years ago due to my vocal disorder, the success of last weeks' album launch is very hard for me to comprehend! To see that venue full of friends, fans and family, some of whom hadn't seen me perform in over 35 years, had my heart in my throat and tears in my eyes. It awoke a part of me I thought had long since left this world...and to wrap up with one last movie reference I'm reminded of one of the final scenes in the Tom Hanks classic..."Castaway"... where he is reunited with his FedEx workmates and his friend says something like..."now get some sleep... we've got a big day tomorrow... It takes a lot of work to bring someone back to life".

"Thank you from the depths of my heart and soul! Never more sincere",

Tony Johns Feb 2017

That warm Febuary night, in 2017 at Lizottes, may not have resurrected my solo singing career but it certainly ensured my songs would have a

secure and long lasting legacy!

From that night onwards I had a new and positive outlook on life and my career in music. It restored my appreciation for all the beauty that a life in music and song had gifted me. All the warm, loving audiences, friends and family, all the wonderfully talented and caring musicians and all the magical sounds and emotions that songs can evoke.

I went back to gigging in a diverse variety of line-ups - duo's, trio's, bands and tribute shows - revitalised and eager to learn, as if starting from the beginning. One of the new acts I became a part of, exemplified this fresh start of going back to basics. It was a duet called Zodiac Moon with a wonderfully caring woman by the name of Lisa Snowden. Lisa began her singing career late in life but displayed an innocent passion for music, reminiscent of my early years. I resurrected my acoustic guitar for her repertoire which we performed totally live with just our instruments, unaided by drum machines or any other type of pre-recorded backing music. It was raw and a little loose, but full of honesty and emotion- elements that had been absent in my performances for so long.

All of the recent publicity and radio airplay surrounding my album's release revitalised my profile, prompting many of my former followers to attend my new gigs. Believing I had regained my singing voice, many of these people began requesting my original tunes, so it was disconcerting when I had to explain that I still hadn't recovered from my vocal disorder. I didn't let that phase me. I was just happy to be back in the saddle!

Creative Isolation

To further encourage the flow of my creative juices I began a recording and song-writing collaboration with two ex-pat Newcastle musicians living in Europe. Through the wonders of modern computer technology, email, file transfer and desktop recording software, I've been contributing to recording projects with Jeff Dunn and Brett Reid. Jeff, a former band member of the Orphans, now living in France and Brett, a former member of DV8, now residing in Austria. Jeff arranges the foundation for the songs in his home studio, playing drums, guitars, banjo and doing vocals, then emails them to Brett to put down Bass and vocals, then passes it on to me to provide my touch with guitar or harmonica. I'm constantly amazed when he sends me the final mix of the songs, hearing the symbiotic combination of each of our individual talents, resulting in beautiful music, performed thousands of miles apart from each other. Involvement in these projects was a Godsend, particularly during the Corona Virus Pandemic in 2020 when we were all encouraged to isolate in our homes to prevent the spread of the virus. It was at this time that Jeff and Brett began assisting me with the production and recording of a song I'd recently composed called *"Climbing Mountains"*. It was my first in a long time and hopefully not my last, and it's lyrics are printed on the last page of this book. It was special to have Jeff's involvement in this song as he was involved in my first recording project, playing guitar on the *"P.C.A. The easy way"* record back in 1983!

Listen

Today, I find immense satisfaction in knowing that my songs, old and new, are still being heard. On radio and online. Many community radio stations around Australia have my songs on regular rotation on their country music programmes. One particular presenter, Alan Gilmour, at 94OneFM, enabled my song, "Tribute" to be voted most requested song in 2017 on his "Australian Country Songwriters" show! Social media and internet music streaming services have helped market my songs around the world, ensuring their perpetuity.

I decide to write this book when I realised that all of the songs I'd written combined to tell the story of my life. Rather than keeping a diary, I chose a "Song Book" to store my personal experiences. Like an artist illustrating his life, my lyrics were the brush strokes of mine. The canvass was the places and people I encountered. The colours, my emotions.

I hope it's been an interesting yarn for you to read.

Have a listen to my songs sometime. Google my name or the name of one of my songs. They might be a long way down the list of Itune's songs, but they are there! None of them were chart topping hits and, thankfully, some of them never saw the inside of a recording studio, but you might find one or two that are worth a listen. Like them or not, you'll now know they had much more value to me than just rhyming lyrics following a melody in music!

This book is as much a story about my songs as it is about me. They've played a vital role in making my life what it is, what it was and who I am. I hope I've done them justice.

I think we all hope to leave a mark on this world. A good impression. Our footprint. Something to be remembered by.

My songs are my footprints.

In the end, just like each of my children, a part of me lives on....... in song!

Epilogue

Mount Sugarloaf (photo courtesy of Geoff Sidebottom)

I wrote this book over a period of several years [2018-2022], the most interesting time being when the later chapters were written while in isolation due to the Covid 19 virus that was affecting the whole world in 2020 - a concerning, unique event, the consequences of which the world has yet to come to terms with....the virus that is, not my book!

Writing about events in my past, good and bad, right and wrong, happy and sad, has helped me come to terms with myself and my life. It has shaped my attitude regarding my past and future and taught me to face whatever life presents to me, whether it be good or bad, right or wrong, happy or sad. It's taken over sixty years, but I finally concede that it's all just part of life. Life's journey. Up the mountains, down the valleys. It's all part of the journey.

The destination is another story........maybe another song?

Tapestry of Austrian alps made by Elvira Edna Gibbons

Climbing Mountains   Tony Johns 2020

As a boy I climbed a mountain
walking a dog, granma and me
on a hill she called "Molly Morgan"
we sat in the shade of a tree

As a man I returned to that mountain
with my sweetheart, holding hands
carving our names into that tree
shaping a heart, making our plans

My life climbing mountains
mountains of love, mountains of pain
my life climbing mountains
high in my mind
mountains to climb

As a traveller I wandered the Alps
singing praise gliding on skis
hearing the bells from Hohe Salve
down to the Garten, bending my knees

My life climbing mountains
mountains of joy, mountains of fear
my life climbing mountains
high in my mind
mountains to climb

*Little more than moments in time
when time seemed endless to me
like the worries and fear in my life
never as big as they seemed to be*

*As a father in awe of the view
from a hill with the sweetest of names
on mount Sugarloaf overlooking my home
and my children playing their games*

*My life climbing mountains
mountains of hope, mountains of time
my life climbing mountains
high in my mind
mountains to climb
high in my mind
mountains to climb
high in my mind
mountains to climb*

Index of Songs

I Built this House	11
Zeus	16
Doin' Time	21
Falling	24
Train Ride '3801'	27
Haunted	30
My Fire Will Never Die	34
Walkin' Track	41
Too Old to Be	44
Pray in My Own Time	49
Plastic Man.	53
When I Close My Eyes To Sing	59
Oedipus Rex	63
Sad Song of Joy	65
Cold Again	70
Am I really on My Own	72
Restless Man	76
Key To My Cart	81
Be More Than We Were	83
The Name Game	87
Bob's Funeral	91
P.C.A. The Easy Way	96
Moving Away	101
Merv The Perv	103
A Loving Friend	105
Lucky Charm	107
Can I Sleep In Your Bed Tonight	109
To My Friends	111
Wastin'	113
The Typical Australian Backyard Party [circa 1981]	115
Marijuana Cookies	120
Closing Early	124
Ballina	126
Back in the Hunter Valley	130

Lost in My Dreams	132
Campin' in the Barringtons	138
Looking For The Light	140
Walking on Water	145
Hungry Creek	148
Show Us Ya Mota	152
I've Been Robbed	155
Chasing Love	158
Love on the Line	160
Musical Chairs	162
What's The Next Step	166
Sing my Blues Away	170
Average Song	173
You're Never Too Old	175
Shouldn't've Done What I Did	178
Time to Say Goodbye	180
Goin' Back To Europe	182
Talking with Her Hands	185
What We Left Behind	189
In the Catacomb	191
The Eight Days of Ski Lessons	195
The Curse of the Austrian Bellringer	197
April [Fool]	200
Stubbo's Bar	203
Breakfast With The Bitch	206
They've All Gone Home	211
I Know This Road	221
Clique	223
Happy Chap	226
I Can't Wake Up	227
Over The Hill	236
You Only Want Me For My Body	241
Sitting on the Moon	247
Celibate Summer	250

Living in a Hut	253
Slave Trade	255
The Captain's Mad	260
The Way I Live	267
The Ballad of Wallaby Ted	270
What I'm Gonna Do Tomorrow	272
It's Gone	275
Don't You Trust Me	277
Somewhere	279
Already Been Done	286
The Man Next Door	293
Sydney	295
Chew Tobacco Rag *[Billy Briggs][1951]*	300
The Man Who Comes Around *[Bud Green & Tommy Tucker][1937]*	302
Stereo Blonds *[Mark Tinson]*	304
Conscience	306
Hold on to You	308
Natural	312
Belmont Bay	317
Give Me a Chance	319
Sophie	322
One Day Away	324
Fishin' With Jack	327
One of the Family	331
I'm Satisfied	335
Someone Who's Got It All	337
Tradin' Places	339
Tribute	344
Always Be My Child	353
Stop-Go Man	358
Climbing Mountains Tony Johns 2020	378

Acknowledgements

Graham Davidson; [Rack and Rune Publishing]. Formatting and artwork and finally bringing my project into existence!

Michael Brown; Front cover photo and various other photos throughout the book !

Carol Lancaster; Rear Cover photo and others throughout the book, love and support.

Elvira Edna Gibbons; Tapestry on epilogue.

Paul Newey; Initial proof read and encouragement to publish the book.

Mark Tinson; Inspiration, encouragement and "big brotherly"advice.

Peter Anderson; [Rock City Promotions] For seeing my potential and openings doors that I was reluctant to enter.

Steve Pickett; [Eastern Acoustic Organisation & Newcastle Live] Encouragement and endorsement.

Louise Bale; [Australian Dysphonia Network]. Encouragement and endorsement.

My children; Sophie[proof reading and edits], Jack and Brady. For their support and for inspiring me to write this book as a memento for them.

My Family; Mum, Dad, Pam and Lynette for the love, support, encouragement and for being the foundation for the wonderful life I have !

My friends, Associates and Acquaintances; [most mentioned in this book !.. and many more!] who have made my life so colourful and fun !

All the other photographers; who's photos appear in this book-such as Greg Lunn, Trevor Dare, Geoff Sidebottom, [Uncle] Len Charnock[dec] and many more.

Various Journalists and Photographers from the Newcastle Herald and Maitland Mercury, including Leo Della-Grotta, Michael Parris, Chad Watson, Josh Leeson, Simone De Peak and Donna Sharpe.

Maitland library staff.

Hunter Writers Centre.

Ingramspark.

All the pubs, clubs, parties, weddings and social gatherings that had me perform for them.

Best job in the world !

Timeline

Year	Artist/Band
1963-65	Tony Gibbons
1973-76	Khan/Atacama
1977-80	TG/Pure&Simple duo[Helen]
1981-1982	Tony Johns
1983	Tony Johns &Band
1984	Tony Johns
1985	Tony Johns&Colours
1986	Tony Johns & Colours
1987	Tony Johns&Colours
1988	Tony Johns&Colours
1989	Tony Johns &TJ Band & Tex Pistols
1990	Tony Johns & Tex Pistols
1991-1993	Tony Johns & Tex Pistols & Duo with Helen Vandenbruggen
1994	Tony Johns & Tex Pistols
1995-1998	Tony Johns & Tex Pistols
1999-2010	M.T.Pockets Duo with Emil Matla
2010-2015	Tony Johns [instrumental solo] MT Pockets duo, Dreams Trio, Sass & the Boss Trio, Infusion Trio &Band, The Bel-air Boys, The Yaegermisters, Let Loose duo.
2016-2022	Let Loose duo, Infusion trio&band, Neil Diamond Tribute band,MTP, Zodiac Moon. The Associates.

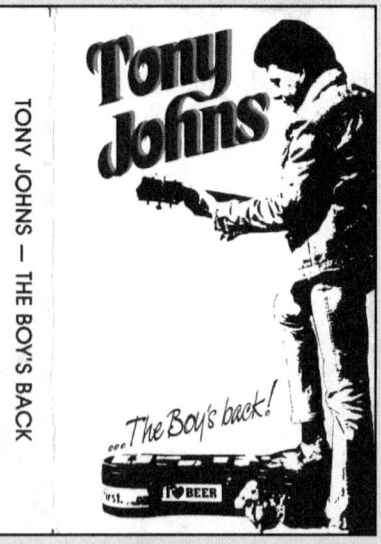

Performance	Album/Single
Sitting on Back Fence serenading neighbours	
Maitland Town Hall/CWA hall/School dances	
Happy Valley/Cessnock Hotel restaurants	
Maitland/Newcastle/NSW&QLD east coast	
Newcastle/Hunter Valley	P.C.A. The easy way[s]
Newcastle/London/Europe	Back in the Hunter Valley[s]
London/Austria/Newcastle	Goin'Back To Europe[Cassette album]
Austria/Greece/Newcastle	The Boy's Back[cassette album]&Dock of the Bay[s]
Austria/Newcastle/Sydney	
Newcastle/Sydney	The Way I live [single & Vinyl album]
Newcastle/Sydney/Austria	Helmut's Pub[cassette Album]
Newcastle/Sydney	Bits of Hits[cassette album]
Newcastle/Sydney/Hunter Valley	
Newcastle/Sydney/Regional NSW	
Newcastle/Sydney/Regional NSW	Never Mind the Bullocks [Tex Pistols}
Newcastle/Sydney/Regional NSW	The Valley [CD/cassette]
Newcastle/Sydney/Regional NSW	S.L.A.P. [Tex Pistols]
Newcastle/Hunter Valley	
Newcastle/Hunter Valley	
"	
"	
"	
"	
"	Natural [album cd]
"	
"	

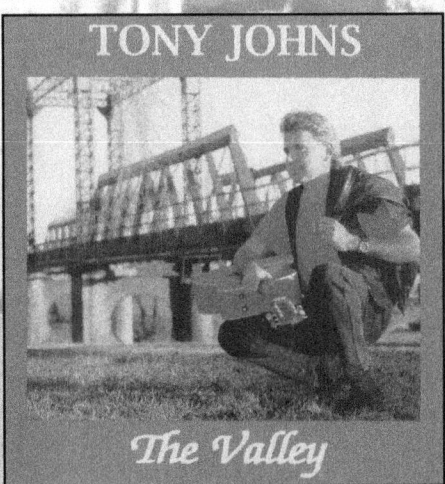